MILTON'S PUNCTUATION
AND CHANGING ENGLISH USAGE
1582–1676

MINDELE TREIP

Milton's Punctuation

AND CHANGING ENGLISH USAGE
1582–1676

METHUEN & CO LTD

11 NEW FETTER LANE EC4

235594

First published 1970
© *1970 Mindele Treip*
Printed in Great Britain
by Butler and Tanner Ltd.
Frome and London

SBN 416 13650 8

PR
3596
77

Distributed in the U.S.A.
by Barnes & Noble Inc.

This title of distinction *reacheth verie far, bycause it conteineth all those characts, and their uses, which I called before signifying, but not sounding, which help verie much, naie all in all to the right and tunable uttering of our words and sentences.*

R. MULCASTER, 1582

... the knowledge of these stops or points is no lesse conducible ... to distinct and ready reading (the perfection of Orthoepie) than to Orthographie, or right writing . . . .

I remember my singing-Master taught me to keep time, by telling from 1, to 4, ... The same course I have used to my pupils in their reading, to inure them to the distinction of their pauses. . . .

S. DAINES, 1640

For
Joan Bennett
and
Douglas Bush

Contents

Preface

Why apparently so minor a matter as Milton's punctuation should deserve a treatment of the present length, might be thought to require some explanation.

Punctuation is a matter not necessarily divorced from the more creative aspects of a poet's style. The pauses made between and the weights placed upon the words spoken or written are matters intimately connected with communication. In addition, pauses are a means of patterning syntax; and pattern was especially important to an earlier era of writing, much more conscious of form than our own. A study of Milton's punctuation may well have something to tell us about his poetical techniques and intentions, and about his and the period's use of language. This study primarily concerns *Paradise Lost*, but its implications are of much broader relevance to Milton. The development of Milton's techniques of punctuation from his earlier poems to the major epic is an index to his maturing versification and rhetorical competence. The punctuation of *Paradise Lost* is therefore a subject which has a bearing on the whole of Milton's poetry and poetical growth.

The history and development of English punctuation have received slight attention from students of English literature. Percy Simpson's short monograph (1911) on Shakespearian punctuation was an outstanding exception, and the present study has been particularly indebted to the illuminating hints thrown out by that work. In the sixty years since, a few essays by other Elizabethan scholars have developed certain of Simpson's views, chiefly those concerning the theatrical use of punctuation in Shakespearian and contemporary Elizabethan drama. A few paragraphs or more rarely pages on the punctuation are to be found in the introductions to some recent editions of Milton's poems and to editions of some other sixteenth and seventeenth century writers (notably Donne and Jonson). One or two essays on pointing (or pointing and orthography) in

Comus and "Lycidas" very nearly complete the list of serious discussions on the subject of earlier punctuation. These few essays or briefer discussions represent a minority of scholarly opinion. To paraphrase very broadly the various (and somewhat diversely oriented) points of view in the studies just referred to, this element of scholarly opinion has tried to suggest that an earlier punctuation might have had its own governing principles and *raison d'être* different from those of modern pointing; that in an earlier use, punctuation might have significantly affected verse structure; that earlier pointing might have been intended to direct the reader's hearing of the rhythms and help his grasp of the emotional content of the verse; that pointing might even have had some parallel rhythmical and elocutionary functions in earlier prose; in short, that punctuation might once have been thought an integral part of the complex mechanism of style. But such views have not been commonly accepted or indeed made generally known. A prevailing attitude has undoubtedly been that varying styles of punctuation in earlier works, if they have any meaning at all, only reflect the vagaries of different authors or the differing conventions between printing houses, and are of little stylistic or linguistic importance, although they may perhaps have a certain antiquarian or typographical interest.

Yet punctuation usage was before the eighteenth century (and indeed still is) fluid and evolving, part of the living organism of language, just as were other aspects of English speech and writing; and the history and development of English punctuation are intimately bound up with the history and development of the language. Punctuation is in essence a means of clarifying and sharpening syntactical organization: a means of defining the varying designs and purposes in the construction of the sentence or other units in writing. Syntactical organization has by no means always been based exclusively on grammar, as it is now. The period between about 1580–1680 (the century which approximately ends with *Paradise Lost*) witnessed a particularly marked evolution away from rhythmical and oratorical, or sometimes theatrically dramatic, concepts of syntactical design, concepts which encouraged individuality and flexibility of expression, toward more logically and grammatically oriented views. The approach was increasingly to the ideal

of 'correctness' in writing: toward regulating all aspects of composition according to universal and logically fixed standards.
Altered practices in punctuation are among the features which
reflect these changes. We might therefore expect to find in the
earlier practice of punctuation some index to the morphological
factors which made an earlier use of written language so different from our own. To study the punctuation of *Paradise Lost*
and of its background is not only to become aware of how
language in the seventeenth century was changing – a matter
which must be of interest to all students of that period – but
also to gain a specific insight into some of the formal factors
which distinguished earlier writing. In punctuation we find a
valuable tool for the analysis of style in earlier prose and verse
and a gauge to some of the puzzling phenomena of stylistic
change.

The general style of punctuation in *Paradise Lost* itself, particularly in the extant Manuscript of Book I, is remarkable in
being a far-reaching though by no means isolated exception to
the increasing trend of the mid-seventeenth century toward
greater correctness in writing. The style of punctuation in
Paradise Lost is in the tradition of the livelier and more dramatic, the more rhythmical and flexible, altogether more poetical
punctuation of the Elizabethans. Of course Milton adapted the
older practices with his usual sophistication. He was not being
merely old-fashioned but presumably recognized the poetical
advantages of the older style. A study of punctuation in
Milton's major poem thus confirms what every other research
into his poetry suggests: his special fondness for the Elizabethans as a fertile and quickening stylistic influence; his
conscious assimilation of certain older models in forming some
elements of his style; his wide range of poetical reference and
his artistic independence; his unique skill at drawing a genuine
poetical expressiveness out of even the most minute or formal
stylistic elements. In other words, we are brought once again
to apprehend the inventiveness, high artistry and integrity of
Milton's style.

A study of the pointing in the original texts of *Paradise Lost*
also brings the important realization that in Miltonic usage
punctuation and verse structure are closely interdependent.
The larger rhythmical plan of Milton's blank verse is controlled

by a skilful manipulation of the pointing as much as by any other factor. The principles according to which Milton moulds and relates his lines, verse periods and verse paragraphs, the way in which he formulates the basic rhythms of his verse, and the way his poetic rhetoric is counterpointed against these established rhythms, are matters which can all be much illuminated by a study of the poem's punctuation. The present study originated as one aspect of a more general criticism on the style of *Paradise Lost*, and it is hoped that the questions here raised about Milton's versification and poetic rhetoric may be of interest to other readers of Milton.

Lastly, a study of the punctuation in *Paradise Lost* has a considerable bearing on some important problems connected with the text of that poem. It has been realized by all who have worked with the texts of the Manuscript of Book I and of the 1667 and 1674 editions that there is little evidence and much uncertainty as to the extent of Milton's personal control in smaller matters, such as spelling and punctuation. The fact of Milton's blindness, which forced him to supervise the preparation of the manuscript and printed copies of his poem through some intermediary person or persons, exacerbates already considerable editorial problems. Editors have usually concluded that the second edition, or that collated with the first, represents the most authentic and fully corrected author's text. This may not be true in all respects. An examination of the punctuation variants between the Manuscript and the two first editions, in Book I, suggests that a distinctive and poetical style of pointing which could well be Milton's own is more fully and consistently illustrated in the Manuscript than in either of the corrected editions, and that the editions' revisions to the punctuation are in a somewhat different general style from that of the Manuscript.

It has been necessary to work toward these conclusions mainly from within the three original texts, by comparing their variant pointings and the differing stylistic traits which these variants seem to indicate. External corroboration of an indirect kind has also been sought through comparing the style of punctuation in *Paradise Lost* with the practice of other authors contemporary with Milton or earlier; with contemporary and earlier theory of punctuation; and with the style of punctuation employed in another work coming out of the publishing house of Samuel Simmons (the printer of *Paradise Lost*). But more direct indications as to Milton's individual and poetical use of punctuation are also to be found in the autograph drafts of his own early poems, especially the mature sonnets.

If the conclusions reached in this study are in any way sound, then a fresh recognition should be accorded to the value of the punctuation in the Manuscript of *Paradise Lost*, Book I, both because of its general linguistic interest and also because of its particular importance relative to the text and mature style of *Paradise Lost*. It is also hoped that the findings here may be of some help in studying others of Milton's texts, and that they may indirectly assist in establishing the authenticity and purpose of the punctuation in the texts of other seventeenth century or Elizabethan writers.

However, the main purpose of this study will have been served if it assists in the reading of Milton's verse. We need all the help we can get with that, for Milton's verse although lucid is far from simple. Some knowledge of the poet's habits of punctuation and their historical background is very relevant. Milton's "elaborate metrical plan and his divine ear" (De Quincey) necessitate that the fit audience though few should be an informed one.

I am happy to have this opportunity to make several acknowledgements. Mrs Joan Bennett and Professor Douglas Bush, among many other acts of kindness, read parts of the manuscript of this book. Their generous advice and encouragement over an extended period have been much appreciated. However, they have not seen the manuscript in its final form and are thus unacquainted with at least its later faults. I am greatly obliged to Professor L. C. Knights for his attentive and most courteous consideration of the manuscript and its problems. Lucy Cavendish College kindly made a grant towards the typing expenses incurred. I am grateful to Dr P. Gaskell, librarian of Trinity College Library, Cambridge, who allowed me to consult some of the College's early editions of *Paradise Lost* and also their precious manuscript of Milton's early poems, and equally to Mr Douglas C. Ewing, assistant curator of autograph manuscripts and later printed books at the Pierpont Morgan Library, who was kind enough to consult the original manuscript of

Paradise Lost, Book I, and give his opinion about some doubtful pointings. Mr J. L. M. Trim provided valuable advice on some linguistic matters. My husband's support has been extended in so many forms that I could not now detail it, nor would he wish me to. I must at least say that he read the entire manuscript and discussed it on many occasions, and that I have always found his criticisms searching and salutary. I am very much indebted to the staff of Methuen, whose helpfulness, efficiency and courtesy have been impressive. Finally, I must thank Mrs Joan Ashford, who found time to assist in the proofreading; Mr J. C. Lingard, who helped to prepare the index; and Mrs B. Reeson, my typist.

M. T.

Lucy Cavendish College
   Cambridge
      January, 1969.

I

Introduction

1. *Textual Methods*

The general plan of this study is, first, to establish the broad context of seventeenth-century punctuation practice before Milton and to trace the changing usage of the period up to the time of *Paradise Lost*. Second, an attempt is made to disentangle Milton's own usage, chiefly through comparing the punctuation in the several stages of the text of *Paradise Lost* (the scribal manuscript; the 1667 edition; states, that is, proof changes in the first edition; and the 1674 edition). Milton's autograph handwritten poems, especially the mature sonnets, are crucial in establishing a standard for these comparisons.

In the historical outline presented in chapters II–III the period covered is 1582–1676, the date plus two years of the second edition of *Paradise Lost*. The emphasis of the discussion is as much on the actual practice of punctuation in the period as on punctuation theory. Both printers' and authors' punctuation is thought to be of value in showing the broad evolution of practice during this century. However, authors' manuscripts or author-supervised editions have been used where possible.

Working with the text of *Paradise Lost* itself raises a number of special problems, and a few words must be said about what has been done or intentionally not done.

The analysis of Milton's punctuation in chapters IV–VI centres on the variants between the scribal manuscript of *Paradise Lost*, Book I, and the 1667 edition (first states). That is, the root of the question is the changes made to Milton's manuscript when the poem was edited at the press. To establish an accurate list of these first corrector's or compositor's changes, the collotype facsimiles of the Manuscript of Book I reproduced in Helen Darbishire's edition have been collated with the photographic facsimiles of the 1667 text (first states) published in H. F. Fletcher's edition of *Paradise Lost*. The list of variants

1

thus established is given in a table in Appendix A. It agrees in most but not all particulars with the transcriptions and collations of Fletcher and Miss Darbishire. There were further a small number of pointings which were difficult to read in the collotypes of the Manuscript. Mr Douglas Ewing kindly consulted the original in New York and gave his opinion in these instances. Two of the pointings which he identifies differ from the received transcriptions of Fletcher and Miss Darbishire. This small detail confirms the present writer's impression that in the case of *Paradise Lost* (as also in the case of some of Milton's early poems) editors have regularly misread a few of the more unusual of Milton's pointings.

The next set of punctuation variants arises with differences between the different copies of 1667 – changes evidently made later in the printing or 'in proof'. These are interesting but less vital to the question of Milton's punctuation practice. Fletcher and Miss Darbishire record only slightly more than two dozen of such instances distributed over the entire poem: or an average of 2·8 proof changes per Book. These must be set against more than 130 punctuation variants made at an early stage in Book I alone. It would therefore hardly have been a profitable task, even had it been feasible, to undertake an independent collation of pointing variants in the numerous extant copies of 1667. There are simply not enough proof changes to make such a task worth while. The list of proof changes given in Appendix B has been compiled partly out of the lists and collations recorded in Fletcher's and Miss Darbishire's editions, partly out of direct comparison of alternative states of some pages. (Fletcher in almost all cases prints full alternative photographs of pages known to exist in different states, thus affording an opportunity for independent study of some at any rate of the variants.) No variant recorded by him or Miss Darbishire has been listed here without having been studied in its context in Fletcher's facsimiles, and some effort has been made to ascertain that the states presented by Fletcher and Miss Darbishire as later or earlier, were in fact such. The present writer has found only one punctuation proof change (III, 35) not given in these editors' lists, and this omission was rectified by Fletcher in the note to that line in his edition of the 1674 text. In general Fletcher's collations in that edition are much more complete than are those in his edition of the 1667 text. The Trinity College Library copy of the 1667 edition (first title page) exhibits about two thirds of the variants listed in Appendix B.

The question of the different issues or title pages of the 1667 edition might be raised. Although this matter has been a subject of much interest to bibliographers, it is not very relevant to the present study. It is generally accepted that the text of the 1667 edition, or nearly all of it, was printed off all at one time; parcels of the stored pages were then bound up with fresh title pages (or in the later issues, also with added preliminary matter). Only the second title page of 1669 shows any reset pages (signatures Z and Vv). These were reprinted, in a few copies, apparently to make up a shortage of some sheets in the last binding. The various issues of the first edition of *Paradise Lost* therefore cannot show any significant fresh stratum of punctuation changes in the text of the poem. However, the punctuation variants appearing in the two reset signatures are listed separately in Appendix B, with a few comments. The present writer does not altogether agree with Miss Darbishire's interpretation of the Vv signature.

The 1674 edition is the next problem; it represents the final stage of the text of *Paradise Lost*, as far as Milton himself could have had a hand in it. It is known that Milton made some significant verbal or larger changes for this edition; but the number of punctuation changes in it, whether by him or others, is again not large. There are on an average perhaps ten pointing changes per Book in 1674, as compared with 2·8 per Book in states of the first edition – and over 130 earlier pointing changes in Book I alone in 1667. Here also then, it would not have been practical to undertake a separate full collation of the 1667 and 1674 punctuation. However, the variants are tabulated and discussed in some detail in Appendix C. The list there is based on Fletcher's collations given in his textual notes to the 1674 text. All variants were studied in their contexts in the photographs Fletcher gives of the relevant pages in both the 1667 and 1674 editions. Some thought has been given in this Appendix to the question of which punctuation variants are true ones and which may be unintentional compositor's or printing errors. In general the 1674 is worse printed than the 1667 text; it was

B

a popular, cheap edition with which the printers took less
trouble. It has been thought that there is some basis for establishing at least the grosser of the printing or compositor's errors
in 1674. Gross errors apart, the possibility that a change
(especially an omitted mark) in the 1674 text may be accidental
and of no significance has always been allowed for; but so also
has the converse and equally important possibility, that a
change may be meaningful even though unconventional. These
considerations have of course been kept in view in the discussion of the 1667 text; but such problems arise somewhat less
often and less pressingly in 1667, because the punctuation
changes there are on the whole homogeneous, conventional and
show few omitted marks.

The textual methods which have been indicated above may
possibly have allowed a few variants within the first edition or
in 1674 to pass unnoticed, but these would not alter the general
picture. The methods followed give a reasonably full history
of punctuation changes to the text of *Paradise Lost* during
Milton's lifetime, and in those particulars which concern this
study most, the earliest pointing changes made when Milton's
manuscript was edited at the press, the picture is more or less
complete.

The punctuation of some of Milton's early poems has been
considered in this study; but the punctuation of Milton's late
poems and on the whole of his prose has not, because of the
difficulties raised by the nature of the printing of these works.
In the cases of *Paradise Regained* and *Samson Agonistes*, the
lack of adequate controls over the text (no extant manuscripts;
no substantial numbers of meaningful variants in errata to or
different states of the first edition; no revised edition printed
during the author's lifetime) make discussion of Milton's
possible part in the pointing uncertain. Much of the prose raises
similar difficulties, magnified by an often poorer printing. However, the prose punctuation is touched on briefly in chapter II.
Even though full textual study of the prose and the late poems
may be difficult, our apprehension of the style and purpose of
their punctuation must inevitably be sharpened by our more
complete understanding of the practices in *Paradise Lost* and
the early poems.

The question of spelling variants arises. Spelling variants in the various editions and printed states of *Paradise Lost*, and spelling practices and corrections in the scribal Manuscript of Book I, as well as spellings and spelling changes in the manuscripts or printed texts of the early poems, have an obvious bearing on criticism of Milton's punctuation. J. T. Shawcross has made a detailed study of Milton's spelling and its textual implications, and some of his conclusions will be considered in chapter VIII, where there is also a brief independent discussion of spelling variants between the Manuscript, Book I, and the 1667 text (first states only). This discussion is not intended to be exhaustive, but rather gives a rapid impression of some of the principal kinds of spelling changes made in the Manuscript and in the 1667 text, what poetical implications these may carry and how they may correspond to the punctuation changes. As Shawcross' detailed work on the subject makes clear, Milton's spelling is not a matter which can be discussed authoritatively without extensive study of his usage at all stages of his life and work. His usage was based on several and sometimes complicated principles; it was in certain aspects inconsistent (more so than his punctuation); and his distinctive practice was slow to evolve. To establish Miltonic orthography it is necessary to survey a wide area of manuscript and printed material, such as would have been quite beyond the range of the present study.

Appendix D gives a table of comparisons of the average number of punctuation marks, per hundred words, in Milton (the various texts) and the other authors quoted in this study. The results may confirm the impression, which even a rapid glance will convey, that Milton's punctuation was much more sparing than that of many of his contemporaries or predecessors; this despite the fact that punctuation was becoming generally heavier and more profuse during the course of the seventeenth century. There are other interesting features to emerge from the data. For instance, the figures suggest that punctuation in the texts of *Paradise Lost* on the whole stays closer to Milton's autograph practice than does the pointing in some of his earlier printed texts. But it is important to make the reservation that tables of comparisons of this kind are by themselves an inadequate index to pointing practice. In the case of Milton especially, each punctuation variant or indeed each stop in a given passage has to be studied individually and in its complete context, in order to decide what significance it may hold and what style of pointing it may contribute to. Only after this kind of close study can meaningful analysis be made. Chapters V–VI draw inferences about the text of *Paradise Lost*, after considering the relative numbers within the different groups or types of punctuation changes made by the 1667 edition. This is statistical study of a kind; but it is hoped that it is the more meaningful because it rests on full prior assessment of the context of each variant and close comparison of each variant with the style of Milton's Manuscript.

Readings from *Paradise Lost*, in chapters IV–VII, except where otherwise indicated follow the 1667 text in H. F. Fletcher's facsimile edition. The 1667 edition, together with the Manuscript of Book I, forms the basis for the discussion in chapters IV–VI, and for the sake of consistency this same text has been quoted from throughout. Any variants between the first and second editions, in punctuation or in Book and line numbers, if they arise in material quoted, are indicated in the text or the notes. The punctuation given in presenting all quotations, whether from Milton or other authors, is (excepting for ellipses) always the punctuation of the original only; I have omitted or put outside quotation marks any of my own punctuation which might fall in immediate juxtaposition with the originals and so possibly cause confusion. In all collations, the earlier readings are given first.

In the ensuing chapters no time will be spent on conjectural emendation or reconstruction of the original punctuation. It has seemed much more useful to interpret that existing.

2. *Milton's Control over the Punctuation*

Supposing the original punctuation of *Paradise Lost*, and even, that punctuation as partly preserved in the partially altered text of the first edition, to be both purposeful and distinctive, whose are we to think it, Milton's or somebody else's? How much warrant may there be for assuming Milton's control or influence over the punctuation of written manuscript or printed text, when he could not see either? As will be proposed, the strongest arguments for the poet's control lie in the impression of a strong poetic sensibility operating in the punctuation of the poem, especially that of the Manuscript, and in the fact that the printer so largely retained this pointing or respected its general style when correcting, although it was unrepresentative of the period.

There is little of more direct evidence to prove that Milton directed the pointing at any stage in the composition or printing of *Paradise Lost*. There may be some indirect evidence, in certain metrical spelling changes in both the manuscript and printed texts. Helen Darbishire was impressed by these spelling corrections and thought they derived from Milton himself.[1] She argued that, if thus much of Milton's spelling survived (or even was, as she felt, carried through more consistently) into the printing, Milton must have exercised a comparable control over the punctuation. Her argument is stronger for the following reason: one would think that punctuation, as both a grammatical and possibly also a rhetorical signal system and a matter which can be intimately associated with verse structure, could not have seemed to Milton less important than spelling. Indeed, one might think that he would have regarded it as of more importance. Many older alternative spellings (for example, idle final *e*, doubling of end consonants) were merely matters of convention or personal habit; they make no difference to the sound of the verse. But almost all punctuation, regarded as a system of pauses, can make a considerable difference to how a line is read; even the most casual insertion or deletion of a comma may tell.

There is no reason to suppose that Milton would not or could not have supervised punctuation. He took great pains with the editing of his own works, especially *Paradise Lost*, and his supervision of his texts extended to quite small mechanical details when these affected the reading of his verse. Instances of his care are the marking of line indentations, and word elisions so as to indicate the correct number of syllables and hence the desired rhythms. All this we can observe from his manuscripts and from certain minute corrections which are still being made (evidently by Milton) as late as in the errata to the first edition, and in the second edition of *Paradise Lost*. Why then should he have been indifferent only to punctuation, a matter also and greatly affecting the reading of his verse?

No one else concerned with the preparation of the poem at any stage was indifferent to the punctuation; nor, apparently, was anyone ever totally unaware of the poetical relevance of punctuation. Are we to imagine that, of all the people involved in the production of the text, only Milton did not care about the punctuation; or that, if he really had not cared about it, anyone else would have taken so much trouble over it, or at any rate would have punctuated the text for him in anything but a perfunctory and standardized way, according to prevailing contemporary practice?

The fact of Milton's blindness need not have raised any insuperable difficulty as regards getting his own punctuation into the text. The poem was dictated, and Milton could have named some of the stops as he recited (anybody dictating a letter now might do as much). Alternatively, a secretary who had become familiar with Milton's versification and style might have learned to transcribe punctuation approximately from the pauses, weights and inflections of the poet's voice. Again, the poem must have been read back to Milton many times, during and after its composition, for correction. In this process also, a practised reader could have indicated the stops by length of pause or named some, while Milton corrected the punctuation by ear, querying certain pointings and correcting others as he listened.

Milton could have had the help, in preparing his manuscript, of a number of persons familiar with his stylistic practices: Edward Phillips (who said that he corrected punctuation in the drafts of *Paradise Lost*); John Phillips; Daniel Skinner; Thomas Ellwood; or Milton's own daughters. Perhaps the most likely possibility is that there took place some form of close collaboration between Milton and an amanuensis familiar with his style; such a person (or persons) might have punctuated along the poet's known lines, with some guidance from the poet himself. If more than one amanuensis was concerned in preparing the first drafts of *Paradise Lost* (as seems probable), that would account for the fact that some parts of the Manuscript now seem better, or more 'Miltonically', punctuated than others. The scribe who prepared the fair copy could have been instructed to treat the punctuation with respect; and his copy was certainly corrected as to pointing, possibly by one of the original amanuenses (see chapter V, section 1, where Miss Darbishire's evidence of two handwritings is discussed). However, the possibility cannot be dismissed that a few un-Miltonic pointings may have crept into the Manuscript at the time of its final transcription, just as a number of old-fashioned spellings did.

As regards the printing, the possibility of Milton's indirect supervision of the punctuation is not ruled out, although the situation is complicated by the number of new hands possibly concerned in correcting (the printer, the press corrector, compositor, etc.). But even at this stage Edward Phillips or some other assistant of Milton's could have acted as emissary to the printer, at the very least exerting some restraint over the nature and number of changes made to the punctuation, and perhaps inserting an occasional pointing himself. Or the person who undertook the bulk of the early corrections at the press could have been made conversant with some of Milton's main practices.

All these are mere speculations; but they point out the possibilities for Milton's control (even if indirect) over the punctuation of his text. Further, evidence exists to show that printers of Milton's period or earlier could sometimes be quite scrupulous about following an author's punctuation, if it seemed reasonable. Percy Simpson[2] in his book on English proofreading has noted that "In earlier times the treatment of punctuation varied: in most of the copy here described the printer followed it [that is, the author's punctuation] as a general rule . . .". It is true enough that the first edition followed the Manuscript's punctuation "as a general rule". We have no justification for assuming that the printer felt free to do otherwise, or that he thought the Manuscript's pointing of no consequence.

It was, then, by no means impossible or unlikely that Milton should have directed the punctuation of his manuscript and retained at least some general influence over changes to the punctuation made in the edition. Whether he personally directed any specific pointing changes in printer's copy or in proof is another question. It might seem reasonable to assume that the printed edition, taken as a whole, would reflect Milton's personal practice to a lesser degree than the author's own manuscript. The rather haphazard nature of the proof arrangements at the press and the larger number of hands (some strange) possibly involved in the correcting do make all natural probabilities point that way.

3. *Milton's Early Manuscripts*

More direct indications that Milton cared about punctuation and had evolved distinctive practices concerning its use are to be found in the extant autograph manuscripts of his early poems. A cursory inspection of these might seem to contradict any notion that Milton ever took much trouble over punctuation, for the pointing in his autograph poems or in other manuscript poetry dating from well before his blindness is sometimes very incomplete. The drafts of his minor poems in the Trinity College Manuscript, and the Bridgewater Manuscript of *Comus*, which was a scribe's fair copy of the acting version of the masque,[3] are punctuated in parts with surprising scantiness, portions, especially of "Lycidas" and of *Comus* (in Milton's hand) in the Trinity Manuscript, being virtually without punctuation, as Masson[4] noticed. In the Bridgewater *Comus* more pointing was supplied. However, closer study of these manuscripts does much to dispel these first impressions of Milton's apparent neglect.

For instance, it might be said that what punctuation there is in the Trinity *Comus* is often dramatically expressive: as if the poet had felt it especially necessary to give the pointing in some dramatically important places. He inserted an odd pointing, so to speak, just as an individual line occasionally struck him, perhaps to show the actors how he heard the line. It was more important to him to mark these than other pointings, these being personal and poetic matters, less self-evident than grammar. Some passages in *Comus* which are punctuated more fully so as to convey some inflection or emphasis are found (choosing almost at random) at lines 23, 37–8, 52–3 and 2–3 on, respectively, pages 11, 12, 16 and 17 of the Trinity Manuscript; also lines 55–63 on page 17 (to which we may compare the dramatically less appropriate readings of 1637, 1645 and 1673, cited later).

Occasional pointings of fine rhetorical value are to be found in the non-dramatic poems also. One example is seen in "Lycidas", line 9 (Trinity MS, page 32), where a colon boldly underlines the sweeping contrast toward the conclusion of the poem between Lycidas' drowned body and his exalted spirit in heaven. Another instance is seen in Sonnet 11, end of line 8 (Trinity MS, page 40), in the contemptuously emphasizing semi-colon after the word *hogs;* . . . .

In Sonnet 14, line 4, the Trinity Manuscript (page 41) also shows an evident semicolon after *life;* appropriately emphasizing the antithesis which follows (" . . . death, call'd life; wch us from life doth sever.") Again in *Comus*, page 12, lines 37-8, a colon is used to indicate suspense or a break:

> Breake off, breake off, I *heare* feele the different pace
> of some chast footing neere about this ground: . . .
> run to yor shrouds . . .

W. A. Wright's transcriptions, followed by Fletcher, give neither of these heavy stops, but they seem plain in the original. Such cases presumably arise because editors tend to read an unusual pointing into something more expected and conventional; there are some similar instances in the Manuscript of *Paradise Lost*.

What is also perfectly obvious, in the Bridgewater *Comus* and in Milton's own drafts of *Comus* and "Lycidas" (more strikingly in Milton's drafts, because they have generally so little punctuation), is that the existing punctuation is largely metrical. The one place where the poet most consistently took the trouble to mark the stops (whether commas or heavier marks) was at the caesura. He obviously wished to show how the lines run over and where the verse is breathed. Some typical examples are "Lycidas", lines 15-16 (Trinity MS, page 32), and *Comus*, lines 40, 41 and 44 (Trinity MS, page 17). In these and similar instances the punctuation tells how Milton was hearing his lines and how he meant them to be read out. He evidently regarded such metrical pointing as of more importance than, say, marking full stops at the end of a line when a sentence finishes there, or writing capitals to introduce a new sentence or start new lines, all these being obvious matters which anybody could easily put right later.[5]

In addition, there are clear signs of a rhythmical and structural use of punctuation in some of the autograph sonnets in the Trinity Manuscript. In these, punctuation helps in particular to define the stanzas and to show the flow of the thought in relation to the sonnet pattern. Sonnets 11, 14 and 13 in its second draft are fully and sensitively punctuated along the rhythmical and rhetorical lines evident in the Manuscript of *Paradise Lost*, Book I, with almost no omissions of stops in terms of the Miltonic scheme. The punctuation of these sonnets will be discussed in greater detail later.

It is important to remember that none of these early manuscript poems were intended for printer's copy and that their punctuation may therefore not be in a final form. The Trinity Manuscript was Milton's workbook, in which the poems were written often in rough or early drafts, and their punctuation might have been deliberately left open for future revision. (Indeed it often had to be, in view of the unfinished or undecided state of many lines.) Different drafts of poems suggest that Milton pointed more fully as poems approached a finished state. The two drafts of Sonnet 13 to Lawes in the Trinity Manuscript show this very clearly. The earlier draft has little pointing, but the second draft is fully punctuated so as to indicate the rhythmical modulation of the lines, the pattern of the argument, and (counterpointed against this) the shape of the stanzas. Again, the Bridgewater Manuscript, although a fair copy, was taken from an acting copy, in which Milton could well have relied on the speakers' voices to supply some pauses and inflections, knowing that the syntax itself would give the actors any needed clues to the stops.

Certainly, these early manuscripts suggest one thing plainly: that Milton had little interest in rendering a merely conventional or formally correct punctuation. He must surely have had in view that, before the ultimate publication of these poems, some further transcription or editing would supply some of the more obviously lacking grammatical stops. Perhaps he meant himself, in later drafts or copies of some of these poems, to supply further punctuation along more personal lines.

It is also worth noting that the manuscript of *Paradise Lost*, unlike Milton's earlier manuscripts, was first written to dictation. The amanuensis could therefore have recorded through the punctuation some of the particular accents, pauses and inflections of the poet's voice (and equally, the absence of pauses), even if the poet had actually had the earlier habit, not unknown to authors in the heat of composition, of neglecting to mark all the stops into his manuscript as he wrote. But it is also quite possible that with the manuscript of his major and later work Milton took more pains to indicate the punctuation fully, or that he had by then fully formed his personal style of pointing, a rhythmical and rhetorical system which evolved along with the distinctive blank verse and the rhetorically heightened language of his mature epic manner. Milton's later spelling shows greater individuality and flexibility,[6] and perhaps his punctuation developed in the same way. Such a development might seem to be confirmed by the fuller and rhythmically more sophisticated punctuation of the Sonnets cited, as compared with that of *Comus*, which is of earlier date.

To sum up, then, there is enough possibility that the original punctuation of *Paradise Lost* may be Milton's or substantially his, and this punctuation is distinctive enough and in itself of enough poetic interest, that it surely merits more serious attention than it has had in the past. We may now turn to a closer analysis of punctuation with examples, drawing first (in chapters II–III) from other works of Milton's period or earlier; next (in chapters IV–VI) from the alternative written and first printed versions of Book I of *Paradise Lost*; and lastly (in chapter VII) from the twelve Books of the printed poem, taken as a composite whole.

II

Elizabethan and Earlier Seventeenth-Century Punctuation

1. The Early System. Theatrical Punctuation

It need scarcely be cause for surprise if Milton chose in matters of punctuation to subordinate minor grammatical correctness to the rhythmical and dramatic demands of his verse. In so doing he would only be following the older, Elizabethan tradition, to which in so many of its aspects he was devoted. As Percy Simpson[1] noted in his valuable short study some sixty years ago, it is only modern punctuation which is, or "attempts to be, logical; the earlier system was mainly rhythmical." The word "mainly" and Simpson's actual basis of analysis (partly grammatical) suggested that there was also a logical or grammatical element in Elizabethan punctuation. The two aspects (Simpson did not make this clear) overlapped or sometimes collided; but Simpson seems to have meant to imply that the rhythmical element was the more distinctive aspect of Elizabethan pointing and that it often took precedence over the grammatical.

To illustrate his thesis, Simpson took as points of departure the 1623 Folio of Shakespeare's plays and the 1609 edition of the Sonnets; in these he found various instances mainly of a dramatically expressive punctuation. Simpson's theory was subsequently developed and modified by the work of A. W. Pollard and other Shakespeare scholars, and more recently by the valuable work of A. C. Partridge.[2] These scholars have expressed the opinion that Elizabethan punctuation represented a scale chiefly of time values rather than grammatical or logical values. The classical derivations of this concept, and its historical background in Elizabethan and Jacobean grammatical theory, have been partially explored by W. Ong and

14

earlier, C. Fries – the latter with more negative conclusions than Ong, who found evidence that Elizabethan pointing was intended to serve *"the exigencies of breathing* in discourse" (especially oratory).[3] Other scholars found that the time-value theory of pointing shed much light on the 'elocutionary' style of punctuation in Elizabethan drama before about 1616 (punctuation intended to show how the lines might be delivered by the actors). These scholars and Simpson considered that Elizabethan lyric poetry also shows some evidence of an elocutionary style of pointing, but their concern has been mainly with dramatic verse.

The word "rhythmical", which Simpson chose to describe the early pointing, is a term of wide implications and one not to be confined to the playhouse. The broadly rhythmical system of punctuation of which Simpson and others wrote undoubtedly had a specifically metrical aspect also, an aspect perhaps even more basic to the system than were the elocutionary features. The concept of pointing as a scheme of time values and as a breathing system divorced from or only loosely related to sense meant that punctuation could be used to help show the metrical structure and larger rhythmical movements of verse. It could even be used to show comparable rhythmical organization in prose. That is, stops could be used to help display various formal elements of structure in literary writing, just as they might indicate the contours and hiatuses or the stresses of spoken language in the theatre. The metrical and elocutionary aspects may thus be thought of as the twin faces of Elizabethan punctuation. However, the scholars cited above did not stress the metrical element in Elizabethan punctuation or deprecated its significance.[4]

Later scholars have put the stylistically limiting dates earlier than Simpson did. They thought that English punctuation had largely changed its character by 1616, and they found that the earlier, dramatic style of pointing was more fully illustrated in the 'good' Shakespeare Quartos or in the Sonnets than in the First Folio, which they believed to contain a modified system of punctuation, partly still elocutionary, but partly revised into a more grammatical form.

Relatively late in date though *Paradise Lost* is, its punctuation appears to be substantially in the early poetical tradition.

Or it might be truer to say that Milton with his usual sophistication appears to have succeeded in fusing elements of both the
earlier and later styles. Certainly he succeeded in adapting the
old metrical-elocutionary system to the peculiar needs of his
heroic blank verse; and he assimilated the older style with no
sign of its former clumsiness.

Probably Milton's punctuation from his earliest writing had
retained some affinities with the Elizabethan system. Probably,
too, this metrical-elocutionary system remained in at least
partial (but accredited) use for longer than some of the scholars
earlier cited have indicated. It will for example be seen in the
1623 Shakespeare Folio that, despite certain grammatical modi-
fications of the punctuation, there is a more deliberately metrical
and oratorical use of stops than in some of the earlier Quartos.
Again, the rhythmical and elocutionary theories of punctuation
seem to have received their most complete theoretical formula-
tion as late as 1640, in the grammar of Simon Daines.

It would appear, further, that a similar relation exists,
vis-à-vis the Manuscript of *Paradise Lost*, Book I, and the first
edition of that poem, to that which is thought to have existed
between the Shakespeare Quartos and the collected Folio of
1623. The punctuation in the earlier text of Milton's poem
is dramatically and rhythmically founded, but in the later
text it seems to have been partly modified and made a little
more grammatical, according to the newer, prevailingly logical system. The earlier rhythmically and rhetorically founded
punctuation of the poem was not obliterated, but it was partly
overlaid. And just as Simpson found that the earlier, expressive
Elizabethan style of pointing gave a clue to many apparent
anomalies in the First Folio edition of Shakespeare's plays or
in the 1609 edition of the Sonnets, so, it is hoped, those rhythmical and dramatic habits of pointing into which Milton's
Manuscript gives an insight will be found to explain many
seeming eccentricities of pointing throughout the twelve printed
books of *Paradise Lost* – such unorthodox punctuation as, one
might surmise, had often been retained intact from the original
copy and had not been subjected to a smoothing down process
at the press.

The change in English punctuation from its early largely
rhythmical to its later more purely logical orientation took

place more fitfully, in some cases, and the two different styles remained mingled in use for longer than scholars have sometimes thought. Nevertheless, the general course of the change may be clearly traced in the seventeenth century – in prose even more clearly than in verse. Verse punctuation is of first interest because of its relevance to *Paradise Lost*; but prose punctuation of the period also has an unexpected relevance to *Paradise Lost*, since the organization of Milton's blank verse is in many ways modelled on prose rather than verse forms.

2. *Verse Punctuation*

In speaking of rhythmical punctuation in Elizabethan poetry, Simpson seems to have thought rather incidentally of a metrical punctuation: that is, the frank marking of the caesura or the line ending by a stop. However, such a metrical stressing of the main pauses of the verse by means of pointing was very usual in Elizabethan verse. Portions of Sir John Harington's[5] translation of the *Orlando Furioso* (1591), a work carefully punctuated by its author, still exist in an autograph manuscript copy which had passed through the printer's hands. The following excerpt shows how consistently the author marked the metrical pauses (especially the caesura) by punctuation, and the printed version, given afterwards, also shows that the printer sometimes followed this metrical punctuation closely, in this passage once adding and once leaving out a caesural mark. However, he usually dropped Harington's significantly structural practice of marking the middle line of the stanza with a colon. The printer's care in respect of the metrical punctuation is more to be remarked since, as Simpson showed in his book on English proofreading, where he reprinted the passages here quoted, Harington's printer freely revised the author's spelling and was less conscientious in some ways about his author's punctuation than were other printers of the period.

> others report, som saynt did him that grace:
> to save his lyfe, and heale each broken lim,
> and to the shore, to bring him in short space.
> the lykelyhood heerof, who lyst may way,
> for now of him I have no more to say.

Others report, some saint did him that grace,
To save his life, and heale each broken lim,
And to the shore did bring him in short space.
The likelyhood hereof, who list may way,
For now of him, I have no more to say.

Simpson might have stressed this matter of metrical punctuation in Elizabethan writing more than he did, since his discussion was so largely directed to poetry (dramatic or lyric),
where metrical considerations would be expected to predominate. A metrical orientation in the pointing does in fact account
for certain seeming inconsistencies between examples which he
cites: why, for example, only one rather than two commas
should sometimes be used to define a phrase (see *Shakespearian
Punctuation*, sections 19–21); or why defining commas are shown
first as omitted at the ends of short phrases and next at the
beginnings (see the examples in section 19 as compared with
those in section 10). What seems to be happening in such
instances is that stops are being inserted or left out for metrical
reasons. The intentions seem to be as follows: to stress the
caesura or the end of the line (but more especially the caesura);
to preserve fluency, that is, not to allow two or three even of
metrical stops to fall in close conjunction within two consecutive
lines; and as a last consideration to follow minor proprieties
of sense.

Shakespeare's sonnets as punctuated in the 1609 edition and
some of the Quarto and First Folio texts of the plays[6] offer
interesting comparisons with Harington's punctuation. The
sonnets show a more flexible use of metrical punctuation and
a more sophisticated adapting of the pointing to the total
pattern of each poem. The strongly caesural pointing employed
in the *Orlando Furioso* is capable of creating (if end-stopped
lines are correspondingly reduced in number) a strong forward
movement which is suited to a long poem; for example, this is
the pattern of pointing adopted in *Paradise Lost* and in Milton's
late sonnets, which are constructed rhythmically as if they
were brief portions out of some long poem. On the other hand,
the 1609 sonnets are treated distinctly as brief lyrics. The lines
are predominantly end-stopped, with pauses often purely
metrical, and midline punctuation is used more sparingly to
give variations in rhythm and feeling. But it frequently happens

that one or both lines of the concluding couplet are also pointed at the caesura, thus creating a slower, more deliberate and suitably final effect. The following sonnets are not untypical:

33

Full many a glorious morning have I seene,
Flatter the mountaine tops with soveraine eie,
Kissing with golden face the meddowes greene;
Guilding pale streames with heavenly alcumy:
Anon permit the basest cloudes to ride,
With ougly rack on his celestiall face,
And from the for-lorne world his visage hide
Stealing un[s]eene to west with this d[i]sgrace:
Even so my Sunne one early morne did shine,
With all triumphant splendor on my brow,
But out alack, he was but one houre mine,
The region cloude hath mask'd him from me now.
   Yet him for this, my love no whit disdaineth,
   Suns of the world may staine, whẽ heavens sun staineth.

54

Oh how much more doth beautie beautious seeme,
By that sweet ornament which truth doth give,
The Rose lookes faire, but fairer we it deeme
For that sweet odor, which doth in it live:
The Canker bloomes have full as deepe a die,
As the perfumed tincture of the Roses,
Hang on such thornes, and play as wantonly,
When sommers breath their masked buds discloses:
But for their virtue only is their show,
They live unwoo'd, and unrespected fade,
Die to themselves. Sweet Roses doe not so,
Of their sweet deathes, are sweetest odors made:
   And so of you, beautious and lovely youth,
   When that shall vade [sic], by verse distils your truth.

Not only the use of commas, but also the heavy punctuation, is of great interest. The sonnet is in each case treated as a rhetorical whole – there are no full stops until the end, or at any rate not until the closing couplet. (The full stop in the middle of line 11, Sonnet 54, is a dramatic exception.) Semicolons occasionally show smaller balances, as in Sonnet 33, line 3.

Colons mark the stanzas; heavy stops distinguish sestet from octet, as in 35. Two or three of such heavy stops, skilfully deployed, link the parts of the thought into one sustained argument, throwing the three quatrains and final couplet or the octet and sestet into close relation; cast a larger pattern of syntactical symmetries over the whole sonnet; and at the same time display the sonnet structure itself.

The 1623 Folio likewise tends to emphasize oratorical symmetry by substituting colons for some full stops. This we may note by comparing the two last speeches of the Duchess of Gloucester, *Richard II*, I, 2, in the Folio edition with the same speeches in the earlier 1598 Quarto. The printers also added too many commas at the caesuras, with some consequent loss of rhythmical flexibility in the lines.

By "rhythmical" punctuation in the Elizabethans, Simpson seems to have meant something much more like a rhetorical than a truly metrical or structural punctuation. He implied a pointing which emulates the rhythms of speech: some free means of phrasing the verse so that it flows easily, moulding itself to the actor's or reciter's voice. As he said, the earlier mode was a "flexible system" which enabled the poet "to express subtle differences of tone". He showed that the Elizabethan poet might hold back a comma (or any stop), or omit one, or insert one unexpectedly, in order to suggest a particular speech inflection and so bring out some subtle shade of meaning. The poet might for similar reasons sometimes use emphasizing stops heavier than grammar or the general pattern of pointing in the context seems to require; or at other times he might use stops lighter than expected – the weight of such expressive stops being determined by contrast (they are heavy or light in relation to the other stops around them).

Shakespeare's sonnets, as Simpson abundantly showed, or Donne's poems are full of beautiful and expressive pointings contrived along the lines just indicated. "Corona" and the "Holy Sonnets" offer many examples of how much meaning can be conveyed by pointing alone, through its rendering of speech accents, intonations or breaks in speech. H. J. C. Grierson and Evelyn Simpson have shown that the punctuation in at least some of Donne's manuscripts is authentic,[7] and both believed that this original punctuation was rhythmical and rhetorical in basis and of significant poetical value. Mrs Simpson suggested that Donne's punctuation was always carefully expressive and delicate, but was sometimes misunderstood or crudely altered by his copyists and printers.

It is of great interest to find, at still later dates, techniques of punctuation in *Comus* and in *Paradise Lost* similar to those in Donne or Shakespeare. And it is noteworthy that in Milton's poems, as in Elizabethan verse, a dramatically expressive punctuation is the natural accompaniment of a prevailingly rhythmical punctuation – a flexible and fluent pointing more easily admitting occasional sharp rhetorical variations than would a more fixed, grammatical system encumbered by a large number of logically differentiating stops.

Examples of dramatic or elocutionary pointing in Elizabethan verse need not be given here, since Simpson and others have covered that ground. But it is worth pausing on the passage Simpson took from *Comus* to illustrate the Elizabethan practice of stopping lightly "for rapid or excited speech". Simpson quoted from the 1637 edition, but it is more instructive to follow the history of the punctuation in the passage from its earliest version, written in Milton's hand in what is now the Trinity Manuscript, to its last appearance during the author's life in the 1673 edition of the minor *Poems*:[8]

2 Bro. heav'n keepe my sister. *yet* agen, agen & neere.
1 Bro. best draw, & stand upon our guard [.] 1 Bro. Ile hallow
if he be freindly he comes well, if not *a just Defence is a* . . .
defence is a good cause & heav'n be for us,
(Trinity MS, ll. 55–8, p. 17)

2 bro heav'n keepe my sister: agen, agen, & neere
best drawe; & stand upon our guard, *El: bro.* Ile hallowe
if he be freindly he comes well, if not
defence is a good Cause, and heav'n be for us
(Bridgewater MS, ll. 473–6)

2 Bro. Heav'n keepe my sister, agen agen and neere,
Best draw, and stand upon our guard.
Eld: bro. Ile hallow,
If he be friendly he comes well, if not
Defence is a good cause, and Heav'n be for us.
(1637, ll. 486–9)

> *2 Bro.* Heav'n keep my sister, agen agen and neer,
> Best draw, and stand upon our guard.
>   *Eld. Bro.* Ile hallow,
> If he be friendly he comes well, if not,
> Defence is a good cause, and Heav'n be for us.
>   (1645, ll. 486–9)

> *2. Bro.* Heav'n keep my sister, agen, agen, and neer,
> Best draw, and stand upon our guard.
>   *Eld. Bro.* Ile hallow,
> If he be friendly he comes well, if not,
> Defence is a good cause, and Heav'n be for us.
>   (1673, ll. 485–8)

As Milton first wrote the passage, the punctuation is very dramatic, at least as much so as in the opening line of the version Simpson quotes. Milton uses both a rhetorically heavy or emphasizing stopping (in the full stop after *neer*.) and a rhetorically light or hasty stopping (in the omission in the same line of the comma after the second *agen* and omission of full stops or comma at the ends of the next three lines, as well as in the middle of the last line). W. A. Wright transcribes a full stop after *guard* but in the smudged state of the line it is difficult to tell whether there is any stop at that point or not.

The scribal Bridgewater Manuscript stays fairly close to Milton's pointing, but spoils the alarmed effect of the first line and a half by adding a grammatically correct comma after the second *agen,* . . . . In the 1637 version the pointing of the first line and a half only, is again dramatic though lighter. It suggests a somewhat different delivery for the actor, less startled, more hasty or excited. But the addition of the two end stops in the second and fourth lines has begun to damp down the total effect of excitement in the passage. Following this cue, the 1645 edition adds another pause, here at the end of the third line; and the 1673 edition completes the damage by adding a last, dragging comma after the second *agen,* of the first line.

As each version adds or alters pauses to improve the grammar the dramatic impact of the original punctuation diminishes, until by 1673 there is very little of it left. The process affords a miniature history of the development of English punctuation during the course of the seventeenth century, away from an expressive style towards a flatter, correct usage. And yet 1673 is still not entirely grammatical in its punctuation; it 'lacks' several heavy stops. How the lines would read, rewritten with a fully logical modern or late seventeenth-century punctuation, may be left to the reader's imagination. At any rate, Milton's verse in its original version or Donne's verse suggests that some writers long resisted the new logical emphasis in punctuation, with its deadening stylistic influence.

3. *Prose Punctuation, and Punctuation Theory*

The theatrical blank verse or prose of the Elizabethans and the conversationally styled sonnets of Shakespeare or poems of Donne might understandably take as one of their aims the imitation, through rhythms and stresses conveyed partly by the punctuation, of the natural pauses and inflections of speech. But non-theatrical verse of the Elizabethan period also has a strong rhythmical foundation in punctuation (in the adaptation of pointing to metrical structure or other poetical effects). Non-theatrical prose of the period before about 1620 similarly often shows a predominantly rhythmical punctuation. In formal written prose of this earlier period it is usually a different kind of rhythm that we find conveyed through pointing; instead of the rhythms of speech or of metre, we find those of oratorical symmetry.

Especially in any prose with a Euphuistic tendency, the punctuation often seems intended mainly to throw into relief all possible parallelism, antithesis or balance in the construction – even to the extent sometimes of creating false balances and antitheses. The creation of such symmetry is itself a rhythmical matter, the oratorical 'period' being partly or often mainly a rhythmically conceived unit which aims to arrange the parts or 'members' symmetrically around a central member in a 'round' design. This design is ideally both complete or internally connected in thought and rhythmically ample: full, finished and pleasing to the ear. A rhythmical period of this kind may well embrace several grammatical sentences and have no full stop before the end. Its pointing often therefore will not bear grammatical analysis. The punctuation cannot exhibit the

relative importance of all the parts in the grammatical construction of the sentence (since the total construction is not primarily
grammatical); nor is it intended to show all the logical interdependencies between the various parts. The pointing mainly
serves to highlight the shape of each member in the larger
oratorical design of the period. The punctuation of this early
prose also sometimes seems to be rhythmical merely in the
sense of breaking the prose into shorter portions of roughly
equal length, or cadencing it evenly so as to provide a regular beat for the ear. This might be said to constitute a
rough equivalence of marking the line or the half-line in
verse.

Nash's prose, in an edition of 1592, is strongly marked by
both such rhythmical elements in punctuation, as the passage
below well illustrates:[9]

> Having spent many yeeres in studying how to live, and liv'de a
> long time without mony: having tired my youth with follie, and
> surfetted my minde with vanitie, I began at length to looke backe
> to repentaunce, & addresse my endevors to prosperitie: But all in
> vaine, I sate up late, and rose eraely [*sic*], contended with the
> colde, and conversed with scarcitie: for all my labours turned to
> losse, my vulgar Muse was despised & neglected, my paines not
> regarded or slightly rewarded, and I my selfe (in prime of my
> best wit) laid open to povertie.

The above passage uses colon freely (and without grammatical
discrimination), alternating this stop with comma so as to bring
out larger and lesser parallels and antitheses in structure. The
priority which Nash gives to rhythm is evident in the way he
will overrun the normal ending of a sentence or break up a
compound which ought to form a natural grammatical unit in
order to bring out some further balance, as for example in:
" . . . to prosperitie: But all in vaine, I sate up late, and rose
eraely . . .: for all my . . .". In the pursuit of such cadences
and symmetries, our sense of the sentence becomes submerged.
The prose unrolls in an ampler stream comparable to that of
blank verse. Like blank verse, it moves with a larger ebb and
flow than that of the sentence, and has its formal patternings
overlying a simple rhythmical groundbeat.

Donne's early prose, in a manuscript of the *Biathanatos*,[10] described and in part reprinted by Evelyn Simpson and dated by her as of around 1612, also shows a strongly rhythmical punctuation. This manuscript was annotated and authorized by Donne, and Mrs Simpson has demonstrated that it was carefully punctuated by the author himself. The printer of 1647 followed Donne's punctuation on the whole with care (although he inserted a few semicolons, as the usage of that date would lead us to expect). Donne's punctuation does not show the elaborate oratorical symmetries of Nash's; for example, colon hardly occurs, whereas Nash or his printer used this stop copiously to mark antithesis or balance. Donne instead relies in a more individual way almost entirely on commas to build a regularly cadenced prose, to supply appropriate speech stresses ("... y^t dore worst lockd against him, in mee, ..."), and even to bring out some balance ("... in the glory, and noone of Learning, as others were in the dawning, & morning, ..."). The passage which follows is illustrative; the brief second sentence affords a beautiful contrast to the mellifluousness of the rest.

Beza, A man as eminent and illustrous, in the glory, and noone of Learning, as others were in the dawning, & morning, when any, the least sparkle was notorious, confesseth of himselfe, that onely for the anguish of a skurfe, wch over ran his head, he had once drownd himselfe, from the Millers bridge in Paris, if his Uncle, by chance, had not then come that way. I have often such a sickly inclination. And, whether it bee, because I had my first breeding, and conversation wth men of a suppressd and afflicted Religion, accustomed to the despite of death, and hungry of an imagin'd Martyrdome, or that the common Enemy find y^t dore worst lockd against him, in mee, Or that there be a perplexity, and flexibility in the doctrine it selfe, or because my Conscyence ever assures me, that no rebellious grudging at Gods guifts, nor other sin-full concurrence accompanies these thoughts in me, Or that a brave scorne, or that a faint cowardlynesse beget it, whensoever my affliction assayles me, me thinks I have the keyes of my prison in myne owne hand, and no remedy presents it selfe so soone to my heart, as mine owne sword. Often Meditation of this, hath wonne me to a charitable interpretacion of theyr Action, who dye so: and provok'd me alitle to watch, & exagitate theyr reasons, wch pronounce so peremptory iudgements uppon y^{em}.

There is nothing in the very brief discussion of punctuation
in the earliest notable Elizabethan grammar, Richard Mulcaster's *Elementarie* (1582),[11] to counteract one's impression
that for that period punctuation was largely a rhythmical or
oratorical matter. Mulcaster's chapter "Of Distinction" opens
by defining punctuation as a means of "tunable uttering" – an
aid to breathing or measuring out the sentence (as in music).
The style of his own writing confirms such an emphasis; like
Donne, Mulcaster relies almost entirely on commas, a certain
sign of a cadenced prose:

> This title of *distinction* reacheth verie far, bycause it conteineth
> all those characts, and their uses, which I called before signifying,
> but not sounding, which help verie much, naie all in all to the right
> and tunable uttering of our words and sentences . . . . *Coma*, is a
> small crooked point, which in writing followeth som small branch
> of the sentence, & in reading warneth us to rest there, and to help
> our breth a litle, as *Who so shall spare the rod, shall spill the childe.*
> *Colon* is noted by two round points one above another, which in
> writing followeth som full branch, or half the sentence, as *Tho
> the daie be long: yet at the last commeth evensong. Period* is a small
> round point, which in writing followeth a perfit sentence, and in
> reading warneth us to rest there, and to help our breth at full,
> as *The fear of God is the beginning of wisdom.*

Mulcaster's description of the functions of the stops is grammatically very vague. A logical distinction is indeed found in
the description of period as a mark concluding "a perfit sentence". Another could be implicit in the description of comma
as a mark following "som small branch of the sentence,"
whereas colon is a mark which follows "som full branch, or
half the sentence". However, Mulcaster relates this distinction
not to syntactical categories but more to length. Nor do his
examples make the implied difference of use between the two
marks at all clear. Why is the noun clause (given comma),
"Who so shall spare the rod", a lesser "branch" than the
adverbial clause (dignified by colon), "Tho the daie be long"?
The illustration which Mulcaster chooses for colon suggests that
its real function, in his mind, was to mark antithesis, while his
example and own use of comma seem to relate the stop mainly
to breathing. The references to length of member also suggest
the breathing function of comma.

The rhythmical application of punctuation, only hinted at by Mulcaster, must have been a commonplace in Renaissance practice and theory. Puttenham[12] is specific about the metrical function of punctuation in verse and implies a partial analogous function for pointing in prose. The main use of the comma in verse is to mark the midline (although he says that comma may also *sometimes* be used to show the sense, especially in a short line without caesura). Puttenham uses the actual terms, *Comma* and *Cesure*, interchangeably: "our Poet when he hath made one verse, hath as it were finished one dayes journey, & the while easeth him selfe with one baite at the least, which is a *Comma* or *Cesure*, in the mid way . . . ". The 1623 Shakespeare Folio amply illustrates such purely metrical use of the comma at both the midline and end of the line. Puttenham does not actually say that heavier stops than the comma may also be used to mark verse structure, but his scheme leaves such a possibility open. For example, in Harington's verse (see above) colon is used to mark the middle point of each stanza. Heavy stops can be used in similar ways to mark other rhythmical units larger than the half-line. For instance, George Wither, discussed later, evidently uses semicolon or colon (not always grammatically) to close many of his couplets, while the 1609 Shakespeare Sonnets, like some of Milton's, use full stop or other heavy stops (often, ungrammatically) to mark the stanzas.

In prose punctuation, Puttenham continues, the sense must be a greater consideration. The ancients invented the three pauses (comma, colon, period) "for a treble distinction of sentences or parts of speach, as they happened to be more or lesse perfect in sence." However, the pauses are *in addition* used for "easment to the breath" and "for a commodious" as well as "sensible distinction of clauses in prose . . . ". He continues: " . . . since every verse is as it were a clause of it selfe, and limited with a *Cesure* howsoever the sence beare, perfect or imperfect . . . ". Puttenham here clearly relates prose punctuation to breathing (hence rhythm) and to 'commodious' (easy, agreeable) delivery as well as to 'sensible' (intelligible) division of clauses. It must follow that, since verse punctuation is to meet both the sense and metre in Puttenham's scheme, prose punctuation similarly should have a dual, logical and rhythmical function. His slightly obscure comparison of verses to clauses also implies this; commas in prose play the part filled by caesura (the metrical pause) in verse lines.

The grammarian Charles Butler half a century later was to differentiate much more logically between the marks of punctuation than had Mulcaster or Puttenham, by showing comma for qualifying phrases, semicolon with most subordinate clauses, and colon for independent clauses. Mulcaster (like Puttenham) does not mention semicolon; around 1580–90 that stop must have been seldom employed. (Even much later some grammarians, for instance James Howell, still did not admit the mark, while others like Simon Daines merely adopted the stop into the older time-value system.[13]) Yet without semicolon a full differentiation of logical function between the parts of the sentence is scarcely possible. Jonson and Butler both knew this and consequently later stressed its use. Simpson[14] has described the history of the stop:

> The semicolon is not recognized by Mulcaster and Hart; according to Ames [*Typographical Antiquities*], it was introduced into England in 1569, but began to be used about 1580. When once it came into regular use, it brought a new element into punctuation. . . . The semicolon, bringing in a finer grading of the stops, started the logical system in use at the present day.

More lately A. Baugh[15] has said that:

> Refinements in the use of subordinate clauses are a mark of maturity in style . . . the loose association of clauses (parataxis) gives way [that is, as language develops] to more precise indications of logical relationship and subordination (hypotaxis). . . .

Hypotaxis in construction depends on the help of semicolon as a more finely distinguishing stop. For a period after it was first introduced, of course, writers tended to use the semicolon interchangeably with the old metrical-rhetorical colon.

The most complete exposition of the rhythmical-elocutionary system of punctuation appears to be that given, almost fifty years after Mulcaster's and Puttenham's accounts, in the work of Simon Daines.[16] Daines' analysis is of particular interest. Since it is not readily available in print, a long portion of it is reproduced opposite.

... the knowledge of these stops or points is no lesse conducible,
... to distinct and ready reading (the perfection of Orthoepie)
than to Orthographie, or right writing: . . . .

The *Comma* . . . The use onely in long sentences, in the most convenient places to make a small pause for the necessity of breathing;
or in Rhetoricall speeches (where many words are used to
one effect) to make a kinde of Emphasis and deliberation for the
greater majesty or state of Elocution.

The *Comma-colon*, . . . to the Ancients was not knowne; but now
in no lesse use than estimation, especially among Rhetoricians. Who
in their long winded sentences, and reduplications, have it as a
constant pack-horse, to make some short deliberation as it were of
little sentences, as the *Comma* doth of words; the time of pause
about double that of the *Comma* generally, which yet is very
small.

The *Colon* . . . is chiefly used in the division of sentences, and
exacts halfe the pause of a *Period*; and halfe as much againe as a
Comma-Colon.

The *Period* . . . is altogether used at the end of every speech or
sentence, . . . and signifies *conclusion*. The pause or distance of
speaking hereto appropriate is sometime more, sometime lesse:
for . . . when in the middle of a line it cuts off any integrall part of
a complete Tractate, which goes not on with the same, but begins
a new line, it requireth double the time of pause, that it doth when
the Treatise persists in the same line: being then foure times as
long as a *Colon*, which in the same line is but twice.

I remember my singing-Master taught me to keep time, by
telling from 1, to 4, ... The same course I have used to my pupils
in their reading, to inure them to the distinction of their pauses, ...

[Example follows:] 'Travellers, Merchants, Historiographers,
report, assure, relate, partly what themselves have seen; partly
what approved in their wofull companions, left to be entombed in
the bellies of those monsters: while they themselves with much
adoe escaped, onely to be the dolefull narratours of so sad a
story.'

Almost every feature of the rhythmical-elocutionary system
of punctuation is stressed in the above account. First, as to
rhythmical features. The title itself of Daines' work relates
punctuation to oral and oratorical considerations rather than
to those of prose written for the eye – to *Orthoepie* or *ready reading* as distinct from *Orthographie* or *right writing*. The stops form
a complete time scale lengthening out from one (comma), two

(semicolon), three (colon), to six (period) or in some cases twelve (period at the end of a paragraph). The musical count of four prescribed by Daines' singing master does not in fact fit his pupil's scheme, or does so only if semicolon is left out and colon given the count of two instead. No doubt this defect indicates Daines' uncertainty as to how to deal with the new stop: whether to take it as a logical value only, or whether to force it into the older time scheme. Daines' time system must be presumed to relate to emphasis in reading or to structure in a broad oratorical sense; his system is too vaguely defined logically to be related with any precision to grammatical structure.

Considering the stops separately, we see that comma is specifically cited as for use "in the most convenient places" for "necessity of breathing", and *only* in "long sentences"; these instructions cannot be interpreted grammatically and evidently relate to periodic rhythm. Similarly a rhythmical value is imputed to semicolon, which is said to be of use in showing the larger aspects of oratorical organization, in particular balances (*reduplications*) in the "long winded" sentences of the "Rhetoricians". In Daines' illustration, further, colon neatly divides a very long sentence into two antithetical parts, while semicolon marks a smaller balance.

Thus Daines establishes a full rhythmical basis for punctuation in prose, in complement to Puttenham's views concerning metrical punctuation in verse. Punctuation used as a scale of values in time, partly divorced from or only very loosely connected with sense, and used also as a breathing device in long sentences and to mark oratorical balances, can hardly fail to have a profound connection with periodic rhythm. Prose rhythm depends chiefly on two factors: on a regular phrasing or breathing of the sentence and on syntactical symmetries of various kinds. In Daines' view punctuation can provide or help to accentuate both of these features. Pointing can create regular musical intervals or help to mark broader patterns in prose, in just the same way as it can be used to mark the half-line and the line or to indicate larger rhythmical units (stanzaic, for instance) in verse.

Now as to the elocutionary aspects of Daines' account. He specifies that both comma and semicolon may in addition be used for particular stresses in delivery of "Rhetoricall speeches".

Comma is suitable for "Emphasis and deliberation" where "many words are used to one effect", semicolon for "some short deliberation as it were of little sentences, as the *Comma* . . . of words". Daines' definition of colon, said chiefly to pertain to sentence division, may imply a logical function for the stop; but a rhetorical function is not precluded, for he may also be thinking of the sentence as a rhetorical entity, with an antithetical or at least symmetrical balance of parts. Lastly (this is Daines' most interesting idea), the period is really two distinct stops under one symbol. One – the shorter – pause is a logical value to show the conclusion of a "sentence"; the other, double in length, marks a paragraph or, as Daines even more broadly puts it, "any integrall part of a complete Tractate". A paragraph or some other portion of a tract may comprise a complete section of thought or argument, but the terms of definition are too large and vague for such a unit to be called grammatical. Such a unit is an oratorical entity, and full stop used to delimit it is a rhetorical mark. Daines thus articulates the rhetorical possibilities of even the logically best defined stop.

Illustrating Daines' views, we shall find various rhetorical uses of full stop in *Paradise Lost*. It is there used occasionally as a stress mark; at the end of the long verse period; and (combining these two functions) to set out the epic simile distinctively. But perhaps the most characteristic rhetorical use of the full stop in *Paradise Lost* is to conclude the long verse period. The mark is used in an exactly analogous way to terminate the lengthy periods of many sixteenth and seventeenth-century prose writers. In their oratorical structures, which like Milton's vastly overflow the grammatical 'sentence', many sentence units are to be found loosely associated. These are linked occasionally by full stops which have not quite the full logical or pause value (this being sometimes indicated by no capital letter following). Or more frequently they are linked by colons which are almost equivalent to the modern full stop and have rather more than the customary value of colon in both logic and emphasis (this being sometimes indicated by a capital letter following, as in Browne, page 33, or Milton, page 115, below). Such punctuation in these prose or in Milton's verse periods seems intended to stress the near independence of each main component, without indicating any complete discontinuity either in thought or delivery until the concluding full stop.

4. *The Continuance of the Elizabethan Style*

A strongly rhythmical punctuation and syntactical construction persists well into the seventeenth century in certain writers of ornate or baroque prose such as the later Donne, Browne and Milton himself. The period 1640–1662 represents a low point in English publishing, as regards both quantity of literary works and printed quality, especially of political writings. Much of Milton's prose was written during this time. The dubious printing of many of his political tracts thus raises problems concerning his punctuation which make brief analysis difficult. However, we may glance at some of the better printed prose, including that of 1641–9 (published by Matthew Simmons, among others).[17]

The polemical opening pages of *Of Reformation Touching Church-Discipline* (1641) suggest a rhythmical punctuation, with colons used to mark large balancing parts (quite independently of grammatical constructions) and commas used regularly to mould and cadence the prose. The prolonged, digressive and quite extraordinary periods here are such that any more logical punctuation would break down, applied to their constructions. On the other hand, the style of the opening pages of *The Reason of Church-governement* . . . (1641) and *The Doctrine and Discipline of Divorce* (1643) is plainer, and in some ways the punctuation seems more grammatical, with mid-century logical usages more consistently in evidence. We need not now attempt to distinguish exactly which elements in the punctuation may be Milton's in texts which in minor matters such as punctuation may well include both author's and printer's uses. Yet one may still carry away a general impression that the pointing in Milton's printed prose is often related to the larger aspects of periodic structure and rhythm.

Details may confirm such an impression. In *The History of Britain* (1670), a fine edition printed by James Allestry, we note that one of two defining commas in a compound is frequently omitted, with the effect that a more rounded phrasing is given to the sentence. (The light, rhythmical punctuation of

Paradise Lost is comparable.) Specific rhetorical usages of kinds characteristic of *Paradise Lost* are scattered throughout the prose works. *The Judgement of Martin Bucer* (1644), *Eikono-klastes* (1649) and *The Tenure of Kings and Magistrates* (1649), all thought by Helen Darbishire to be of particular value in showing Milton's individual spelling, show such characteristic punctuation usages as colon to mark antithesis (*M. Bucer*); emphasizing semicolon and withholding of a comma for rapid or indignant delivery (*Tenure*); possibly rhetorical full stop (*ibid.*); and also emphasizing semicolon to introduce a comparison (*Eik.*) The *Commonplace Book* jottings, many in Milton's hand, show most of the rhetorical or rhythmical usages just named and others, plus generally a very light pointing, interspersed with an occasional exceptionally heavy pointing for stress. (In this combination the style of the *Commonplace Book* is rather like that of the Manuscript, Book I.) To take scattered instances from the *Commonplace Book*, we find rhetorical full stop to introduce speech, or again to introduce comparison or example; and withholding of one of two defining commas in a compound to give a more fluent phrasing. All these Miltonic usages appear somewhat less consistently in the prose than in *Paradise Lost*, but as in the case of the early manuscript poems, the style is evident if we know how to recognize it.

Browne's prose, as punctuated in the first authorized edition of *Religio Medici*, 1643,[18] betrays a constant, rhythmical stressing of both major and minor balances and contrasts which is not unlike Milton's:

> For my Religion, though there be severall circumstances that might perswade the world I have none at all, as the generall scandall of my profession, the naturall course of my studies, the indifferency of my behaviour, and discourse in matters of Religion, neither violently defending one, nor with the common ardour of contention opposing another; yet in despight hereof I dare, without usurpation, assume the honourable stile of a Christian: not that I meerely owe this title to the Font, my education, or Clime wherein I was borne, as being bred up either to confirme those principles my Parents instilled into my unwary understanding; or by a generall consent proceed in the Religion of my Countrey: But having in my riper yeares, and confirmed judgement, seene and examined all, I finde my selfe obliged by the principles of Grace,

and the law of mine owne reason, to embrace no other name but
this; neither doth herein my zeale so farre make me forget the
generall charitie I owe unto humanity, as rather to hate then pity
Turkes, Infidels, and (what is worse) Jewes, rather contenting my
selfe to enjoy that happy stile, then maligning those who refuse
so glorious a title.

Browne, like Nash, breaks up a compound where we would
not punctuate, in order to exaggerate the effect of parallel
structure: "the indifferency of my behaviour, and discourse in
matters of Religion, . . ."; ": But having in my riper yeares,
and confirmed judgement, seene and examined all, . . .". He
also sometimes obscures the normal division between sentences
in order better to bring out the shape of an antithesis: " . . . of
a Christian: not that I meerely owe this title to the Font, . . .
: But having in my riper yeares, . . .". The shape of the sentence
tends to disappear in Browne's prose. Our attention is fixed
upon a different structure: the elaborate, unfolding patterns
of his mounting rhythms.

The use of colon in the above passage to introduce antithesis
is standard Elizabethan practice and is one of the oratorical
usages in pointing which survives longest in the seventeenth
century. (Colon is similarly long used to introduce comparison.)
These practices are found in Milton, who in addition retains
specifically metrical and rhetorical elements in pointing which
did not so commonly survive the Elizabethan period. There are
other still more basic resemblances in syntax and punctuation
between Browne and Milton. Tillyard[19] expressed a commonly
felt opinion, but one which has rarely been analysed, when he
noted that the syntactical structures of the blank verse of
Paradise Lost, in their loose, paratactic and strongly rhythmical
character, seem to be closely connected with the poetic prose
of the seventeenth century. The use of main stops in Browne's
prose to link the successive thoughts into a coherent but supra-
grammatical pattern, enhanced by rhythmical symmetries
which the parallel pointings partly serve to accentuate, has
essentially to do with periodic structure. Similar structures of
speech with associated pointings will be found in *Paradise Lost*.

III

Mid-Seventeenth-Century Punctuation

1. *The Transition of Styles:* 1610–1620

A predominantly rhythmical punctuation is not characteristic of all seventeenth-century writing. One has a distinct impression that in much formal written prose of the earlier part of the century – and certainly of Milton's period – the punctuation used was much less dramatically or rhythmically flexible and expressive, and much more logical or grammatical, than that which Simpson described or which has been illustrated in Nash and Browne. There was distinctly another style of punctuation coming into use toward the end of the first quarter of the century, in which the needs to outline the grammatical construction and stress the sentence as the basic component in writing, to show the relationship of each of the sentence parts to the whole and also show the connections in meaning between the various parts, partially replace the earlier felt needs to show rhythmical structure or give rhetorical emphasis or to accentuate oratorical design. The 1609 Sonnets or, in part, the 1623 Folio of Shakespeare stand as late illustrations of the rhythmical and dramatic style of pointing of the Elizabethans. At almost the same time or just a few years later, grammars, formal prose and sometimes verse show the full development of the more logical system.

Of course the change takes place gradually and is reflected in varying degrees in different authors. Some writers show evidence of both styles together, and some use either one at different times. Even as early as in the 1611 Authorized Version of the King James Bible,[1] the punctuation is in parts probably grammatical as well as rhythmical. (Elizabethan punctuation undoubtedly had a certain grammatical element, although not as systematic nor identical in all respects with the highly logical and formalized pointing of the mid-seventeenth century.) Thus in the prose dedication of the translators commas outline phrases and clauses and show the contours of the sentence, although there is not much differentiation of punctuation according to the grammatical importance of the member. A rhythmical effect is imparted by the recurring light punctuation after the longer subordinate parts: commas (not too many) evenly spaced out so as to make for fluent reading. To some extent these stops are simultaneously showing grammatical structure. Symmetry is seldom striven for through the breaking up of compounds or other natural units of grammatical construction. Semicolon is used to mark introductory but not other dependent clauses; this is as much an oratorical practice as a grammatical one, showing that we have arrived at the main verb and climactic member of the period. The heavier stops, semicolon and more especially colon, are present usually to indicate antithesis, but there also seems to be some attempt to correlate their use with the grammatical importance of the member. More simply, colon introduces antithesis between main members, semicolon between lesser ones. These various points are illustrated in the quotation from the dedication, which is the second passage given.

The prose of the text itself (quoted first) is much simpler and the pointing more definitely rhythmical. Colons and commas predominate. Comma is used for rhythmical breathing and (as Donne uses it) for rhetorical stresses. Colon is abundant and used with strongly rhythmical effect to divide sentences and show balance. This kind of punctuation is to be related not merely to the early poetical tradition but also to an older, musical ('colometric') tradition of punctuation, copied by Milton too when he is echoing the 1611 Bible (see chapter VII, 1). In these parts the translators are consciously emulating Hebrew syntax and constructions. The style and pointing of their own prose is more typical of the more modern aspects of their period.

1. In the beginning God created the Heaven, and the Earth.
2. And the earth was without sonne, and voyd, and darkenesse was upon the face of the deepe: and the Spirit of God mooved upon the face of the waters.
3. And God said, Let there be light: and there was light....
5. And God called the light, Day, and the darknesse he called Night: and the evening and the morning were the first day.

There are infinite arguments of this right Christian and Religious affection in your *Majestie*: but none is more forcible to declare it to others, then the vehement and perpetuated desire of the accomplishing and publishing of this Worke, which now with all humilitie we present unto your *Majestie*. For when your Highnesse had once out of deepe judgment apprehended, how convenient it was, That out of the Originall sacred tongues, together with comparing of the labours, both in our owne and other forreigne Languages, of many worthy men who went before us, there should be one more exact Translation of the holy Scriptures into the *English tongue*; your *Majestie* did never desist, to urge and to excite those to whom it was commended, that the worke might be hastened, and that the businesse might be expedited in so decent a maner, as a matter of such importance might justly require . . . . So that, if on the one side we shall be traduced by Popish persons at home or abroad, who therefore will maligne us, because we are poore Instruments to make *Gods* holy Trueth to be yet more and more knowen unto the people, whom they desire still to keepe in ignorance and darknesse: or if on the other side, we shall be maligned by selfe-conceited brethren, who runne their owne wayes, and give liking unto nothing but what is framed by themselves, and hammered on their Anvile; we may rest secure, supported within by the trueth and innocencie of a good conscience, having walked the wayes of simplicitie and integritie, as before the Lord; And sustained without, by the powerfull Protection of your Majesties grace and favour, which will ever give countenance to honest and Christian endevours, against bitter censures, and uncharitable imputations.

It confirms our view of the increasingly grammatical tendency of English punctuation to observe that, in contrast to what F. H. A. Scrivener[2] called the "too scanty" punctuation of the 1611 Version, a 1683 Cambridge edition of this Bible introduced a "heavier and more elaborate" pointing differing "but little from that in vogue in recent times" (in 1884).

Ben Jonson, writing throughout most of the first half of the seventeenth century, shows some evidence of both systems of punctuation, the rhythmical and the grammatical. There are significant differences in the styles of pointing which he followed at different dates: for example, between some of his works first published just after 1600, then reissued in the Folio of 1616, and printed again in the posthumous Folio of 1640.[3] Simpson sug-

gested that the pointing of the 1606–7 Quarto of *Volpone* was in
its then form dramatic in character; that in 1616 it was recast
by Jonson, partly into a more logical scheme; and that in 1640
(a poorly printed edition, unsupervised by the author) it was
partly 'modernized'. Such alterations, whether or not by Jonson,
fit in with our picture of the change taking place in English
punctuation usage around 1610–25; we might expect more
attention to rhythm or elocution before, and to grammar after,
those dates.

In fact, the punctuation in the editions of his works which
Jonson supervised does seem to be substantially his own. Simpson felt certain, for example, that the extensive alterations
made to the pointing in the Quarto proofs of *Cynthia's Revels*
(1601) or in the revised 1616 *Volpone* were carried out by the
poet himself. It is probable that Jonson never altered his system
of pointing very radically. What we might say, rather, is that
his punctuation always had a certain logical basis (pioneer in
grammar as he was, he might well be expected to have had
strong views, early formulated and consistently held, about such
a subject), but that it varied somewhat along with the current
mode, being more dramatic say in 1601–6 and becoming more
grammatical and systematic by 1616. Elsewhere, Simpson[4] has
described Jonson's pointing as "attempting to combine the
logical and the rhythmical systems", and this seems a more
exact analysis.

The style of pointing which Jonson evolved was, in consequence of its strenuous dual aim, at times a little peculiar, but
it served. The following examples show how Jonson's punctuation serves to give a clear sense of the grammatical structure of
the sentence and of which are its most important parts while yet
retaining, in the dramatic verse a lively conversational rhythm
(as in certain parts of the selection from *Volpone*); in the
"Epithalamion" a metrical sense of the smooth curve of line and
half-line (in the fourth half-line the normal pointing is partly
suspended so as to give a smooth run); and in the prose an
appropriate oratorical accentuation of balance and antithesis.
(Relative to this, there is in the second sentence from *Timber* a
curiously pedantic discrimination between oratorical colon and
oratorical semicolon, so as to mark the pattern and yet keep the
structure of the sentence clear.)

All the wise world is little else, in nature,
But Parasites, or Sub-parasites. And, yet,
I meane not those, that have your bare towne-arte,
To know, who's fit to feed 'hem; have no house,
No family, no care, and therefore mould
Tales for mens eares, to bait that sense; or get
Kitchin-invention, and some stale receipts
To please the belly, and the groine; nor those,
With their court-dog-tricks, that can fawne, and fleere,
Make their revennue out of legs, and faces,
Eccho my-Lord, and lick away a moath:
But your fine, elegant rascall, that can rise,
And stoope (almost together) like an arrow;
Shoot through the aire, as nimbly as a starre;
Turne short, as doth a swallow; and be here,
And there, and here, and yonder, all at once;
Present to any humour, all occasion;
And change a visor, swifter, then a thought!
This is the creature, had the art borne with him;
Toiles not to learne it, but doth practise it
Out of most excellent nature: and such sparkes,
Are the true Parasites, others but their *Zani's*.[5]

See, now the Chappell opens; where the King
    And Bishop stay, to consummate the Rites:
The holy Prelate prayes, then takes, the Ring,
    Askes first, Who gives her (I *Charles*) then he plights
        One in the others hand, . . .[6]

Ill *Fortune* never crush't that man, whom good *Fortune* deceived
not. I therefore have counselled my friends, never to trust to her
fairer side, though she seem'd to make peace with them: But to
place all things she gave them so, as she might aske them againe
without their trouble; she might take them from them, not pull
them: to keepe alwayes a distance betweene her, and themselves.
He knowes not his own strength, that hath not met Adversity.
Heaven prepares *good men* with *crosses*; but no ill can happen to a
good man. Contraries are not mixed. Yet, that which happens to
any man, may to every man. But it is in his reason what hee
accounts it, and will make it.[7]

2. *Punctuation after* 1625. *Butler*

It would seem to be the case that toward the mid-century punctuation, like other practices in grammar or like spellings and word usages, was becoming more standardized, systematic and logical. No doubt the movement setting in strongly toward 1650 to regulate and fix various aspects of the language extended itself to punctuation also. Certainly, the system of punctuation prescribed in 1633 by a manual such as Charles Butler's *English Grammar*[8] is founded on a coherent set of logical rules. And as Masson[9] said, they are good rules, although not altogether like our own. The earlier concern with stressing oratorical design is still present in Butler, but it is less predominant, and there is more concern with reconciling the needs of oratorical design with that of punctuating correctly according to the grammatical importance of the member. The two kinds of demands can be made compatible, if oratorical symmetry is shown only within the sentence and not in the larger period.

The punctuation recommended by Butler is both heavier and more cumbersome, yet in a way plainer, than our own. There is a more liberal use of all the marks of punctuation. Colon and semicolon are more frequent and have a wider range of function than in our use, and also a clearer and more specifically complementary role in partitioning the sentence; commas are used copiously to mark small pauses. Butler's analysis can be summarized as follows.

Full stop (as in modern use) only terminates a sentence. But what *is* a sentence? In Nash's or Browne's prose the task of determining where a sentence really stops or starts is often baffling, for the use of full stop is not necessarily related to the logical termination of each thought. But Butler's use of full stop, as his examples clearly demonstrate, rests on a distinct conception of the sentence as a logically self-sufficient unit and the basic one in writing. To this conception the use of the other stops is related. Butler explains them as a kind of graded scale designed to show the degree of completeness or incompleteness of sense in each component of the sentence.

Colon, somewhat like our semicolon, indicates a major and more independent part within a sentence. (This is quite different from the modern use of colon chiefly to indicate a sequence.)

Comma marks a lesser and much more dependent part; semicolon is something logically intermediate. Butler's examples demonstrate that semicolon is to be used mostly with subordinating conjunctions in dependent clauses. But his rule here is too strict and is never completely accepted by writers of the period, who fail always to reduce semicolon to quite such an inferior status. What we do find in Butler that is absorbed by the writers who follow is a general idea of the semicolon as a differentiating stop distinct from and of lesser importance than colon.

It is notable that Ben Jonson[10] in his *English Grammar* (published in the 1640 Folio but probably written before 1623) should have anticipated what Butler was to say about the logical basis of punctuation and the need for a precise differentiation between the stops. Jonson of the two is probably the pioneer, using a Latin source, Ramus, and in this section of the *Grammar* deserting his earlier authority, Mulcaster. Jonson does not describe or analyse as well as Butler, and there are some confusions in the text (as in the apparent transposition of the functions of semicolon and comma), but we may see the general resemblance of his scheme to Butler's, especially in that both relate the stops principally to sense. Jonson finds an illustration of the correct use of the four points in Sir John Cheke, one of the more austere (and anti-Euphuistic) of Elizabethan writers; he chooses a sentence which is grammatically very well turned, with the balances subordinated to the logical structure, and which does show some logical differentiation in the punctuation.

The grammatical use of colon, the introduction of semicolon as an important and useful mark, and the clear distinction between semicolon and colon (clearly made although not always rigidly followed) are the keys to Butler's scheme of punctuation. In his scheme the pointing is really more closely concerned with illustrating the total plan of the sentence and marshalling its parts into a clearly organized and neatly differentiated grammatical structure than with displaying the meaning unambiguously, as is such an important function of our modern punctuation.

Some of the details of Butler's scheme may now be outlined. Colon is the more important mark than semicolon; and it is mainly a grammatical, not as in Elizabethan use mainly an oratorical, stop. It designates a major unit of thought standing independently within a long sentence. In Butler's words, colon "is a point of perfect sense, but not of perfect sentence": it marks some part which does not constitute an entire sentence but which is yet a "perfect member" or (in thought) complete part of a sentence. Jonson defined colon similarly: ". . . a Distinction of a Sentence, though perfect in it selfe, yet joyned to another". Such a "perfect member" may signify a grammatically independent clause, or one which contains a complete thought even though incompletely or elliptically expressed or joined on conjunctively to the rest of the sentence. So in Butler's examples we may find colon marking a clause or member in which the thought is independent, although the subject may be only referred to or understood (as in the second part of the first example below). Or it may mark a member which begins with a conjunction such as *and*, especially if a new subject is introduced (as in the second part of the second example below). Or again mark what modern grammar calls an independent clause, that is, one standing alone without connecting links in the sentence:

Of him, and through him, and to him, are all things: to whom be glory for ever. (*Rom.* 11, 36)

If the first fruit be holy; the lump is holy: and if the root be holy; so are the branches. (*Rom.* 11, 16)

Butler clearly distinguishes semicolon from colon. Semicolon is the lesser mark, indicating a shorter and in sense more dependent part of the sentence, often a part within a part. Generally, it marks a clause joined on by some conjunction: in practice, more often a subordinating than a coordinating conjunction, and by analogy, sometimes relative clauses beginning *who*, *which*, *that*. Butler's definition of semicolon is less ambiguous than Jonson's, although Jonson knew the value of the stop as a counterpoise to colon, said it was neglected,[11] and used it much himself.[12] Semicolon (Butler must be one of the very first English writers to use the modern name) is "a point of imperfect sense, in the middle of a Colon, or Period" and it is found particularly in a "compound axiom; whose parts are joined together, by a double, and sometimes by a single, conjunction".

That is, semicolon marks a part incomplete in sense: a subordinate clause. Both parts of the second example above and Butler's own syntax in the definition just quoted ("a compound axiom; whose parts . . .") illustrate the rule.

But semicolon may also occasionally serve with more independent clauses, where according to Butler's rule we could expect colon, if the members in question are very short, or closely linked in thought, or especially, in parallel series. Butler himself notes the exception and gives an example:

> A certain Samaritan, as he journeyed, came where he was; and, when he saw him, had compassion on him; and went to him; and bound up his wounds, pouring in oil and wine; and set him on his beast; and brought him to an Inn; and took care of him.

In the passage above, the subject *he* (understood) is the same throughout; semicolon is used for this reason and because the clauses are short and repetitive (the members though "perfect" are "many and short"). Semicolon can be used in the same way even when the clauses are quite disjunct grammatically, as in the next example quoted. These exceptions are really oratorical uses of semicolon in connection with balance.

It is worth observing that in the quotation from *Luke* 10, 33 above (and presumably in his other examples drawn from the Bible), Butler is not using the 1611 Version's punctuation, although the wording is virtually identical. Someone, possibly Butler himself, has modernized the 1611 pointing so as to bring it into line with the logical system Butler is advocating. Some of the sentences are broken up, there are more commas used to frame minor parts, and more semicolons are employed, somewhat monotonously. The total effect is much heavier than in the original.

Comma, in contrast with the heavier and more important marks just discussed, represents a very slight pause. It is a less important mark for Butler than for us, though he uses it much more often. He defines it as "a point of more imperfect sense, in a simple axiom, or in either part of a compound". That is, comma indicates a still smaller and more dependent part of the sentence than does semicolon. It may mark off a short phrase or single word, or divide a number of words of the same sort coming together in a simple statement or within one part of a complex sentence; or else it marks a very subsidiary short clause within another clause. Comma would not suffice, for instance, to divide parts of the sentence equal in value, as we allow with coordinating conjunctions such as *but* or *and* if such clauses introduce a change of subject.

It soon becomes apparent, as Butler explains and illustrates his system, that what he is principally concerned about is that the punctuation should show the place of each part in the plan of the whole sentence – the lesser or greater importance of each member. His aim is to throw into view, through the use of a series of graded and contrasting but logically fixed stops, the entire structure of the sentence in all its main and subordinate parts. Butler's may thus be said to be a logically outlining punctuation (in certain aspects not unlike German punctuation of the present day). The outlining or defining function of his pointing is readily apparent from any of the examples given above, in which each member is marked off by a weight of stop clearly equivalent to its grammatical importance.

Remembering that an average prose sentence of Butler's period was much longer and more elaborately contrived than one of the present day, we may appreciate that a paramount concern of his punctuation should be that the eye may take in the shape and organization of the sentence all at once. There is a logic here, but it is not quite that of modern punctuation. The latter might be said to be more concerned with absolute clarity of meaning, with displaying the logical interdependencies of parts, their due subordination, whether a part is restrictive or not, and so forth, than with showing the relation of each part to the plan of the whole. We use comma for too many purposes and we do not have enough contrast in the use of stops for our modern punctuation to have the same degree of effectiveness as Butler's in displaying the organization of the sentence – which is in any case usually of a much easier and more flowing kind in modern prose than was the case in the mid-seventeenth century.

Inasmuch as the prose of Butler's time was still much more formally structured, more carefully balanced and rounded, than our own, Butler's punctuation needed to be in part oratorical as well as grammatically defining. So Butler takes the time to point out twice in his brief essay that antithesis, when it occurs, may be emphasized by the alternate use of comma and semicolon. He gives the first two of the following examples, to which is added a third of his (already quoted), because it shows a comparable structure and pointing:

> They ate, they drank; they bought, they sold; they planted, they builded. (*Luke* 17, 28)

> I am persuaded, that neither death, nor life; nor angels, nor principalities, nor powers; nor things present, nor things to come; nor height, nor depth; nor any other creature; shall be able to separate us from the love of God, etc. (*Rom.* 8, 38)

> If the first fruit be holy; the lump is holy: and if the root be holy; so are the branches.

The oratorical function here is made to fit in with the grammatical. There is no wresting of the sentences into false or slight balances or antitheses, no overrunning of its boundaries. The main outline of every sentence is kept quite distinct. Contrasting stops highlight the balance and parallelism in the sentence, and in so setting out the oratorical elements of the design actually clarify the grammatical structure; this is evident especially in the third example, with its alternate use of semicolon and colon. Daines in practice (as distinct from his theory) sometimes makes a similar compromise between rhetoric and grammar. He uses pointing to mark stresses and indicate oratorical structure, but usually within a logically well defined sentence rather than a prolonged period.

Bacon's *Essays*[13] in the edition of 1625 show the influence of the outlining or logically defining style of punctuation formulated slightly later in Butler's *Grammar*. The pointing of the *Essays* is such as to keep the structure of the sentence absolutely clear, as a whole and in its main and lesser parts, and yet at the same time to show its oratorical pattern. Semicolon and colon seem nearly but are not quite interchangeable; there is some logical differentiation. Colon marks the most complicated or the most disjunct as well as the obviously antithetical members; semicolon marks simple parallelism, or members somewhat shorter, or linked in thought to what precedes them:

> *Riches* are for Spending; And Spending for Honour and good Actions. Therefore *Extraordinary Expence* must be limitted by the

Worth of the Occasion: For *Voluntary Undoing*, may be aswell for
a Mans *Country*, as for the *Kingdome of Heaven*. But *Ordinary
Expence* ought to be limitted by a Mans Estate; And governed
with such regard, as it be within his Compasse; And not subject
to Deceit and Abuse of Servants; And ordered to the best Shew,
that the Bils may be lesse, then the Estimation abroad. . . . He
that cannot looke into his own Estate at all, had need both Choose
well, those whom he employeth, and change them often: For New
are more Timorous, and lesse Subtile. . . . A Man had need, if he
be Plentifull, in some kinde of *Expence*, to be as Saving againe, in
some other. As if he be Plentifull in Diet, to be Saving in Apparell:
If he be Plentifull in the Hall, to be Saving in the Stable: And the
like.

It is rather striking that the same passage in the original
version in the edition of 1597[14] is punctuated much more lightly,
using (besides full stop) only commas, and fewer of those. In
this version there is no oratorical stressing of antithesis or
balance through a heavier and contrasting pointing. Whether
or not both versions of punctuation derive from Bacon, they
clearly reflect two quite different styles. The earlier and lighter
pointing seems to be more in the cadenced Elizabethan style,
though not in a prevailingly rhetorical or oratorical style. It is
a restrained and not ungrammatical, yet a logically not well
differentiated usage. The 1625 heavier pointing would seem to
reflect the prevailing practice, part logical, part oratorical, of a
slightly later period.

George Wither's *History of the Pestilence*,[15] a long moralizing
poem of the same date, also shows some influence of the new
logical punctuation, although Wither appears to be confusing
this with the old metrical system. Wither's punctuation is on
the heavy side, and stops of all kinds are profuse. One has the
sense that the stops, especially commas, are intended partly to
outline the sentence constructions. There may also be some
logical differentiation between semicolon and colon (semicolon
marks more dependent, colon more independent members, as
Butler was to recommend). Sometimes Wither contrives that
the correct grammatical use of the heavier stops coincides with
their oratorical or even metrical use. Often, however, logical
elements are badly confused with others. Colon veers wildly
between showing antithesis, marking main members, and mark-

ing the close of the lines or couplets. The pointing when metrical
is uninspired; Wither's dogged couplets have little rhythmical
variety or dramatic vividness. His monotonous use of end colon
might remind us of the less imaginative kind of Elizabethan
metrical punctuation, when every line has its "cesure" and its
end stop.

In the passages below, the prose (from the dedication to the
History) shows much confusion of purpose in its pointing, semicolon being insufficiently distinguished from colon, the shape of
the sentences tending to become lost, and any sense of logical
structure receding into a vaguely rhythmical prose. But the
verse passage (it is the rubric to Canto I), despite its over-
working of metrical colon, shows a clearer logical differentiation
of stops within the sentence and, especially in the revised printed
version, an increasing stress upon distinctness of sentence form.
Like Jonson's, Wither's punctuation and syntax seem to have
become increasingly grammatical – although in Wither's case
much darkness preceded the light.

> In the meane tyme, I rest pleased with my Lott; and though I
> never compasse my attemptes; yet something it will content mee,
> that hee is no lesse then the greatest king of Christendoome, to
> whose regard I have aspired: And if your Majestie will not please
> to accept of my humble services, No man els shall; ffor whether
> you regard them or noe, I have long since vow'd myself yours: . . .

> Our Aucthor, first, with God beginns:
> Describes his Anger for our Synns:
> Of all his Judgments, muster makes:
> Declares how Mercy undertakes
> The pleading of this Kingdomes cause,
> To bring God's wrath unto a pawse:
> And, then, with ferventnes she prayeth
> For Charles, whose virtue she displayeth.
>   Next, he sterne Justice introduces
> Complayning on our grosse abuses;
> Who proveth so; our Synfull Nation
> To merit utter desolation;
> That all God's plagues had us enclosed
> If Mercy had not interposed:
> But, after pleading of the Case
> With Justice, Mercy doth imbrace;

> Who, (that our Sinnes may punish't bee)
> To send the Pestilence agree,
> And other plagues a while suspend
> To prove how that will us amend.

An interesting feature of the expanded version of Wither's poem published three years later (*Britain's Remembrancer*, 1628)[16] is that in print Wither tends to reduce the heaviest pointings. Along with these downpointings, which diminish both the outlining and metrical functions of the punctuation, he occasionally feels the need to break up a long sentence. Here is the same passage of verse in the altered version; the pointing is lighter, essentially grammatical and less obviously oratorical or metrical, and to us it has a more modern and familiar appearance:

> Our Author first with God beginnes;
> Describes his anger for our sinnes;
> Of all his Judgements muster makes;
> Declares how Mercy undertakes
> The pleading of this Kingdome's Cause,
> To bring God's wrath unto a pawse;
>
> . . . .
>
> He Justice also, introduces,
> Complaining on our grosse abuses,
> Who proveth so, our sinfull Nation
> To merit utter Desolation,
> That all Gods Plagues had us enclosed,
> If Mercy had not interposed.
> But, after pleading of the Case,
> With Justice, Mercy doth embrace,
> Who (that our sinnes may punisht be)
> To send the Pestilence agree;
> Their other Plagues a while suspending,
> To prove how that will worke amending.

The printed version of the poem is of interest because Wither had, for some reason, to set all the type for the edition himself.[17] Why he should have made the changes mentioned is an intriguing question. One can readily understand why the repunctuation in the first edition of *Paradise Lost* might have a different character from the pointing of the Manuscript, since the two almost certainly derived in part from different hands; but it is more difficult to see why Wither should have chosen to use a different style (in spelling as well as pointing) in the later version. He may of course be exaggerating his own part in the printing. But one could alternatively surmise that his personal habit in composition had been to use a heavy style of punctuation (partly based on the logically and oratorically outlining pointing then in vogue, partly based on the older metrical pointing). But when putting his poem into the press he may well have felt that this heavy style was rather clumsy (or even, in its metrical aspect, too old-fashioned), and so may have thought it advisable to modify it in favour of a lighter style which combined grammatical distinctness with greater ease.

Wither's punctuation is scarcely comparable to Milton's. Yet the first edition of *Paradise Lost*, in a not dissimilar way to Wither's edition, reduced some of the Manuscript's heavy stress pointings in the Elizabethan rhetorical style, which by 1667 might well have seemed hopelessly old-fashioned to the printer; and the 1674 edition (see Appendix C) made certain further changes from heavier, cumbersome grammatical usages to lighter and more modern ones. Even as early as 1628, the changes made by Wither to the punctuation of his book suggest the increasing pressure of the grammatical upon English writing, just as the press changes to which Jonson's work was subjected between 1600 and 1640, by himself and his printers, suggest a similar pressure and development.

Perhaps, in these three cases of press correction in Wither's, Jonson's and Milton's works, we can detect the evolution of English punctuation through the variety of styles existing in the earlier seventeenth century toward something approaching our modern, more uniform usage. The change (though of course not followed by all writers with strict chronological consistency) seems to have been broadly, from a mainly rhythmical and elocutionary to a more systematic grammatical practice. In the mid-century usage still related equally to logical organization and to oratorical pattern; but it subsequently dropped the emphasis on oratorical design in a growing concern with directness and clarity of meaning. The aim shifted, in short, from an early interest in rhythm and expression for their own sakes, to a greater concern with strict grammatical logic and clear sentence form and oratorical pattern only secondarily, to, finally, an exclusive emphasis on correctness, intelligibility and ease.

Such changes in the practice of punctuation of course reflect wide changes of stylistic purpose in writing. Modern writing, prose especially, has tended to set up the ideals of clarity and fluency of construction over any ideals of formal pattern (whether such pattern relates to elaborate grammatical structure, or to oratorical or other rhythmical design). There is a very direct link between the style which has evolved as the ideal of modern composition and the changes which were taking place in syntactical design and correspondingly in punctuation in the seventeenth century.

The writing which we associate with the period after 1660, the Restoration, is that of the plain style, the style of Dryden. But Dryden's prose or verse and its punctuation is (though not chronologically so) outside the area of survey of this chapter. Instead, we might turn to a late illustration of the kind of grammatically outlining or defining punctuation which Butler advocates – heavy, cumbersome, but clear, emphatic and also oratorically effective. This is still in evidence in the later part of the seventeenth century, after the civil war, and is well illustrated in such a work as Joseph Caryl's *Exposition . . . upon the Book of Job*,[18] published in 1676–7, almost contemporaneously with *Paradise Lost*. This work is of interest both for its near date to *Paradise Lost* and because the printer was Samuel Simmons, who also published Milton's poem.

Caryl's exegeses or reflections on *Job* had been coming out piecemeal over a number of years, through various printing associations of the Simmons family. They were then collected and printed anew in two large folio volumes by Samuel during the same decade in which he was occupied with the printing of the second and third editions of *Paradise Lost* (the first edition having preceded the collected *Job* by seven or eight years). The two handsome volumes were printed with unusual care; they are remarkably correct in mechanical respects and very fully and carefully punctuated. Indeed, as H. F. Fletcher has said,[19] this was Simmons' *magnum opus* and altogether a notable printing achievement of the time. Yet it is of interest to note that the punctuation of these carefully prepared volumes, produced by the same printer and at about the same time as was *Paradise*

Lost, has very little in common with Milton's. The differences are more far-reaching than can be accounted for by the different characters of the two books.

Caryl's pointing is essentially of the same part logical, part oratorical kind as Butler's. Like Butler's, it is in general much heavier than our own and makes use of many more stops. The numbered examples from the first few pages of Caryl's preface and "Exposition" illustrate Butler's main rules adequately. It can be seen that Caryl, like Butler, tends to reserve colon to mark the longer, more important and more independent members (as in the second, third and especially fifth examples). Semicolon (or comma), on the other hand, more often marks the more dependent or connected members, such as subordinate or relative clauses (as in the second and fifth examples), or co-ordinate clauses if the subject does not change (as in the second and fourth examples), or disjunct clauses if they are short, closely linked or in a series (as in the fourth example). Colon is in addition used to mark antithesis or introduce a comparison. The examples also illustrate Caryl's prevailingly outlining style of punctuation, with its use of numerous defining commas (as in example one) to mark off all subordinate parts, and its regular contrasting of heavier with lighter stops to differentiate major from minor elements within the sentence and, concurrently, point up syntactical symmetry.

1.   I find, that this is not the first time, that this Book hath been undertaken by way of Exposition, in such a time as this.

2.   When these glorious issues of our Troubles shall be, is in his Hand, who held Job's Estate in his Hand, so fast, that Satan could not touch a Sheep or a Shoo-latchet, till himself willed; and who, when his time came, restored Job's Estate double, to a Sheep and a Shoo-latchet, whether Satan and his Sabeans would or no. We have already seen, in Job, an Epitome of our former prosperity and of our present Troubles: the good Lord hasten the latter part of our National likeness unto him, in the doubled . . . restauration of our Peace and Truth.

3. But now in my very Entrance upon it, the Storm grows so black, that I see you amazed, dejected, and almost desperate: Some are flying, others are preparing to flye; and in this great

Calamity, no man is found to comfort his Brother: But every
one increases his Neighbours fear, by his own fearfulness.

4. It had been much to say, he was a great man amongst the men
   of the *East*; for the men of the *East* were very great men, and
   very rich men. As to say, one is a rich man in the City of
   London, where there are so many rich men; one that goeth for a
   rich man there, is a rich man indeed. But here is more in this;
   he was not only a rich man, or a great man amongst the men of
   the East; but he was the greatest, he was the richest of them:
   as to say, that one is the richest in the whole City, cries a man
   up to the height of riches.

5. Thus, we may look to be restored (not only as Job) to more in
   kind, but to better in kind, I am sure to better in degree: We
   may look, that, for Brass we shall have Gold, or our Gold more
   refined; that, for Iron we shall have Silver, or our Silver more
   purified; that, for Wood we shall have Brass, or our Brass
   better furbished; that, for Stones we shall have Iron, or our
   Iron better tempered; We may look, that, our Officers shall be
   Peace, and our Exactors righteousness, that Violence shall no
   more be heard in our Land, wasting nor destruction within
   our borders, but men shall call our Walls Salvation and our
   Gates Praise.

Caryl's pointing is not identical in every respect with Butler's.
Caryl uses semicolon and colon less abundantly; his sentence
constructions tend to be looser, so that the distinction between
the two stops is sometimes more fluid than in Butler; he is
particularly fond of antithesis, parallelism or other balance,
these being often accentuated by the pointing, and goes beyond
Butler in his prolonged uses of such oratorical devices. For
instance, in the second and fifth examples it may be felt that the
symmetries are tending to obscure the sentence outlines, and
that the prose is verging upon periodic prose. At such moments
only (and in the rare traces of rhetorical elements, colon to mark
antithesis or introduce comparison) does Caryl's prose show any
similarity to Milton's. But generally speaking, Caryl's pointing
has nothing of the cadenced character and dramatic orientation
of Milton's. In the main Caryl's prose (and this is reflected by
his punctuation) is of the particularly elaborate and formally

structured kind characteristic of the period of 1625 and after, in which the stamp of a logical design is too rigidly imposed upon the construction. Unlike the earlier prose of Browne or Milton, Donne or Nash, Caryl's composition lacks living movement and the vitality communicated by rhythmical flexibility and variety.

It is apparent, then, that despite some differences, Caryl's style of pointing is closer to Butler's than to what we shall find in *Paradise Lost*. Although Caryl's and Milton's works came out of the same printing house, their punctuation appears to have derived substantially from two different sources or at least traditions. Of the two works it is Caryl's which in pointing seems to be more representative of its period, following the logically and oratorically defining style, the evolution and modification of which has been traced in this chapter. And it is the pointing of *Paradise Lost* which seems more original and distinctive in its time, hearkening back as it does to the frankly metrical and expressive pointing of a much earlier period.

The foregoing illustrations of punctuation in prose and verse at dates ranging from 1582 to 1676 provide a useful background for assessing the punctuation of *Paradise Lost*. It is particularly against the opposing styles represented by the pointing of Butler's *Grammar* and Caryl's *Job* on the one hand, and the Shakespeare Sonnets and Nash's or Donne's prose on the other, that we must consider the punctuation of Milton's poem. In the intervening period there has been a radical reorientation of English punctuation. Nevertheless, the punctuation of *Paradise Lost* (in the Manuscript of Book I especially) seems to adhere substantially to the earlier tradition, retaining or reviving many of the best features of the poetical punctuation of the Elizabethans. Our analysis must begin with a scrutiny of the Manuscript of *Paradise Lost*, Book I, itself.

IV

The Punctuation of the Manuscript of 'Paradise Lost', Book I

B. A. Wright, Helen Darbishire and M. Y. Hughes in the introductions to their editions of *Paradise Lost* provided some useful comments about Milton's punctuation.[1] Wright's more detailed discussion was the most valuable contribution, and contained many insights into the primarily poetical (and especially, the prosodic) basis of Miltonic punctuation. However, the remarks of these scholars, and in particular Miss Darbishire's earlier analysis, did not take account of the changing character of English punctuation from Elizabethan times to the later seventeenth century, nor differentiate in any way between mid-century grammatical usages (not necessarily Milton's) in the text of *Paradise Lost*, and an earlier-deriving style of rhythmical and expressive punctuation (more likely the poet's). Nor has it apparently been recognized how and when these two diverse styles of pointing come into conflict in the poem – as they occasionally do, particularly in its printed texts.

J. Diekhoff,[2] in an early illuminating study of the punctuation of *Comus*, more clearly distinguished in that poem "a double or triple principle of grammar, verse, and rhetoric". He seemed to consider that all three principles were of equal importance in the poet's usage, without however attempting to explain how the three principles in question might interdepend, or why they sometimes apparently clash. He also accepted the bulk of the often grammatically directed corrections of the two first printed editions (up to 1645) as deriving from Milton, although the changes were by no means uniformly apt.

Similarly, in the case of *Paradise Lost* Miss Darbishire (despite a few reservations in favour of Manuscript readings) and other scholars have accepted the bulk of the 1667 edition's grammatically revised punctuation in Book I as corrections sponsored by Milton, and therefore to be preferred to the readings of the

Manuscript, although the latter are often rhythmically or rhetorically more appropriate. 1674 (see Appendix C) largely follows the first edition's pointing (more closely, despite some errors, than 1667 does the Manuscript's). Editors have varied as to which of the two first editions they prefer to rely on; but most have taken one or other as the basis of their texts, in punctuation as in other matters.

The suggestion might be put forward that there has been an undue reliance on the early editions (especially the first) in minor details of the text such as punctuation, and an exaggerated estimate of the extent to which Milton may have been personally responsible for the revisions to the punctuation executed in 1667. A scholar who has recently questioned Milton's close control over minor pointing changes in at least one text, that of "Lycidas", is J. T. Shawcross.[3] He finds some evidence in that poem of various layers of printer's and possibly scribal interference in punctuation, as in matters of orthography (his principal concern). He rightly directs our attention to the importance of the punctuation and spelling in the original manuscript. However, like Diekhoff, Shawcross overemphasizes grammatical considerations and does not differentiate between the relative importance to Milton of grammatical and metrical principles of pointing in "Lycidas". For instance, he considers the proportion of cases when stops are included medially or conversely at the ends of lines in "Lycidas" and earlier poems (a matter of basic importance); but he then cites apparently as of equal significance Milton's use or omission of stops in compound constructions. These are not entirely appropriate methods to apply to Milton's punctuation. Any analysis into grammatical categories is likely to lead to an impression of much inconsistency and confusion in Milton's practice, since Milton is continually subordinating grammar to structural and rhythmical considerations.

The punctuation of the Manuscript of *Paradise Lost*, Book I, needs to be re-examined, for it holds the key to these various problems. A thorough comparison of the punctuation variants between it and the 1667 edition furnishes some interesting observations.[4] Of the two texts, it is the Manuscript which consistently shows the more distinctive and more poetical habits of punctuation, and in various important practices is closer to what may be Milton's personal usages. (The variants to be discussed in the next two chapters were – all but one at I, 569 – corrections executed, as far as present known states of the first edition reveal, at the press either preparatory to or initially during type-setting. Proof or later corrections are discussed separately in Appendix B.)

1. *Rhythmical Punctuation*

One of the most striking features of the Manuscript pointing, as compared with that of the first edition, is the more exclusively metrical or rhythmical handling of the stops. Marks of punctuation tend to be so arranged in the poem as to fall at a natural pause – at the end of the line or at the caesura. This is a matter of considerable significance for the structure of the verse. Especially often marks fall at the caesura, thus emphasizing primarily the movement of the verse from midline to midline, and setting this long, forward movement against the other basic movement of the recurring pentameter line. (The line is sufficiently emphasized by the manner in which blank verse is set out and by the predominant final accent, and has less need of heightening through the punctuation.) Most pages of the Manuscript show a proportion of anything up to three times as many stops at the caesura as at the ends of lines; in 1667, where some 'missing' stops were supplied at the ends of lines, the ratio has diminished, but there is still a great predominance of midline over end-of-line pauses. Almost any passage from the Manuscript, Book I, illustrates the predominance of caesural pointing; for instance the following (MS, pages 2–3; Miss Darbishire, page 5). The hand corrections are shown (save in *ethereal*, 45, where the final *e* is written over *i*):

> Mov'd our grand parents in that happie state,
> 30 Favour'd of heav'n so highly, to fall off
> From thir Creator, & transgresse his will
> For one restraint, Lords of the world besides?
> Who first seduc'd them to that fowle revolt?
> Th' infernal Serpent; hee it was, whose guile
> Stirrd up with envy & revenge, deceav'd
> The Mother of Mankind; what time his pride
> Had cast him out from heav'n; with all his host
> Of rebell Angells, by whose aide aspiring

To set himselfe in glory above his peeres,
40   Hee trusted to have equalld the most **High,**
If he oppos'd; & with ambitious aime -
Against the throne & Monarchy of God,
Raisd impious warr in heav'n & battell proud
With vaine attempt. Him the Almighty power
Hurld headlong flameing from th' ethereal skie
With hideous ruine & combustion downe
To bottomles perdition, there to dwell
In adamantine chaines & penall fire
Who durst defie th' Omnipotent to armes.
Nine times the space that measures day & night
To. mortall men, hee with his horrid crue
Lay vanquishd, rowling in the firy gulfe
Confounded though immortall: But his doome
Reservd him to more wrath; for now the thought
Both of lost happiness & lasting paine
Torments him, round he throws his balefull eyes
That witness'd huge affliction & dismay
Mix'd with obdurate pride & stedfast hate:
At once as farr as Angells kenne, he views
60   The dismal scituation wast & wilde
A dungeon horrible, on all sides round . . .

In the above passage the Manuscript shows eighteen pauses
(mainly commas) at the caesura, eight at the ends of lines. The
first edition supplies two more commas at the ends of lines 48
and 60, and misses or leaves out one comma at the end of line
42. It is much less often that the edition has to supply midline
stops; in this passage it in fact leaves out one needed medial
stop (in line 59). Thus, in total, the edition shows seventeen
pauses at the caesura, nine at the ends of lines. There is only one
line, in either text, which shows a pause elsewhere than at these
two metrical places; that additional stop (line 34) is obviously
an emphasizing pause. Further, most of the heavy stops fall at
the caesura: an additional, important means of emphasizing the
midline. Seven out of eleven heavy stops in the Manuscript are
placed internally; the edition's substitutions at lines 36, 37 and
56 slightly lessen this preponderance. From this representative
passage it can be seen that punctuation, besides assisting meaning or grammar, has an important rhythmical function in the

poem: that of showing the structure, phrasing and main movements of the verse.

Such rhythmical effects in the punctuation arise partly from
the poet's moulding of the members of the sentence (hence their
accompanying stops) into the verse structure – syntax is made
to coincide naturally with metre. But such structural habits of
pointing also require, to assist them, a severe economy and
selective disposition especially of commas. Here the Manuscript
differs noticeably from the first edition. Where minor stops
might be required to assist the sense or grammatical structure,
the Manuscript tends to insert mainly those which conveniently
fall at the end of the line or at the caesura, and to leave other,
unmetrical stops out. The 'metrical' punctuation of the Manuscript hinges, that is, not on inserting at the caesura or line
ending a great many commas unrelated to sense or syntax, but
rather by a negative principle on putting in those only which
fall naturally, according to the normal logic of the syntax, at
these two places. Elsewhere in the line the Manuscript discreetly
omits minor stops even though a normal syntax seems to require
them (for example, in lines 45, 53, 54 and 59). Very occasionally,
the Manuscript gives commas whose grammatical function is
negligible and whose main use seems to be to emphasize or only
show the caesura or line ending (as, possibly, in line 51). This
was on the whole the old-fashioned system; in much early
Elizabethan verse there is a profuse and often monotonous use
of purely metrical commas. However, purely metrical pointing
is a much less frequent and less distinctive occurrence in the
Manuscript than is the omission of stops which would interfere
with the verse. Stops which would fall unmetrically are simply
left out, unless they are particularly needed for meaning,
emphasis or clarity. The first edition's variant pointings will
show that it is not guided to the same degree by such metrical
considerations.

There are some further variations in the Manuscript on the
general principle of metrical or structural punctuation. Sometimes there is no punctuation for several lines. The rhythms
spoken of, midline to midline or beginning of the line to the end
(or some permutation of these two) then overleap several lines
with a longer span, as happens with good dramatic effect in
lines 44–9. Sometimes a single line, apparently in need of

punctuation at either midpoint or end, is left open, entirely
unpunctuated. The effect is then as if the verse pause itself were
lightly supplying the place of the missing syntactical stops.
(This principle of equivalence probably also operates in regard
to prosody and punctuation, but in reverse. Stops occasionally
seem to compensate for a missing or displaced accent.) The
proportion of lines in the Manuscript thus left unpunctuated at
the end is much larger than of lines left unpunctuated at the
caesura. (Contrast the lack of stopping at the close of lines
34, 43, 45, 48, 52, 57 and 60, with the lack of caesural pause
only at lines 43, 45 and 46.) The edition by no means supplies
all of such missing stops, although it gives a few. Either the
caesura was thought to stand more in need of being stressed by
means of punctuation than was the end of the line (since the
voice tends to pause naturally at the latter place in reading); or
more probably, the intention was deliberately to stress the
midline to midline movement over the movement by whole lines,
and thus keep the verse flowing onward.

Lastly, a final important refinement, it is the exception to
find any single line punctuated at both the caesura and the end
(or indeed twice in any way), double metrical punctuation
generally being reserved for emphasis or structural variety. This
the passage quoted rather strikingly shows. Neither text has a
double metrical pause, or any double pause, except at lines 32
and 34 – although lines 29, 34, 43, 45, 52 and 56 could have had
two metrical pauses, and lines 53 and 59 similarly could have
been given an additional pause. Lines tend to be punctuated
only at one or the other place, so that there is a constant interplay between the two main rhythmical movements of the verse
– midline to midline, beginning of line to the end. (It is also to
be noted that the general avoidance of two metrical stops within
the single line means that the half-line is never unduly emphasized at the expense of the whole: the movement of the verse is
kept long.) This like other rhythmical effects needs to be assisted
by leaving out some minor stops. Therefore the Manuscript may
omit a comma at the end of a line if there must be one at the
caesura; or it may do the opposite, omit a caesural stop if a line
must be punctuated at the end. For this reason, minor grammatical elements in the sentence (for example, appositives,
vocatives, interjections, short qualifying phrases as in lines 34

and 52 above, brief relatives or coordinates) frequently appear as only half punctuated – defined by stops at one end only (which end, may vary). These omissions do not usually much affect the sense; but it is apparent that they make grammatical analysis of Milton's practice in such constructions meaningless. The first edition's variants show an urge to tidy up the grammar in such instances.

To summarize what has been said. The general pattern of pointing in the Manuscript (especially as regards the number of lighter stops admitted) is such as to leave a skeleton outline of the grammatical construction of the sentence, with the rhythmical structure of the verse emphasized by contrast, because so few pauses are allowed to fall at other than metrical places in the line. And the relative distribution of stops is also such as to stress the midline to midline shaping, the whole verse line, and lastly the half-line, in that respective order of importance, setting these three elements into rhythmical interaction. The final shaping in this complex interplay of rhythms is provided by the use of semicolons or colons to mark the main divisions, and full stops to mark the total dimensions, of the verse periods (normally much longer than sentences). In these weightier pauses or closes (always metrically positioned) the main, surging, forward rhythms of Milton's verse find natural resting places.[5]

Not cluttering up the verse with a great number of minor stops has the added advantage of setting off those heavier stops which are occasionally used (especially in the Manuscript text) as points of sharper poetical inflection. Unexpectedly heavy rhetorical pointings used for special effects show up better not only by their contrast with the surrounding context of more ordinary punctuation, but also by contrast with a prevailingly sparing and fluent punctuation. Even these rhetorical pointings are almost invariably held within the main metrical framework; that is why such a revision as the following by the first edition seems so wrong (the added exclamation mark which breaks the half-line):

> If thou beest he, But oh how fal'n how chang'd
> (MS, I, 84)

> If thou beest he; But O how fall'n! how chang'd
> (1667, I, 84)

2. *Prosody*

Something must be said however briefly about the possible relationship between Milton's punctuation and his prosody. Here we are concerned with the metrical structure of the single verse line, as distinct from the larger rhythmical structures of Milton's blank verse.

Among the numerous learned controversies over Milton's versification, two main interpretations of his prosody stand out fairly clearly. The first (summarized earlier by J. H. Hanford[6]) is that Milton's line is based on five stresses arranged into an iambic pattern, with complicated substitutions and reversals of accents constantly taking place. The second view (as recently expressed by Douglas Bush[7]) is that the basis of Milton's line is syllables rather than stresses. The Miltonic line is taken to be founded on ten syllables (a virtually constant factor), with a free fluctuation of between three and five stresses in each line.

However different critics may theorize about Milton's line, it is probable that many readers in practice tend to hear it with an iambic, five-stress groundbeat at least in the background. As they read, a series of shadowy equivalences is likely to be continually taking place. Thus when we test a 'weak' line to see if it can be made to show the right metre, we may mentally stress syllables which we would not stress in reading aloud. (At most, we might stress such weak syllables only very lightly in reading out.) We realize that in such instances Milton is withholding stresses and is relying on the established iambic pentameter pattern to make itself tacitly heard. Similarly, when we find irregularities of accent (a reversed foot, or a weak foot, or a strong foot with two accents), we may often feel that the normal five beats are merely being redistributed within the line – that there may be compensating irregularities elsewhere. Mentally in such cases we may still be hearing the usual five accents in the usual rising pattern. Our sense of the normal pattern will help us to arrange the line in reading it aloud so that it takes up more or less the same total time and has more or less the same total accentuation as the pentameter norm. No doubt many of Milton's metrically most exceptional lines do not fit into this description, but even these draw some of their impact from our continuing sense of the standard accentual pattern and of their differences from it.

In the series of shadowy metrical equivalences we may be making when reading Milton's verse, the punctuation probably plays a certain part. It is tempting to try to relate the Elizabethan time-value system of pointing (varying numbers of beats for the different stops) directly to Milton's prosody and to see if the pointing may not in some way be making up beats (like a rest in music) in metrically defective or irregular lines. But Miltonic punctuation is not identical with the early time system out of which it grew (although both are related to metre); and even the early system did not use stops in quite that way. Milton's chief aim in punctuation is to stress not single lines but larger structural units: to weld lines together. This aim is not compatible with the use of pointing as a system of close metrical correspondences within the individual line. For instance, we cannot expect to find that in lines defective in one or more stresses there should always be a compensating punctuation (perhaps commas) to supply the missing beats, or that a line which has a heavy pause such as a semicolon should perhaps have one syllabic accent less to make up. Metrically defective lines in *Paradise Lost* are not always punctuated, and many lines written in the normal five-beat pattern are. Similarly in the cases of lines containing reversed accents, weak feet, feet with doubled accents, etc.

It is, of course, the case that the marking of caesura and line ending by punctuation means that in effect stops are usually falling in conjunction with a strong syllabic stress at either the fourth or sixth syllable and the tenth syllable of the line (normally fixed points for accentuation). That is to say, punctuation is regularly heightening the iambic rhythm at these points.[8] In this respect, punctuation is cooperating with metre within the line (although as was earlier remarked, the rhythmical pattern established by midline and end-of-line pointing cannot be assessed solely in terms of the individual line, but is part of a larger rhythmical structure in the verse.)

The strong tie of the punctuation with the iambic or rising stress pattern does however have one notable effect which is reflected within individual lines on occasion. When metrically defective or irregular lines do have punctuation (especially if the stops are adjacent to the irregular feet), the effect is sometimes unusually forceful. In these cases, probably, we cannot help reading the lines as if the nearby stops partly supplied the missing or the displaced beats. The punctuation becomes a kind of compensating or regularizing factor. As it were, we have to take an extra breath with the comma or other stop associated with the irregular foot, so as to make up the required metrical time. Some instances may be observed at lines 36, 38, 41, 42, 47, 49, 52 and 53 in the passage from the Manuscript (pages 2–3) given previously. Individual readers of course will vary in their rendering of these lines; but the present one would give the stops in these lines a somewhat longer pause than usual. Ultimately such interplay of two different kinds of beats (syllabic accents and punctuation pauses) seems to give unusual rhetorical emphasis to the lines. The metrical variation naturally calls attention to itself; it is then partly corrected by the punctuation, so that the normal rhythm reasserts itself. This pattern of variation followed by check or reversal is bound to be strong. No one could read the following line without exceptional emphasis:

| Ŭnrés|pited, | ŭnpi|tied, ŭn|repreevd, |　　　(II, 185)

The accentual pattern here (partly the three syllabic stresses, partly the pauses of the commas) is like a muffled drumbeat.

Of course there are for Milton an unusual number of stops in the above line, which partly accounts for its force. But in the following lines, where there is only the usual single internal pause, there is still great weight at the beginnings. At least in part this is because a pause falls in close conjunction with an accentually irregular opening foot:

| Láy ván|quisht, rów|ling in | the fi|ery Gúlfe |　　　(I, 52)

| Dáy, or | the sweet | appróach | of Ev'n | or Mórn, |　　(III, 42)

The commas somewhat unusually placed after the third or first syllables respectively, act as a sort of accentual balance to the doubled stress and reversed stress, respectively, of the opening feet. The effect we may get from the actual reading of the lines might be in the opening parts much slower than the scansion suggests, something more like this:

| Láy ván|quisht, | rówling in | the fí|ery Gúlfe |

| Dáy, | or the sweet | appróach | of Ev'n | or Mórn, |

The supernumerary beat, in the second and first feet respectively of the lines as rescanned above, represents the felt effect of the commas, pulling the rhythm back to the rising pattern. As a consequence of reading the opening syllables more slowly, we have to race the tempo in the syllables which follow, as if both lines had a foot (the third and second respectively) containing an extra weak beat. The fine opening of Sonnet 13 is another example:

| Hárry, | whose túne|full & | well-méa|sur'd sóng |

This reads more slowly at the opening than the metrical pattern marked would indicate:

| Hárry | , whose | túnefull & | well-méa|sur'd sóng |

We might summarize the total effect by comparing it to 'rubato' in music. We tend to make up the required time for the line by dwelling longer on certain parts and hurrying over other parts. Another partial analogy is Beethoven's emphasized rests. The pauses are significant because they seem to be trying to reestablish the expected pattern of musical beats. As in these musical instances, the verse emphasizes where it delays or provides an unusual kind of accentuation. It might be suggested that in such cases punctuation and syllabic stresses are acting in an intimate prosodic cooperation.

3. *Milton's Autograph Sonnets*

All of the individual features of punctuation which were earlier described in the Manuscript of *Paradise Lost*, Book I, are illustrated, if anything more clearly, in the final drafts of the mature Sonnets punctuated by Milton's hand. Sonnets 11, and 13 and

14 in their second drafts, quoted below (Trinity MS, pages 40–1), show in particular the use of pointing as a broad structural and organizing device, of service in shaping the complex overall pattern of the sonnets with their characteristic play of sequacious argument and syntax against formal stanza divisions.

13

To M^r: Hen: Laws on the publishing of his Aires

    Harry, whose tunefull & well-measur'd song
      First taught our English Music how to span
      Words with just note & accent, not to scan
      with Midas eares, committing short & long,
5   Thy worth & skill exempts thee from ye throng,
      with praise anough for Envy to look wan;
      To after-age thou shalt be writt the man
      That with smooth aires *couldst* cou'dst humor best our
        tongue.
    Thou honourst Vers, & Vers must lend her wing
10   To honour thee, the Preist of Phœbus quire
      That tun'st *th* thir happiest lines in hymn, or story.
    Dante shall give Fame leav to set thee higher
      Then his Casella, whom he woo'd to sing
      Met in y^e milder shades of Purgatory.

11

On the detraction wch follow'd ^{up}$_\wedge$on my writing certain treatises

    I did but prompt the age to quit thir clogs
      By the known rules of ancient liberty
      when strait a barbarous noise environs me
      of Owls & buzzards, asses, apes & dogs
5   As when those hindes that were transform'd to frogs
      Rail'd at Latona's twin-born progeny
      which after held the Sun & Moon in Fee.
      But this is got by casting pearl to hogs;
    That bawl for freedom in thir senseles mood,
10   And *hate the truth wherby they should be free;*   /still revolt
      Licence they mean, when they cry liberty,   when Truth
    For who loves that, must first be wise, & good;   would set
      but from that mark how farr they roav, we see   them free.
      for all this wast of wealth, & loss of blood.

14

When Faith & Love wch parted frō thee never,
Had rip'n'd thy just soul to dwell with God[,]
meekly thou didst resigne this earthy load
of death, call'd life; wch us from life doth sever.
5 Thy Works & Almes, & all thy good Endevor
staid not behind, nor in the grave were trod
But, as Faith pointed with her golden rod,
follow'd thee up to *Joy* joy & bliss for ever.
Love *Love* led   on   Faith   knew
Faith‸*shew'd* the‸*way*, and‸*she* who *saw* them best
10   thy handmaids, clad them o're with purple beames
and azure wings, that up they flew so drest,
And spake the truth of thee in glorious theames
before the Judge, who thenceforth bidd thee rest,
And drink thy fill of pure immortal streames.

In the above we may see:

(1) The almost complete avoidance of unmetrical stops, except for emphasis, as the comma after *death,* in S. 14, line 4, and that after *wise,* in S. 11, line 12, and in one other instance, probably also emphatic, in S. 11, line 4.

(2) A conspicuous emphasis on internal punctuation, in the sense that no grammatically needed stops are omitted at the midline, although line endings are not infrequently left so unpunctuated (as for example in S. 13, lines 10, 13; S. 11, lines 2, 4; S. 14, lines 5, 6); in the sense also that stops are sometimes almost forcibly transposed from their syntactically expected places at the end of the line to the caesura (as in S. 11, line 13, and S. 14, lines 6 to 7).

(3) The avoidance of double metrical stops within a single line, or one stop, usually the end one, left out (as for example in S. 13, lines 10, 13; S. 11, line 4; S. 14, lines 5, 6).

(4) The use of rhetorically emphasizing punctuation, as in the semicolon (not so transcribed by Wright) after *life;* in S. 14, line 4 or in the heavy pointing at S. 11, line 8.

(5) The general subordination of grammar, or of strict consistency of usage with any specific grammatical construction, to the rhythmical and structural principle of punctuation. To take one instance, it has been suggested that Milton frequently

uses comma before *and, or,* or *nor* in a brief compound. (Earlier practice often was to precede and follow such constructions with commas.) If Milton has this habit, it is at least modified according to the rhythmical plan of the lines. To illustrate: in S. 14, lines 5 and 6, the first of the defining commas, that falling at the midline, is given in each instance with a compound construction; but the second comma, which would fall at the line ending, is both times omitted. However, in the same construction in S. 14 the first defining comma (before *and*) is omitted, since it would here fall at the end of a line (10), and both that line and the next have medial punctuation. Apparently the principles named in (2) and (3) are the guiding rules. Occasionally a full defining punctuation is given with short compounds, especially if the end stop is a heavy one which cannot easily be omitted. Sometimes when two defining stops are shown, it seems that the intention is to indicate great emphasis: as in S. 11, lines 12 and 14, and S. 14, line 4.

(6) The use of punctuation in a highly individual way as a counterpoint to stanza structure. Thus sometimes punctuation is used to suggest the shape of the stanzas when the actual syntax does not. In S. 11, line 8, which contains no real break in the syntax, ends nevertheless with a semicolon, partly emphasizing, partly metrical or indicating the end of the second stanza. Again, in S. 14 the grammatically expected stop is not given at the end of line 6 (certainly not in the amended line of the early draft, and probably not in the fair draft; a mark which could possibly be read as a misplaced full stop after *trod* is most probably the disjointed end of the tail of the *d*). The thought is instead made to flow over into line 7 as far as the comma after *But,* . . . . Thus the four-line stanza is welded into a continuous rhythmical unit. On the other hand, where a pronounced break in the syntax does coincide with the end of a stanza, the punctuation is frequently used in just the reverse way, to avoid too closed a stanza and to give the opposite effect that the argument is forcing its way across the sonnet divisions. Thus in S. 11, line 4, the expected concluding full stop or colon at the end of the first stanza is omitted; and in S. 13, end of line 4, the grammatically expected semicolon is moved forward to the end of line 6, so that the thought comes to a rest halfway through the second stanza instead of at the close of the first. The effects of these

F

evidently contrary practices are in fact the same: to suggest a kind of constant interplay or counterpoint between the thought or syntax and the formal sonnet divisions. The 1609 Shakespeare Sonnets or Harington's Ariosto show a similar metrical use of heavy pointing to mark stanzaic structure, but less subtlety in juxtaposing stanza pattern against syntax.

Milton's earlier very tentative draft of the sonnet to Lawes (Trinity MS, page 40) shows the punctuation left much more open in the poem's unfinished state, but a key pointing (that in line 6) already indicated. Something, possibly a comma, has been deleted by the author at the end of line 2. The two drafts of Sonnet 14 (Trinity MS, page 41) show Milton experimenting with the punctuation. One line (11) is left unpointed at the end in the earlier version only, but in others, 1, 5, 2 (?), the pointing of the later version seems deliberately to be pruned. The comma at the end of line 8 in the early draft becomes a full stop in the later version; Milton here decided to make the stanza 'closed'. The transcripts of Sonnets 13 and 14 in other hands (Trinity MS, page 42) suggest possible scribal interference with the punctuation, as seen in the conventional regularizing of the pointing in S. 13, end of line 4; S. 14, end of line 6 and medially, line 7. Milton's effective comma after *Harry,* at the opening of Sonnet 13 is also omitted.

The rhythmically based style of punctuation employed in the Manuscript of *Paradise Lost*, Book I, is thus visible in rudimentary form in the extant autographs of *Comus*, "Lycidas" and other early poems, and the same style is to be found fully formulated in the autographs of the mature sonnets. It is apparent that this Miltonic style of punctuation represents a great refinement over the rather mechanical type of metrical stopping found in certain Elizabethan verse. The system of punctuation illustrated in the Trinity Manuscript or in the Manuscript of *Paradise Lost* not only provides a finer discrimination of rhythms and moulds itself to verse of more complex rhythmical organization; it also affords a more effective compromise between rhythmical and grammatical modes of pointing, so often conflicting or confused in earlier usage. In Miltonic punctuation as much grammar is allowed, on the whole, as will easily fit the metre and broad rhythmical plan of the verse. The structural principle is kept dominant, and the limited number of exceptions allowed (for clarity, meaning or emphasis) need cause no confusion. Rhetorical or elocutionary pointings can in limited numbers also be accommodated to the underlying rhythmical scheme.

An understanding of how deeply the Manuscript's punctuation is related to rhythm may do much to explain the general scantiness of the Manuscript's pointing in certain contexts and its apparent neglect to mark stops in some places. There are undoubtedly certain errors and defects of punctuation in the Manuscript text; some passages seem insufficiently punctuated by any standards, and there appear to be a few gross errors of pointing and perhaps even an occasional rhythmical error. This does not mean that all the punctuation in this text which does not meet conventional standards is necessarily wrong. It may readily be understood that if more than one person had helped Milton with the dictation and correction of the early drafts of *Paradise Lost*, there would almost certainly be some degree of variation and error in the punctuation, since not all the assistants could have been equally skilled or equally familiar with the poet's habits. It would also be odd if an occasional pointing error had not crept into the text from the scribe who prepared the fair copy. But despite occasional omissions and errors, it is seldom that the Manuscript's punctuation is inadequate to show the main movements and larger structure of the verse, or the phrasing of individual lines. In the 1667 edition, where more regard was evidently paid to the minutiae of grammar and in general more stops were used, the rhythmical treatment of punctuation is frequently obscured. But it still remains as an underlying habit, and an understanding of the rhythmical techniques of the Manuscript can therefore do much to illuminate a certain kind of punctuation (or sometimes, a lack of punctuation) in parts of the printed text.

V

The Manuscript of Book I and the 1667 Variants: Rhythmical Punctuation

1. *Corrections to the Manuscript*

Before turning to the first edition's variants, it is instructive to glance at corrections made within the Manuscript, Book I, itself. It is of interest to see that of the nineteen commas which Helen Darbishire detects as having certainly or probably been added to the Manuscript text by a correcting hand different from the scribe's,[1] sixteen (all but two of three commas in line 584) fall at the end of a line or at a caesura. These sixteen additions, all of which are grammatical as well as metrical, are given in the notes.[2] Line 584 is altogether a rhythmical exception. It contains only three syllabic stresses, and the three commas added by the corrector complement these stresses so as to give unusual weight to the place-names listed: "Damasco, or Marocco, or Trebisond,". . . . With the exception of line 584, the corrector never adds commas at other places in the line, although there are many other instances where the grammatical need seems as pressing as in these sixteen. Further, of these added commas, two only are second metrical pauses in the line: 88 (removed in 1674) and 312 (necessary to avoid a misreading).

It is also interesting to observe that the scribal or some other correcting hand occasionally deletes commas which, though grammatically acceptable by seventeenth-century standards, interfere with the rhythmical phrasing. In the passage below, the comma after *shout,* (but not the comma after *concave,* which is a caesural pause) has been struck out:

A shout/ that tore hells concave, and beyond . . .
(542)

Three similar deletions have been made elsewhere.[3]

70

The Manuscript's corrections to its own punctuation therefore conform to the broad structural principles of punctuation which were earlier noted in that text. There will be seen similarly a few rhetorical heightenings of the punctuation within the Manuscript, along the elocutionary lines of the early poems.

2. *Appositive-Vocative Constructions*

The Manuscript's pointing with vocative and appositive constructions supplies an apt introduction to its rhythmical plan of punctuation. It sometimes omits the two defining commas in such constructions and at other times it inserts them both, or more often the second alone. What appears to be the guiding consideration in such omissions or inclusions is again the rhythmical phrasing of the line. Certain variant pointings between Manuscript and first edition plainly give the clue to this. In the two appositives below, the Manuscript marks only the second comma, that which falls at the caesura; while the edition, more awkwardly for the rhythm though consistently with seventeenth-century practice, points at both ends of the minor phrase:[4]

> ; in Hesebon
> And Horonaim Seons realm, beyond . . .

> ; in *Hesebon*
> And *Heronaim, Seons* Realm, beyond . . .
> (408–9)

Astarte queen of heav'n, with crescent horns;

Astarte, Queen of Heav'n, with crescent Horns;
(439)

Punctuation with interjections is similar; the defining comma is left out by the Manuscript if it interferes with the smooth phrasing of the half-line. We again find a variant in this regard in the 1667 edition. The Manuscript omits the unmetrical comma after the interjection (a practice often followed in Milton's prose), but the edition meticulously puts the stop in:

> Between the Cherubim; yea often plac'd

> Between the Cherubim; yea, often plac'd
> (387)

One needs to turn to the complete poem for further illustration. Where the second of the two defining commas in, for
example, a vocative or appositive construction would fall outside and weaken a main metrical pause, the practice is to omit
both stops. The first comma is not usually given alone even
when (as in the next examples shown) it might fall at a metrical
pause, since to do so would create a grammatically strained
reading:

> Whatever Earth all-bearing Mother yeilds . . .
> (V, 338)

> For of Celestial Bodies first the Sun
> A mightie Spheare he fram'd, unlightsom first, . . .
> (VII, 354–5)

But the defining commas, either the second alone or both, may
be given according as they happen to fit into the pattern of
end-of-line and caesural pauses:

> But thou O Father, I forewarn thee, shun . . .
> (II, 810)

> Long after to blest *Marie*, second *Eve*.
> (V, 387)

> . . . when *Raphael*,
> The affable Arch-angel, had forewarn'd . . .
> (VII, 40–1)

> Stand still in bright array ye Saints, here stand
> Ye Angels arm'd, this day from Battel rest;
> (VI, 801–2)

> . . . to receive our King
> The great *Messiah*, and his new commands, . . .
> (V, 687–8 [Ed. 2, 690–1])

It will be noted that commas are not given at the ends of lines
801 and 687 in the last two examples, although these could be

appropriate according to the explanation just offered. Such a variation is probably due to the desire to lighten the punctuation, in view of the double stops in each of the following lines. As usual, it is the pause at the end of the line rather than the medial pause which in such a context is sacrificed.

One of the most significant consequences of this type of light, rhythmical punctuation is that the regular and expected verse phrasing may sometimes be interrupted with great effect. For instance, we may compare Messiah's injunction to his armies (VI, 801-2 above), unemphatic because the vocatives were unpointed, with his command to the deeps of Chaos here, where the vocatives are completely defined:

> Silence, ye troubl'd waves, and thou Deep, peace, . . .
>
> (VII, 216)

Grammatical clarity requires the extra commas, but the unusual number of pauses in the line also lends a fine weight and impressiveness to the Son's command.

3. *Comma Variants in* 1667

To turn now to the main body of the 1667 punctuation variants and their metrical relevance. There are about one hundred and thirty-one alterations made to Milton's copy by the first edition at an early stage in the printing; possibly one or two more (see chapter VI, 1). This number include some sixty-five commas added to the Manuscript text and about eighteen others deleted. Among these are many useful and some necessary corrections, but generally speaking this group of changes shows much less consistency of rhythmical purpose than does the comparable group of scribal corrections, the twenty-two additions or deletions of commas within the Manuscript itself. It will be helpful to break down this group of comma variants in 1667 in more detail. The process of tracing out the changes is slow, but an important question is involved: whether or not the edition is punctuating according to the rhythmical and structural principles of the Manuscript.

In twenty-two instances which will not be discussed in detail but are given in the notes, the edition supplies commas at the end of the line.[5] In fourteen others, similarly listed, it adds

commas at the caesura.[6] In most of these particular changes the
logical and in varying degrees the rhythmical articulation of
the line are both improved (although in a few instances doubled
metrical pauses in the line might be questioned, as for example
444, 517 and 628, where second commas are added further to
define short relatives or other brief, minor constructions).

In some further instances the deftness of rhythmical touch is
notable, and might well make us wonder just who the corrector
was:

> And cheifly thou O Spirit that dost prefer
> Before all temples th' upright heart & pure
> Instruct me, for thou know'st;

> And chiefly Thou O Spirit, that dost prefer[7]
> Before all Temples th' upright heart and pure,
> Instruct me, for Thou know'st;
>   (17–19)

> Nigh on the plain in many cells prepar'd
> That underneath had veins of liquid fire
> Sluc'd from the lake a second multitude . . .

> Nigh on the Plain in many cells prepar'd,
> That underneath had veins of liquid fire
> Sluc'd from the Lake, a second multitude . . .
>   (700–2)

> For who can yet beleive though after losse . . .

> For who can yet beleeve, though after loss, . . .
>   (631)

In contrast, there are some disturbing instances when the
edition inserts commas in an obvious attempt, which nevertheless fails, to correct defective pointing in the Manuscript. For
example, at lines 59–60 the edition removes the Manuscript's
comma following *kenne,* and inserts instead a comma after *wilde,*
whereas what was probably needed was the original comma
following *kenne,* plus, certainly, a heavier stop after *wilde,*[8] . . . .
The edition adds a comma after *renown'd,* 507, but again a
heavier stop such as a colon is required. Also the edition adds
a comma after *seat's,* 796, whereas commas after *themselves* 793
and *sat* 795 are more conspicuously lacking.

Sometimes the edition's alterations do active damage. Here it might be thought that they spoil a delicate and right sequence of stops:

> . . . [   ] that pigmean race
> Beyond the Indian mount, or Faerie Elves
> Whose midnight revells, by a forrest side
> Or fountain, some belated peasant sees,
> Or dreams hee sees, while over head the Moon
> Sits arbitress, and neerer to the earth
> Wheels her pale course:

> . . . like that Pigmean Race
> Beyond the *Indian* Mount, or Faerie Elves,
> Whose midnight Revels, by a Forrest side
> Or Fountain some belated Peasant sees,
> Or dreams he sees, while over head the Moon
> Sits Arbitress, and neerer to the Earth
> Wheels her pale course, . . .
> (780–6)

In the Manuscript pointing the lines move easily and gracefully from caesura to caesura, until just at the right moment a shorter breathing indicates an appropriate hesitation: "Or fountain, some belated peasant sees,/Or dreams hee sees, . . .". There seems scant gain to the grammar and none to the poetry in the changes made at lines 781 and 783.

In other instances there are sharper rhythmical improprieties in the edition's alterations. It once or twice inserts grammatically incorrect commas, which if meant to be metrical stops are inept;[9] more often, it adds commas which embarrass the rhythm, although they may be of some slight grammatical use according to the contemporary habit of fully punctuating even minor sentence elements:

> Of Oreb or of Sinai didst inspire . . .

> Of *Oreb*, or of *Sinai*, didst inspire . . .
> (7)

> Still urges, & a fiery deluge fed . . .

> Still urges, and a fiery Deluge, fed . . .
> (68)

Glory of him that made them to transform . . .

Glory of him, that made them, to transform[10] . . .
$$(370)$$

Whither upheld by strength or chance or fate;

Whether upheld by strength, or Chance, or Fate, . . .
$$(133)$$

T'wixt upper, nether and surrounding fires;

'Twixt upper, nether, and surrounding Fires;
$$(346)$$

The Manuscript characteristically omits one or both of the dividing marks of punctuation in series such as those in the last two examples, in order to keep the lines fluent. The printed 1667 text also often shows similar practices, presumably retained from the original copy.

The following changes similarly are atypical of the style of the Manuscript, which tends to avoid doubling metrical pauses in a single line and would be unlikely fully to punctuate such minor sentence elements as those below, particularly the coordinates:

One next himselfe in power & next in crime, . . .

One next himself in power, and next in crime, . . .
$$(79)$$

Hath scath'd the forrest oakes or mountain pines, . . .

Hath scath'd the Forrest Oaks, or Mountain Pines, . . .
$$(613)$$

Cornice or freeze with bossy sculptures grav'n, . . .

Cornice or Freeze, with bossy Sculptures grav'n, . . .
$$(716)$$

It is to be noted in line 79 that the light pointing of the Manuscript would seem to have been deliberate, since, as Helen Darbishire[11] detected, the comma after *crime,* was itself a correction, by a different hand from the scribe's. The line had therefore been revised, yet it had not been thought necessary to add more than the one comma.[12] One further comma added by the edition might be questioned, depending on what kind of emphasis one chooses to give in reading the lines. The comma inserted at the end of line 465 after *Ascalon,* is a second metrical pause, and it is uncharacteristic of Milton to use commas before *and* in a series. 1674 returns to the Manuscript's reading.

To summarize so far. In almost all cases where the first edition adds commas to the Manuscript text, a grammatical purpose is evident. In most instances the edition refines the grammar while yet paying some regard to the structural pointing of the Manuscript. That is, grammatically useful commas are added mainly at the natural pauses in the verse line. But sometimes the edition can be seen to be punctuating grammatically yet across the metre; in a few instances it adds metrical stops which confuse the syntax; and more frequently it adds commas which, though grammatically acceptable and metrically placed, nevertheless spoil the rhythm by over-punctuating – making too many pauses in a single line. It has already been remarked that the Manuscript's habit (not a rigid rule, but a prevailing practice) is to avoid double punctuation in the same line. It is clear that, if too many lines in the poem were punctuated twice, it would be the half-line which dominated the rhythmical plan of the verse, and we should lose our sense of the whole line as the basic rhythmical component.

Some eighteen deletions of commas by the edition also suggest a mainly grammatical concern. Eight marks, listed in the notes, all grammatically slight, might have been purposely taken out.[13] In the Manuscript six of these eight commas fall at the caesura (146, 245, 394) or at the line ending (201, 245, 404) and were probably intended chiefly to mark the verse pauses. In accordance with the rhythmical habit already explained, these 'redundant' marks only half define some minor sentence element. So presented the punctuation is illogical, and the edition is more logical in leaving out the half defining punctuation altogether. The Manuscript's comma at 245 in addition to being a metrical mark is probably meant to carry a contemptuous stress on *he*, ... The Manuscript's commas at 146 and 295 are important for phrasing, and the altered lines

in the edition do not read well. However, the two other commas
listed (398 and 611) are both unmetrical and grammatically
negligible, and the edition could have deleted them partly on
rhythmical grounds. Also, the commas at 201, 245 and 404 are
second metrical pauses in the lines, so that these deletions
too could be preferred for rhythmical as well as grammatical
reasons. But the edition shows no rhythmical consistency in
these matters, since elsewhere it removes rhythmically needed
or appropriate commas from the text or inserts unmetrical
commas.

It is harder to say whether five other omissions by the edition
were intended or accidental.[14] Although the deletions at 21,
218 and 651 are grammatically not incorrect, there is little to
recommend any of the changes. The Manuscript's grave pause
after *Abysse,* (line 21) seems right for both the rhythmical
phrasing and the feeling of the line. The edition's removal of the
comma following *God,* (line 42) creates a confusing double
reference and an unpleasant run-on of four lines. The Manuscript's pointing at 218 represents Milton's normal punctuation
in a series, and the deleted comma also marks the true caesura,
which in the altered reading is wrongly made to fall after *good-
ness, ...* The absence of a comma in line 366 is confusing;
and finally, the edition's deletion of the comma after *Heav'n,*
(line 651) again makes several lines run on without a pause. In
nearly every instance the rhythms of the verse are damaged,
and at 42 and 366 the sense also.

Three further omissions also seem uncertain in purpose.
Two commas in line 383 and the single one of line 362, all
deleted by the edition, were probably intended by the Manuscript to carry special emphasis. At any rate their omission,
although not unrhythmical, is ungrammatical and so contrary
to almost all the edition's other corrections.

Allowance has to be made for a certain amount of negligence
at the press. The compositor most likely missed a few commas,
as perhaps in the eight instances immediately preceding; he or
the corrector deleted others, probably mainly on grammatical
but perhaps to a limited extent on rhythmical grounds. But the
most important inference is to be drawn from the very small
total number of such omissions. The Manuscript's pointing was
evidently considered by the press to be so scanty as to require

that commas much oftener be added than removed. The rhythmical basis of this sparing punctuation could hardly have been fully apparent to the press correctors.[15]

What has been said so far on the minor punctuation variants thus confirms that the Manuscript's general intention (especially plain in its handwritten corrections to the pointing) was to punctuate with main reference to the rhythmical structure of the verse. The Manuscript inserts or omits commas according to whether or not they fall at a natural verse pause; it tries to avoid making too many pauses in any one line; and it apparently allows exceptions to these principles chiefly where sense or emphasis urgently require them. The edition, on the other hand, seems to be punctuating with a much more persistent concern for grammatical regularity. The number of its changes is statistically not large; but their emphasis is different. The edition often contrives to accommodate its grammatical corrections to the verse structure; but it does not show an invariable regard for the Manuscript's rhythmical habits of pointing, and sometimes (as in making too many even of metrical stops in a line) it has evidently failed to understand those rhythmical principles in full. There are just enough differences between its style of punctuation and the Manuscript's to tell us something of importance about each.

VI

The Manuscript of Book I and the 1667 Variants: Rhetorical Punctuation

1. *Emphatic Punctuation*

A second individual feature of the Manuscript punctuation, clearly brought out by the 1667 variants, is its frequent use of a heavy or emphasizing punctuation. That is to say, the Manuscript often uses stops heavier than ordinary grammar, whether ours or that of the seventeenth century, would seem to require. These heavy stops, metrically placed like most of the punctuation, stand out by reason of their greater weight relative to the other stops in the context. Such emphatic stopping has every appearance of being deliberate in the Manuscript. Three times these heavy stoppings are corrections to the written copy, once by a different hand from the scribe's:[1] *Mankind; what time* 36 *empire; that* 114 *Innumerable. As when* 338. The last instance is a heightened pointing to introduce epic simile.

Such heavy stoppings are, like the structural punctuation, primarily aural in intention. They are guides to vocal emphasis and inflection in the reading aloud of the verse. They help to supply the narrative spontaneity and constantly changing intonation, the cherished illusion of the speaking voice, all of which form part of the 'unpremeditated' effect of Milton's verse, just as the light rhythmical punctuation supplies much of the verse's 'ease'.

It is very noticeable that the edition tends to reduce such rhetorical stops. Perhaps they were thought to be illogical; perhaps the general effect of so much heavy stopping was found to be cumbersome and old-fashioned. At any rate, these unusually heavy pointings seem to have disturbed the press correctors, who no doubt were paying chief regard to the correctness of the punctuation as it would be seen on the printed page. They would have been reading the lines rather than hearing them. In modernizing these along with other elements in the punctuation, the correctors failed to realize what special emphasis the stops carried.

There are about thirty-four instances, including the following illustrative passages, corrected in this way by the edition:

1. Thither, if but to prie, shall be perhaps
   [ ]r first eruption; thither or else where:

   Thither, if but to prie, shall be perhaps
   Our first eruption, thither or elsewhere:
   (655–6)

2. If such astonishment as this can seise
   Eternal spirits: or have ye chos'n this place
   After the toyle of battell to repose . . .

   If such astonishment as this can sieze
   Eternal spirits; or have ye chos'n this place
   After the toyl of Battel to repose . . .
   (317–19)

3. Yet to their Generalls voice they soon obai'd;
   Innumerable.

   Yet to their Generals Voyce they soon obeyd
   Innumerable.
   (337–8)

4. Regions of sorrow, dolefull shades, where peace
   And rest can never dwell; Hope never comes
5. That comes to all: but torture with out end
   Still urges, . . .

   Regions of sorrow, doleful shades, where peace
   And rest can never dwell, hope never comes
   That comes to all; but torture with out end
   Still urges, . . .
   (65–8)

6.   . . . , to support uneasy steps
   Over the burning Marle, not like those steps
   On Heavens azure; and the torrid clime
   Smote on him sore besides, vaulted with fire;

> . . . to support uneasie steps
> Over the burning Marle, not like those steps
> On Heavens Azure, and the torrid Clime
> Smote on him sore besides, vaulted with Fire;
> (295–8)

7.   : hee through the armed files
Darts his experienc'd eye, and soon travers
The whole battalion views; thir order due,
Thir visages and stature as of Gods,
Thir number last he summs.

> : He through the armed Files
> Darts his experienc't eye, and soon traverse
> The whole Battalion views, thir order due,[2]
> Thir visages and stature as of Gods,
> Thir number last he summs.
> (567–71)

8.   ; his forme had yet not lost
All her original brightnesse; nor appear'd
Lesse then Archangel ruin'd, and th' excess
Of glory obscur'd:

> ; his form had yet not lost
> All her Original brightness, nor appear'd
> Less then Arch Angel ruind, and th' excess
> Of Glory obscur'd:
> (591–4)

9.   . . . , while night
Invests the sea, and wished morn delayes.
So stretcht out huge in length the Arch-fiend lay . . .

> . . . , while Night
> Invests the Sea, and wished Morn delayes:
> So stretcht out huge in length the Arch-fiend lay . . .
> (207–9)

Most of the changes recorded above are grammatically more correct by seventeenth-century or indeed by any standards.[3] Nevertheless, these alterations all take away something of the characteristic movement of Milton's verse, and the ear familiar with his syntax quickly senses that they are wrong. The Manuscript pointings clearly demonstrate Milton's use of a strong stopping to indicate sharp qualification, contrast, or antithesis, as in examples one, two and five. Also to give emphasis to some particular word, or to set off a significant statement, as in examples three and four. And lastly, to block out the narrative in clearly marked, emphatic steps, as in examples six to eight. The practice of 'blocking out' by a strong punctuation is a consistent habit in the poem; it is less in evidence in the early autograph poems, but perhaps the parallel there is the use of heavy pointing to define sonnet stanzas. This type of heavy pointing in *Paradise Lost* relates to narrative action and to periodic structure rather than to sentence logic; the use of semicolon and colon in such contexts has not necessarily much reference to the independence of the sentence element.[4]

We may compare with examples one, two and five above, the pointings to indicate contrast or a break which were previously cited in "Lycidas" and *Comus* (Trinity MS, page 32, line 9 and page 12, line 38). Similarly we may compare with examples three and four above, the emphasizing pointings of Sonnet 11, line 8 and Sonnet 14, line 4 (Trinity MS, pages 40–1). Milton's distinctive usage in these respects has not altered between the early and the later poems; nor, evidently, have the negative reactions of his editors. It was noted in chapter I, 3 that two at least of these rhetorical stops in the early poems apparently have been mistranscribed by modern editors. The first editors of *Paradise Lost* also reacted with embarrassment to the unusual punctuation, often reducing Milton's heavy stops; and most modern editors of *Paradise Lost* have followed the first edition.

In this context may be mentioned two Manuscript pointings (listed separately in Appendix A). The marks at lines 362 and 467 were given in 1667 as commas and have been so transcribed by Miss Darbishire and others.[5] However, the photographs of the Manuscript show a distinct dot well placed in each case over the comma, and consultation of the original confirms that these are inked marks and that the stops are intended semicolons. There seems no reason to regard these semicolons in the Manuscript as other than rhetorical stops, similar to those in examples three and four above (emphasizing punctuation) and examples six to eight (blocking-out punctuation), and similarly reduced by the edition.

G

The first edition shows a considerable number of down-pointings of heavy stops, along lines similar to those indicated in examples one to eight above. These are listed separately.[6] Helen Darbishire restored to her edition of *Paradise Lost* the original punctuation in five of the passages quoted at length (namely in lines 297, 318, 569, 592 and 656); also that in all the parallel instances cited (note 6) except for lines 37, 540 and 640. There seems no reason why the remaining pointings should not also be retained. The only exception is MS *Fearless;*] Ed. *Fearless,* 131. This pointing seems unsuitably emphatic and may be a mistake – perhaps an old-fashioned heavy metrical pointing.

It may be mentioned here that the first edition shows a few changes only to a heavier pointing. Half of these involve in-dications of a rather obvious and mechanical kind where the Manuscript text is or was thought to be defective. Once a full stop is marked in at a place which is obviously intended as the end of a sentence.[7] Once a colon is altered to full stop to introduce speech – a usage followed more or less consistently throughout the first edition.[8] Once an exclamation mark is added after an ejaculation, and earlier in the same line comma becomes semicolon to show a syntactical break in speech.[9] Possibly in this line the compositor missed or merely ignored an existing Manuscript correction of semicolon to comma after *he,* . . . . Also, two question marks are substituted for other marks at 183 and 380 (in the latter, wrongly). These few alterations are mostly matters of differing printers' conventions or forms as regards special marks, rather than matters of true rhetorical or expressive significance. We should now with the Manuscript prefer colon to full stop to introduce speech. Our own practice would however agree with the printer's in his substitution of the exclamation mark in 84 (although it is ruinous to the phrasing of the line) and, in one case, of question mark. The Elizabethans sometimes exchanged question with exclamation mark, so the scribe had not necessarily been in error. But we should probably use the dash instead of semicolon (as in line 84) to show an obvious interruption in speech. The alternative signs mean the same thing; once the convention has been decided, the signification of each mark stays constant.

On three occasions of a different kind the edition substitutes heavier dividing marks between the main clauses of a long sentence, in the logically outlining way illustrated earlier in Butler or Caryl, giving semicolon for Manuscript's comma.[10] Once a heavier pointing in the edition turns out to be an error where the compositor missed a scribal correction in the Manuscript.[11]

In only one instance could the edition be said to have heightened a pointing possibly for rhetorical emphasis – a case when a simile is introduced: MS *clusters, they*] Ed. *clusters; they* 771. Three other heightened pointings, similarly associated with epic similes, must be accepted as in fact grammatical changes, since the edition's downpointings in other parts of these similes necessitate adjusting and weighting the pointings in these places. Thus the changes at 202, 229 and 238, taken in conjunction with the changes at 208, 230 and 237, are all merely regularizing changes designed to reshape the syntax so that colon always introduces independent clauses. In no other instance in Book I except 771 has the first edition introduced heavier rhetorical markings of any of the other kinds (not associated with similes) illustrated in Manuscript examples one to eight. In contrast, several times the 1674 edition makes such apparently rhetorical emendations (see Appendix C, section 8); and possibly once the first edition does so in a *proof* change (see the reading at III, 630, discussed in Appendix B).

It is apparent, then, that when the first edition does heighten the punctuation it does so almost exclusively for grammatical reasons. It is also evident that the printed text is far readier to lighten than to increase the weight of the stops (some thirty-four pointings are reduced, as compared with less than half that number raised), and that in doing so it obscures something of the Manuscript's distinctive, emphatic style in pointing. Here is another matter, therefore, in which the 1667 variants offer a valuable guide to distinctively Miltonic habits in punctuation, habits which are still evident and of basic importance throughout the printed poem, although less consistently followed there. The Manuscript has a particular value in conveying so clear an impression of poetical purposes working through its punctuation, and in offering a text less overlaid with contradicting intentions than does either of the first two corrected editions.

2. *Heavy Pointing in Epic Similes*

The pointing of example nine from the Manuscript, quoted earlier, is most conveniently discussed now. The first edition repeatedly reduces the weight of especially heavy markings such as the colon in line 208 of this passage – marks most often found in the Manuscript in association with epic similes. What the Manuscript may be trying to convey by such unconventional pointing is best gathered from a rapid survey of its punctuation of similes throughout Book I.

Milton works out similes with varying degrees of elaboration; therefore he presents them with different degrees of emphasis. Among the similes in the Manuscript Book I we may distinguish roughly four forms. All characteristically make use of a heavy pointing, varying in weight exactly according to the length and prominence of the simile. Such pointing is usually rhetorical, that is, heavier than the grammar requires or heavier than the general pattern of pointing in the context.

(1) First, there are shorter comparisons or sometimes series of brief comparisons (or analogies). These are normally introduced by semicolons, and if more than one are separated by semicolons. Such punctuation serves sharply to draw attention to the short or passing comparison which might otherwise be lost in the flow of the narrative. Examples are the following:

> ... up they sprung
> Upon the wing; as when men wont to watch
> On duty, sleeping found by whom they dread,
> Rouse and bestirr themselves ere well awake.
>   (331-4)

> And now his heart ...
> Glories: for never since created man
> Met such imbodied force, as nam'd with these
> Could merit more then that small infantry
> Warr'd on by Cranes: though all the giant brood
> Of Phlegra with th' Heroic race were joyn'd ...
> Mixt with auxiliar Gods; and what resounds
> In fable or Romance of Uthers sonne ...;
> And all who since, baptiz'd or infidell

> Jousted in Aspramont or Montalban, . . .
> Or whom Biserta sent from Afric shore . . .
> (571–85)

(2) When worked out at any length, similes are usually presented formally by the familiar *As when* and are preceded and followed by full stops. The heavy pointing makes the comparison stand out very clearly from the rest of the narrative, yet at the same time the grammatical incompleteness forces a reading continuous with what precedes and also probably with what follows, the full stops giving the effect not of terminations in the thought but rather of particularly pronounced pauses which, after their initial hesitation, only throw the reader more strongly on to the next part. Examples are these:

> . . . , yet faithfull, how they stood,
> Thir glory witherd. As when Heavens fire
> Hath scath'd the forrest oakes or mountain pines,
> With singed top thir stately growth though bare
> Stands on the blasted heath.
> (611–15)

> Thither wing'd with speed
> A numerous brigad hasten'd. As when bands
> Of pioners with spade and pickaxe arm'd
> Forerun the royall camp, to trench a field,
> Or cast a rampart.
> (674–8)

If the similes are not presented formally by *As when*, the pointing may be lighter (but may still be rhetorical); these features are seen in the next two examples, which are approximately of the same length as the two just given:

> . . . ponderous shield . . .
> Behind him cast; the broad circumference
> Hung on his shoulders like the moon whose orb . . .
> (284–91)

> . . . down they light
> On the firm brimstone, and fill all the plain;

> A multitude, like which the populous North
> Pour'd never from her frozen loyns, . . .
>   (349–55)

(3) The most elaborate, longest similes have two distinct
parts, comparison and application (the *As when* and the *So*),
both normally introduced by full stops. This (to us) unusual
pointing has the advantage that it marks the simile very
strongly off, both in its substance and its application, compel-
ling the mind to reflect on each part and giving the whole
simile a prominence which suits its epic character and the
deliberate care with which it has been formulated. At the same
time, the logical incompleteness of the presentation forces the
mind to build its own bridges, to carry the thought on over the
full stops and to recognize all three parts (object, comparison,
and application) as together forming one natural, complete unit.
By analogy, the correct way to read the simile aloud would be
as an emphatically inflected but continuous rhythmical structure. Examples of this form of simile in the Manuscript are
given below. (The double simile in the second passage is introduced by somewhat lighter stops, colon and semicolon, to
indicate the joint and auxiliary status of the two comparisons.)

>   . . . obai'd;
> Innumerable. As when the potent rod . . .
> Wav'd round the coast, up call'd a pitchy cloud
> Of Locusts, warping on the Eastern wind,
> That . . . dark'n'd all the Land of Nile.
> So numberless were those bad Angells seen . . .
> T'wixt upper, nether and surrounding fires;
> Till, as a signal given, . . .
>   (337–47)

>   . . . th' excess
> Of glory obscur'd: As when the sun new ris'n
> Looks through the horizontal misty air
> Shorn of his beames; or from behind the moon
> In dimme eclipse disastrous twilight sheds
> On half the nations, and with fear of change
> Perplexes Monarchs. Dark'n'd so, yet shon
> Above them all th' Archangel: but his face . . .
>   (593–600)

. . .
Brusht with the hisse of russling wings. As bees
In spring time, when the sun with Taurus rides,
Poure forth thir populous youth about the hive . . .
New rub'd with baume, expatiate and conferr
Thir state affairs. So thick the aerie crowd
Swarm'd and were straitn'd; till the signal giv'n . . .
(768–76)

(4) The fourth form of simile is similar to that just shown,
except that the comparison instead of being formally introduced is arrived at more indirectly. It may be worked into the
syntax of the preceding sentence, or may perhaps be arrived
at by means of a short preliminary comparison. But the same
emphatic presentation is used, in that when the real gist of the
comparison or the main comparison is arrived at there is again
a strong rhetorical stop, usually colon, to set it off. Semicolon
or colon is probably used in such cases because of the more
continuous nature of the syntax, which renders the use of the
full stop, even as an emphasizing stop, awkward. The devious
way in which the comparison or the important part of it has
been arrived at gives an impression that the effective analogy
has been hit upon by some happy chance; all the same, the
pointing does not allow us to pass it over too quickly. Such
markings are seen, in the examples next shown, at ; Him 202–3
: or 304   : they 786. The first edition changes the semicolon at
202–3 to colon – possibly for rhetorical heightening, more likely
because the clause introduced is independent. But the lighter
pointing is consistent with Milton's practice in such contexts.
And there is usually at the close of such comparisons a coda-like
application (as there was in the third group), introduced by
full stop (or once, in the examples given, by colon), and merging,
as the simile concludes, into the resumed narrative.

. . . , in bulk as huge
As whom the fables name of monstrous size,
Titanian, . . . , or that Sea-beast
Leviathan, which God of all his works,
Created hugest that swim th' Ocean stream;
Him haply slumbring on the Norway foame
The Pilot of some small night-founderd skiff, . . .

Moores by his side under the Lee, while night
Invests the sea, and wished morn delayes.
So stretcht out huge in length the Arch-fiend lay
Chain'd on the burning lake, nor ever thence . . .
(196–210)

. . . , hee stood and calld
His legions, Angell form's, who lay intrans't
Thick as Autumnall leaves that strow the brooks
In Vallombrosa, where th' Etrurian shades
High overarcht imbowre: or scatterd sedge
Afloat when with fierce winds Orion arm'd
Hath vext the red-sea coast, whose waves orethrew
Busiris and his Memphian chivalry . . .
And broken chariot wheeles. so thick bestrown
Abject and lost lay these, . . .
(300–12)

Throng numberless [   ] that pigmean race
Beyond the Indian mount, or Faerie Elves
Whose midnight revells, . . . , some belated peasant sees,
Or dreams hee sees, while over head the Moon . . .
Wheels her pale course: they on thir mirth and d[   ]
Intent, with jocond music charme his eare;
At once with joy and fear his heart rebounds.
Thus incorporeal spirits to smallest forms
Reduc'd thir shapes immense, . . .
(779–90)

Two general features emerge from the above survey of epic
similes. The first is that for the sake of emphasis the Manuscript
regularly marks off with a stronger pointing the beginning and
end of each main formally presented simile, or each of the two
parts in a long formal simile (comparison and application, the
As when and the *So*), or each element in a multiple comparison,
or else the most essential aspect of an indirectly introduced
simile when the real bearing is arrived at. It uses for these
purposes heavy or rhetorical stops directly proportionate in
weight to the length, prominence and formality of the comparisons. The use of the full stop as a rhetorical marking in the
context of similes is particularly striking – it is used as if it
represented a pause something like a colon but rather heavier.

The beginning and often the end of the longer, formal comparisons, or else the beginnings of both their main parts, are normally marked by such rhetorical full stops (as in groups two and three).

A second feature is that, in the longest similes which might because of this unusual weight of pointing become too much separated from their context, the Manuscript contrives at the close of the comparison (after the *So*) to mould the simile back into the ensuing narrative by the use of a punctuation now *lighter* than one would expect. This is seen in most of the long, formal similes (the similes in two parts). In particular, the third group of examples have in every case the second or *So* part directly tied to the subsequent narrative by a semicolon or a colon, just where one would expect a full stop. In the fourth group also, the coda-like application is sometimes directly tied to the ensuing narrative by a lighter punctuation.

The way, then, to read the long Miltonic epic simile is as a single, extended verse period, punctuated not grammatically but rhetorically, the unusually heavy pointing making the comparison or all its parts stand out distinctly, yet without detaching it completely from the narrative in which it is embedded.

A good deal of the Manuscript's original style of pointing of similes survives into the printed first edition. For example, the simile at II, 635–43 illustrates all of the distinctive features noted above: the formal comparison introduced by a full stop; the most essential aspect of the comparison set off by another heavy stop (a colon); and the second part of the simile, its application, again set off by a full stop and at its conclusion tied to the ensuing narrative by a relatively light punctuation. But it is apparent that the printer or his corrector did not like the particularly heavy stops associated in the Manuscript with epic similes, and in Book I we can see that he proceeded (in accordance with his general tendency to lighten all unusually heavy punctuation) to reduce a large number of such markings.

The rhetorical full stops were the printer's chief target; these he often read as approximate to, and rendered as, colons. He most often altered the full stop introducing the second part (the *So* or application) of the formal simile. This was an obvious correction to attempt, since it regularizes the syntax: *So* or *Such* now balances and grammatically completes *As when*.

Sometimes this change is accompanied by other regularizing changes elsewhere in the simile, such as those at 202, 238, 304. Thus we have, before *So* or *Such*, four changes down from full stop, listed in the notes.[12] Since in any case such full stops have not been consistently reduced throughout the printed text, there seems no justification at all for these changes.[13] Nor does there seem any justification for the edition's two lesser downpointings of rhetorical colon or semicolon, used to introduce each element in a double comparison;[14] nor again for its downpointing of rhetorical colon, beautifully used to set off the essential part of a simile.[15] No more can one justify its downpointings of rhetorical semicolon or colon used to introduce a shorter comparison, or, as in line 230, a long comparison if the flow of the syntax is such as to make the use of the full stop unsuitable.[16]

In the case of the simile beginning at line 229 the first edition regularizes the pointing both at the opening and close of the comparison: MS "fire, . . . hew; as when"] Ed. "fire; . . . hue, as when" 229–30; MS ". Such resting . . . feet: him followd"] Ed. ": Such resting . . . feet. Him followed" 237–8. What is the correct punctuation has been somewhat disputed.[17] But an unnecessary difficulty has been made over the passage. The Manuscript's pointing throughout is entirely in accord with Milton's normal practice when presenting such similes. We have a heavy rhetorical pause (colon, not full stop, because the comparison is arrived at circuitously) to introduce the *As when* of a long comparison. This is only an emphasizing pause and does not prevent the reader's making the connection which Milton obviously intended between the *hew* or aspect of the fiery land and the image of the volcano which follows. Then we have rhetorical full stop before the *Such* or application of the simile; and lastly we have a relatively light punctuation (colon instead of full stop) to tie the simile at its close back into the ensuing narrative.

In all of the changes recorded above the printer sacrificed much of the rhetorical impact of the Manuscript's unusual punctuation. Indeed, in Book I the press changes are numerous enough seriously to obscure the main lines of Milton's rhetorical punctuation of epic similes. These lines are remarkably consistent when one looks at the Manuscript in isolation. In the light of this original punctuation, such heavy pointing of similes as survives in the text of the first edition is much more meaningful.

3. *Milton's Punctuation and Butler's*

It is of interest to compare the style of punctuation in the Manuscript of Book I and also of the 1667 variants with the more typical style of pointing of the middle seventeenth century. On the one hand the Manuscript's pointing is much lighter and freer than, say, Butler's or Caryl's, in its rhythmical character regularly making use of far fewer minor stops than they and using a heavy punctuation with much less regularity. And on the other hand the Manuscript's pointing is occasionally much stronger than theirs, in its dramatic or rhetorical character occasionally making use of a weight of emphasizing punctuation which would not be permissible according to Butler's rules of logical expression.

As regards the first point of difference, it will be seen at once that the ample rhythms and surging momentum of Milton's verse are utterly incompatible with Butler's analytical style of punctuation, which tends to chop up every sentence into small logical compartments. The scanty, metrically oriented pointing of the Manuscript is intended to help shape the larger rhythmical structure of Milton's long verse periods and verse paragraphs. Designed to mould these longer curves and cadences, such pointing is opposed by nature to Butler's logically outlining punctuation, which multiplies commas in order to define all the smaller parts of every sentence and multiplies heavy stops to distinguish between major parts.

As regards the second point of difference, we have to realize that Milton's heavy pointing is usually serving a quite different function from Butler's. The latter habitually uses a graduated punctuation with many heavy stops in order mainly to differentiate the internal grammatical structure of his sentences. But Milton uses occasional heavily weighted stops chiefly in order to convey a variety of emphatic or dramatic effects in his representation of action, conversation or places – to provide a steady force of expression in his narrative. Or else he uses a rhetorical pointing to outline the organic structure of event and incident, without consistent reference to grammar or syntax. Thus he enables the reader to read his verse aloud with an appropriate emphasis on salient details of narrative, with a sense of the total structure of experience in each event, as also with a breathing adequate to the needs of his long verse periods. Milton's punctuation therefore has an altogether wider range of artistic purpose than does that of most of his contemporaries.

Such comparisons as the preceding ones must inevitably appear unflattering to Butler, since they have all been drawn from a poetical vantage point. They do not leave room to say that Butler was a superb logician and a grammatical reformer much in advance of his age. What he was trying to do with English syntax and punctuation was, simply, poles apart from what Milton was attempting.

Nor do the above comparisons mean to imply that Milton's punctuation has no foundation whatsoever in logic and grammar. It would be incorrect to convey any idea that the punctuation of *Paradise Lost* bears no relation at all to the grammatical usage of Milton's own period. To take only one or two examples, we often find in both Manuscript and 1667 texts comma before *and* in a compound; or the typical seventeenth-century logical distinction between semicolon and colon. The practice is simpler than Butler's, semicolon in *Paradise Lost* usually being used before conjunctive clauses if no contrast is intended, while colon is used before fully independent members. But to analyse Miltonic punctuation on a grammatical basis is inevitably confusing, for there is almost no consistency of practice in grammatical respects. Consistency lies rather in the steady subordination of grammar to the needs of the verse and the narrative. We can appreciate that grammatical and rhythmical or rhetorical schemes of punctuation need not invariably conflict. Such schemes may to a certain degree overlap, and there need be no confusion between them if the writer carefully slants his usage so as to give regular priority to the considerations which are most important to him. We might expect that for a poet, and especially such a poet as Milton, poetical considerations should usually be uppermost.

The style of punctuation of the 1667 corrections only, may be just a little closer to the mid-century norm as represented by Butler. The total number of punctuation changes made by the first edition in Book I is statistically far from large: about one correction in seven or eight lines (or, between one and two corrections per hundred words, with a very slight average increase in the total number of stops used). And even in this limited number of alterations there seems to be some degree of overlay or confusion of intention (perhaps interference between two correctors) – as if the edition were trying to repunctuate with some regard for the poetical style of the original and yet at the same time reduce the Manuscript's margin of grammatical error or unconventionality. But in so far as one can generalize, it is true to say that there are very few changes made during the early printing which are not consistent with or indeed obviously called for by seventeenth-century grammar. This is so, even though structural considerations are not entirely absent from the edition's punctuation.

The two smallest groups of changes in 1667 were seen to be omissions of commas and heightening of stops. The most important inference deriving from these two groups of changes is connected with their small numbers. The press correctors obviously felt it to be much more often necessary to put commas into Milton's copy than to take them out, just as they felt it to be more often necessary to reduce than to increase the weights of stops. They were clearly aware of those unconventional tendencies in the Manuscript pointing which have in the present study been called "rhythmical" and "rhetorical", and they felt that the second of these especially needed modification.

Much the largest group of changes consists of those instances where the first edition has added commas to the Manuscript's text. Here the edition's new punctuation stays closest to Milton's, in that most of these added commas (although mainly grammatical in intent) are accommodated to the verse structure. The next largest group of changes is the reduced stops. Considering that there are naturally fewer heavy stops than commas used per page, downpointings occur in at least an equal ratio to commas added. In this group of downpointings one can see very clearly that the correctors were being influenced by the seventeenth-century view, evident in such rules as Butler had formulated, about the need to make a clear logical distinction between major and minor parts of the sentence. Subordinate parts of the sentence or incidental words or phrases, whatever weight or value the voice might give to them in reading aloud, were not to be set off by heavier stops than the main members. Here the correctors' judgment was at fault. Like some later editors, they did not take sufficient account of the fact that Milton's meaning is usually plain enough, even though his grammar is frequently vague, elliptical or ambiguous, leaving sentences radically over-extended, wandering and incomplete. The best way of conveying Milton's main ideas and true sequences of thought is in fact as the Manuscript does, by a free rhetorical punctuation adjusted to the narrative context, and not by a pointing referred to logic or grammatical structure. In lessening the weight of stops or in otherwise altering or moving stops the edition not only often obscured something of the dramatic quality of the verse, but occasionally it ran itself into worse tangles of sense than those which it set out to rectify. Modern emendators have sometimes been similarly taxed by Milton's 'confused' grammar.

VII

Miltonic Pointing in the First Edition

The limited number of alterations to the punctuation introduced by the 1667 edition in Book I of *Paradise Lost* implies that in the complete twelve Books of the printed text, as in the first Book, much original Miltonic pointing survives. The poet's rhythmical habits of pointing are in evidence in nearly every line of the poem and need no further illustration. In the present chapter it is chiefly Milton's rhetorical uses of punctuation throughout *Paradise Lost* which will be considered. Using the Manuscript as guide, it is hoped to show that many irregularities and apparent oddities of pointing in the printed text may be justified by poetical considerations alone. Not only do individual unusual instances of punctuation take on meaning in the light of the Manuscript's rhetorical practices; so also do much larger elements of Milton's style and composition.

1. *Heavy Stopping*

A quick run through the scale of heavy stops shows a large number of interesting and unusual usages of punctuation in the first edition. Take the emphasizing comma, lowest in the scale of heavy stops, and an irregularity of pointing which is easily misunderstood:

> Yet not rejoycing in his speed, though bold,
> Far off and fearless, . . .
> (IV, 13–14)

The comma after *bold,* appears to be misplaced; it seems that it ought to have been put after *off* . . . . But read purely for its weight of pause, the questionable comma throws a slight ironical emphasis onto *Far off* . . . ; at the same time, it accentuates the antithesis contained in the first line: "Yet not rejoycing . . . ,

though bold, . . .". Milton's intention here, as so often in the
poem, was surely to emphasize the conflict in Satan's state of
mind; and the further and pointed implication is that now, after
his defeat, it is merely from a safe distance that Satan displays
bravery. (Is this not evident also at the end of Book II and in
Books IV and IX? Evasiveness, the wish to avoid another direct
conflict, is now a key to Satan's action.) Such a complex in-
nuendo could scarcely have been brought out by an ordinary
punctuation.[1]

The semicolon, various unusual and emphasizing functions of
which have already been noted in the Manuscript, may be used
in much the same way as the comma above to put particular
weight on a single word:

> . . . with Power (thir Power was great)
> Hovering upon the Waters; what they met
> Solid or slimie, as in raging Sea
> Tost up and down, together crowded drove
> From each side shoaling towards the mouth of Hell.
> (IX [Ed. 2, X], 284–8)

Here the weight of the semicolon in the second line, with the
emphasis it lays upon *; what* . . . , perfectly suggests the pause
and strain as Sin and Death first collect the mud and slime in
Chaos, then (as with a heave to overcome the inert dead weight)
crowd or shovel it in a heap before them.[2]

The semicolon may be used similarly to throw into unexpected relief a significant phrase or clause, as for instance
the two phrases "; A Wilderness of sweets;" and "; enormous
bliss." which sum up the essence of the description in the
passage below.[3]

> Thir glittering Tents he passd, and now is come
> Into the blissful field, through Groves of Myrrhe,
> And flouring Odours, Cassia, Nard, and Balme;
> A Wilderness of sweets; for Nature here
> Wantond as in her prime, and plaid at will
> Her Virgin Fancies, pouring forth more sweet,
> Wilde above rule or Art; enormous bliss.
> (V, 291–7)

If successive short phrases or clauses are set off by such point-ing, the effect may be more immediately dramatic:

> That under ground they fought in dismal shade;[4]
> Infernal noise; Warr seem'd a civil Game
> To this uproar;
> (VI, 666-8)

A comparable technique of repeated heavy stops (semicolons or sometimes colons), used to block out emphatically the stages of a vigorous action, is seen throughout the extended description of the battle in Heaven (VI, 189 ff.). But this particular type of heavy stopping will be immediately familiar to Milton's reader, for it is a prominent feature throughout much of the poem, regularly contributing a certain excitement to the tenser moments of the narrative. Several illustrations have already been given from the Manuscript.[5] The device relates more con-sistently to dramatic context and to the organic structure of the long verse period than it does to grammatical syntax.

The colon as a heavier stop, in a context where commas and semicolons have already been liberally employed, may serve to register a number of sharper or more abrupt effects – most char-acteristically of a break or contrast in the thought or action. (In a more lightly stopped context semicolon may occasionally perform the same function.)[6] The colon thus used may suggest a moment of sharply suspended action, such as Eve's giddy moment of dream flight:

> Forthwith up to the Clouds
> With him I flew, and underneath beheld
> The Earth outstretcht immense, a prospect wide
> And various: wondring at my flight and change
> To this high exaltation; suddenly
> My Guide was gon, and I, me thought, sunk down,
> And fell asleep;
> (V, 86-92)

The pointing, which throughout follows the feeling of the pass-age so delicately (notice the dream-like hesitation of line 91), also contrives through the colon of the fourth line to suggest the pause of that very moment during which Eve is caught up to

H

the clouds and hangs marvelling – and also the end of that moment, which comes so quickly as, with the semicolon of the next line, she drops back to earth. The marking off of the relevant phrase with heavy stops at both beginning and end gives the reader the feeling that he has experienced the actual span of that prolonged and dizzy second.

A similar effect occurs in this next passage. Colons appear to mark off the actual blast of the archangelic trumpet as it suddenly opens forth, reaches out to the angels scattered in all the corners of Heaven, and is held for the space of three lines – until the angels, who have been as if transfixed by the ringing summons, can collect themselves and start up in response:

> Th' Angelic blast
> Filld all the Regions: from thir blissful Bowrs
> Of *Amarantin* Shade, Fountain or Spring,
> By the waters of Life, where ere they sate
> In fellowships of joy: the Sons of Light
> Hasted, resorting to the Summons high, ...
> (X [Ed. 2, XI], 76–81)

This small but perfect effect of arrested time and action depends mainly on the colon of the fifth line, which seems to put a sudden stop to the trumpet peal and jolt the angels into motion. Reducing this colon to comma changes the character of the entire passage.[7]

The use of colon to suggest an abrupt transition or change is well shown in the following:

> ... , thence many a League
> As in a cloudy Chair ascending rides
> Audacious, but that seat soon failing, meets
> A vast vacuitie: all unawares
> Fluttring his pennons vain plumb down he drops
> Ten thousand fadom deep, and to this hour
> Down had been falling, had not by ill chance
> The strong rebuff of som tumultuous cloud
> Instinct with Fire and Nitre hurried him
> As many miles aloft: that furie stay'd,
> Quencht in a Boggie *Syrtis*, neither Sea,
> Nor good dry Land: nigh founderd on he fares, ...
> (II, 929–40)

Here each colon indicates a sudden change. First, Satan while exploring Chaos drops into an unexpected void (how did Milton know about air pockets?) The pause of the fourth line seems like that very second during which he hangs suspended before plunging downward. Then, without having time to right himself, he is tossed upward (the abrupt stop of the next colon, at the *end* of the clause now, conveys the bump with which the upward fling ends). Again before he can recover, he is plunged into a bog (the elliptical clause here, ending so prematurely with the third colon, is like his gasp of surprise); and it is several moments (so this last colon also suggests) before he is able, shaken up and half drowned, to carry on. Notice too, in contrast to this jarring stopping, how vividly the almost unpointed lines which run on between lines 932–8 convey the feeling of Satan's seemingly endless drop into bottomless void and his balloon-like effortless ascent directly afterwards. It is possible, by changing the final colon to comma,[8] to make a single continuous grammatical unit out of the last three lines of this passage. But this is a much less effective pointing and obscures the contrast which has just been described between the suggestively gliding and the jarring punctuation.

A similar use of colon to indicate contrast occurs in the description of the tortures of the damned in Book II. Here the colon of the third line suggests the abruptness and intensity of the *bitter change* ... :[9]

> Thither by harpy-footed Furies hail'd,
> At certain revolutions all the damn'd
> Are brought: and feel by turns the bitter change
> Of fierce extreams, extreams by change more fierce,
> From Beds of raging Fire to starve in Ice ...
> (II, 596–600)

It was noted earlier that the Elizabethans and many seventeenth-century writers used colon to mark antithesis.[10] However, Milton's use of colon in the ways just described is not tied to oratorical balance; it is a dramatic and expressive device.

Lastly, the colon (like the semicolon as shown earlier) may occasionally be used in a more sustained and regular way and with longer clauses, so as firmly to block out the stages of an action or a description. Often, when colon is so used, some special effect obtains. In the following passage the unusually heavy pauses in repetition give the effect of short, parallel sentences, deliberately echoing the metrical pointing of the 1611 Version:

> Again, God said, let ther be Firmament
> Amid the Waters, and let it divide
> The Waters from the Waters: and God made
> The Firmament, expanse of liquid, pure,
> Transparent, Elemental Air, diffus'd
> In circuit to the uttermost convex
> Of this great Round: partition firm and sure,
> The Waters underneath from those above
> Dividing:
> (VII, 261-9)

Thus both semicolon and colon may be used to convey a variety of sharp or emphatic, abrupt or broken effects, or else in a more continuous way so as to indicate a vigorous succession of events. Both kinds of usages are rhetorical, that is, they relate to the dramatic or descriptive context more than to grammar. Probably the semicolon is used more often in the continuous and the colon in the discontinuous way. But there is no rigid distinction. Which stop shall be used in any specific context depends on the weight of the other punctuation in the context, as well as on the kind or degree of emphasis required.

The rhetorical full stop is found less often in *Paradise Lost*, but when it does occur, its impact is great. (An exception must here be made for the epic simile, with which such stoppings are regularly associated.) An illustration is offered by the passage below, where the frank overriding of the full stop in a heavily partitioned yet continuous syntax gives a structural effect comparable to that found in the epic simile:

> Yet not the more
> Cease I to wander where the Muses haunt
> Cleer Spring, or shadie Grove, or Sunnie Hill,
> Smit with the love of sacred song; but chief
> Thee *Sion* and the flowrie Brooks beneath
> That wash thy hallowd feet, and warbling flow,
> Nightly I visit: nor somtimes forget

Those other two equal'd with me in Fate,
So were I equal'd with them in renown,
Blind *Thamyris* and blind *Mæonides*,[11]
And *Tiresias* and *Phineus* Prophets old.
Then feed on thoughts, that voluntarie move
Harmonious numbers; as the wakeful Bird
Sings darkling, and in shadiest Covert hid
Tunes her nocturnal Note.
(III, 26–40)

". Then feed on thoughts . . ." obviously belongs to the same long sentence which runs without a break through the passage. But if the clause thus strongly marked had been set off by only a semicolon or a colon, it would have had no greater weight than the clauses which precede and follow, and it seems that a much longer and a very pronounced pause was wanted just at this point. The syntactical partitioning is such as to mark off with a progressively heavier pointing each of several stages in the thought. The poet indicates the sequence of his reflections. First he wanders where the Muses haunt (he meditates upon classical poesy). Then his thoughts turn naturally to his religious subject . . . *Sion*. Next, by a still natural association but wandering farther afield (heavier pause of colon here), he thinks about his great poetic predecessors. And finally there is a sharper break in his thoughts – a long pause during which he scarcely thinks at all, but instead broods or *feeds* on thought. This is the pause which bridges the processes of reflection and creation; the moment before thought, in a deeper and less conscious process, becomes spontaneously transmuted into harmonious verse. The weight of the full stop is beautiful just here. It calls a sharp halt to the poet's mental ramblings and suggests the way in which his mind collects itself before sinking into its second state, that of a more intense creative activity. The heavy pause evokes just that moment of suspended thought, in fact, before the mind surrenders itself to the Muse and, from thinking about poetry, begins to make it. If one regularizes the punctuation here and reduces the full stop to semicolon or colon something central to the passage is lost.

To the above passage it is worth comparing the use of rhetorical full stop in the Folio *Macbeth*. Simpson's[12] comment on the passage in question will be given in full.

> ....that but this blow
> Might be the be all, and the end all. Heere,
> But heere, upon this Banke and Schoole of time,
> Wee'ld iump the life to come. But in these Cases,
> We still have iudgement heere, ...
>
> *Macbeth*, I. vii. 4–8

Read these lines as they are pointed in the Folio, and the period
after 'end all' arrests attention. Hanmer was the first to empty
the passage of all its metrical power by printing 'the be-all and
the end-all here,' but the meaning as well as the movement of
the verse suggests the close connection of the words 'Heere, but
heere'. The pause is the most powerful of which blank verse is
capable. At that final monosyllable the rhythm gathers like a wave,
plunges over to the line beyond, and falls in all its weight and
force on the repeated word. The check given to the line fits in
admirably with the brooding, hesitating mood of the speaker. . . .
In no other way could this particular rhythm have been suggested
in print: for its full realization we must go to the actor.

Other instances of rhetorical full stop occur in the Manuscript
at lines 530 and 540, where full stops introduce two incomplete
sentences in a passage which need not be fully quoted here. The
edition somewhat inconsistently downpoints the second of these
marks to colon, though it does not alter the first. But the
two heavy stops each mark one main phase of the military
review taking place in Hell. First, the general, Satan, orders
that the imperial standard be elevated (". Then strait com-
mands . . ."). Next, the army respond with their answering
salute (". At which the universall host upsent/A shout . . .").
Meanwhile the actual unfurling of the flag, a smaller act which
is part of the larger ritual, is marked by the colons of lines 535
and 539 – lesser strong stops, set between the major full stops
which frame the whole event:

> . . . , a Cherub tall:
> Who forthwith from the glittering staff unfurl'd
> Th' imperial ensign , . . . rich emblaz'd,
> Seraphic arms and trophies: all the while . . .

The edition's levelling out of the punctuation spoils this minute
and exact outlining of the incident.

2. *Light Stopping*

All of the passages cited thus far illustrate a heavy or deliberately heightened stopping, used for rhetorical emphasis or to convey certain dramatic impressions. The reverse also sometimes obtains in *Paradise Lost*: a pointing lighter than ordinary grammar requires is deliberately employed in order to convey opposite impressions or effects. Such light, rhetorical stopping is a feature distinct from the poem's habitually sparing, rhythmical punctuation; it is used with more localized intention. For example, commas may sometimes be unexpectedly omitted, just as they are sometimes unexpectedly inserted. Consider the effectively muddled run-ons of "The dark unbottom'd infinite Abyss" (II, 405) and "The black tartareous cold infernal dregs" (VII, 238), or the similar impression of confusion in ", so thick bestrown/Abject and lost lay these," (I, 311–12). Such effects as these seem too felicitous to be accidental.

A step further on the scale of light stops is the comma set in place of semicolon between independent clauses, or in place of full stop between what ought grammatically to be written as complete sentences. It is interesting to contrast with the descriptions of Satan's appearance and his military exercises in Hell, quoted earlier, [13] where a solemn and firm effect obtained through the repeated use of a heavy, blocking-out type of pointing, the following passage where a light pointing simulates speed:

> Forthwith from Councel to the work they flew,
> None arguing stood, innumerable hands
> Were ready, in a moment up they turnd
> Wide the Celestial soile, . . .
> (VI, 507–10)

Or again to contrast with the violence of civil war in Heaven, suggested by the heavy pointing of the passage at VI, 666–9, the ease of reinstated order communicated by the light pointing some lines farther on:

> At his command the uprooted Hills retir'd
> Each to his place, they heard his voice and went

> Obsequious, Heav'n his wonted face renewd,
> And with fresh Flourets Hill and Valley smil'd.
>   (VI, 781–4)

Such hasty pointing is especially effective in imparting a dramatic urgency to the speeches. In the passages below, one could not replace some of the commas by more conventional semicolons without losing all sense of Ithuriel's quick, angry challenge:

> Which of those rebell Spirits adjudg'd to Hell
> Com'st thou, escap'd thy prison, and transform'd,
> Why satst thou like an enemie in waite
> Here watching at the head of these that sleep?
>   (IV, 823–6)

Or of Satan's conspiratorial mutter:

> New Laws from his who reigns, new minds may raise
> In us who serve, new Counsels, to debate
> What doubtful may ensue, more in this place
> To utter is not safe.
>   (V, 677–80 [Ed. 2, 680–3])

Or of the Tempter's rapid 'aside' (like the Elizabethan stage villain's to his audience):

> Then let me not pass
> Occasion which now smiles, behold alone
> The Woman, opportune to all attempts,
> Her Husband, for I view far round, not nigh, . . .
>   (VIII [Ed. 2, IX], 479–82)

The light pointings after *prison, ensue, smiles,* and *attempts,* are plain dramatic directives such as no good actor would miss.[14]

It might be thought normal and natural that punctuation should be made lighter (or heavier) as the dramatic occasion requires. Yet punctuation has for a long while been geared only to a very limited extent to the conveying of such inflections. Light pointings such as those given above are frequent targets for emendation in modernized or reconstructed editions of

Paradise Lost – just as are the heavier types of rhetorical pointing illustrated earlier.[15] Such emendations are made in despite
of the fact that a light rhetorical pointing, like a heavy pointing,
is a recurrent feature not only in *Paradise Lost* but in Milton's
earlier poetry and in Elizabethan poetry generally. We may
recall the passage Simpson took from *Comus* to illustrate the
prevailing earlier practice of stopping lightly "for rapid or
excited speech".[16] The theatrical context of *Comus* makes the
dramatic function of Milton's light pointing a little more
obvious in this instance, but the excited inflection in the voices
of the brothers is exactly the same as that in the voices of
Ithuriel or Satan, and it is communicated in the same way:
by a hasty punctuation.

There is another common function of a light pointing in
Paradise Lost. The comma may be used, where one might expect
a heavier stop, to mark a rapidly passing antithesis, so imparting the feeling of a dramatic acceleration in the speaking or
narrating voice. It seems that while the poet's habit is to make
use of colon to mark a major contrast (or major parallel) in
statement, he often reserves the comma to mark minor and
rapid antitheses. So for example we have, "Hee for God only,
shee for God in him:". But (continuing in the same passage)
where the contrast is developed at greater length, we have:

> . . . Hyacinthin Locks
> Round from his parted forelock manly hung
> Clustring, but not beneath his shoulders broad:
> Shee as a vail down to the slender waste
> Her unadorned golden tresses wore
> Disheveld, . . .
> (IV, 299–306)

The poet tends to use the comma especially with antitheses
which are short and pointed, that is, picked out by word repetitions or verbal plays such as those shown below. It will be
convenient to use italics to draw attention to the devices in
question:

> *He* with his whole posteritie must *die,*
> *Die hee* or Justice must;
> (III, 209–10)

                             Amazement seis'd
            The Rebel Thrones, but greater rage to see
            Thus *foil'd* thir mightiest, ours joy *filld*, and shout, . . .
                             (VI, 198–200)

Some further instances of antithetical comma are listed separately – not all, however, heightened by verbal play.[17]
   The comma is used in the same way with short, pointed reiterations:

            The Monster moving onward came as fast,
            With horrid *strides*, Hell trembled as he *strode*.
                             (II, 675–6)

            Behold *mee* then, *mee* for him, *life* for *life*
            I offer, on *mee* let thine anger fall;
                             (III, 236–7)

And it is used rather similarly between clauses where there is a repetitive or amplifying effect (for example at V, 353; VI, 251; and VI, 774).[18]
   Christ's speech from III, 236 and following amply illustrates the use of both antithetical and reiterative comma. There the effect is emphatic but formal. Elsewhere the same devices may be employed with greater dramatic liveliness. Two further examples may give some idea of the variety of ways in which the simple devices in question may be developed. In Book IV short, balanced lines swinging quickly back and forth on repeated antithetical commas give a charming representation of Eve playing with her reflection in a pool of water:

            As I bent down to look, just opposite,
            A Shape within the watry gleam appeerd
            Bending to look on me, I started back,
            It started back, but pleasd I soon returnd,
            Pleas'd it returnd as soon with answering looks
            Of sympathie and love, . . .
                             (IV, 460–5)

And in this next passage brief pauses (reiterative, then antithetical, comma) alternate with the slower pauses of a heavier stopping in a lovely, rhythmical symmetry. The arrangement

suggests recurring tremors of passion in the voice speaking, and
at the same time a certain formal control which does not make
the note of passion less moving:

> . . . , least the Adversary
> Triumph and say; Fickle their State whom God
> Most Favors, who can please him long? Mee first[19]
> He ruind, now Mankind; whom will he next?
> (VIII [Ed. 2, IX], 947–50)

Such stoppings, at once rhythmical and dramatic, seem a
triumph of decorum in heroic verse. In such rhythmical, patterned structures the poem's punctuation shows elements of
the oratorical symmetry stressed by Elizabethan and some
seventeenth-century punctuation. But, as is so often the case
with a superior artistry, in *Paradise Lost* formal symmetry has
become fused with a deeper feeling.

3. *The Verse 'Sentence'*

We may finally turn from briefer to some lengthier instances of
rhetorical punctuation in *Paradise Lost*. Larger structures of
speech in the poem than the scattered and mainly short passages
hitherto studied, also show varied and effective patterns of
rhetorical or oratorical stopping. The epic simile, with its
sequence of unusually heavy stops followed by a light stop,
was one such larger structure. The epic simile thus presented
resembles a prose period inasmuch as it uses punctuation to
relate (with accompanying rhythmical symmetry) parts which
are organically connected in thought though not in grammar.
Many others of Milton's descriptive 'verse sentences', sometimes
aptly termed 'verse periods', also come to mind. These too show
periodic, that is, organic and rhythmical principles of structure
and punctuation.

By 'verse sentence' is here meant one of those extended passages of narration, of between ten and thirty or forty lines,
defined by or at least compressed between two full stops. These
passages are often and in a random way broken up in modern
editions; but they frequently have their own unity and ought
to be left intact. If the grammatical sentence is to be defined

as one complete thought, Milton's verse sentence may sometimes be described as one complete moment in his narrative. Such a sentence may elaborate a moment of drama in the story, delimiting the extent and tracing the course of one particular event. Or the sentence may amplify and outline a single visual scene, enclosing and setting it off like a picture in a frame. One needs to look at such sentences in full to appreciate the art with which pointing may be deployed throughout.

Two such self-contained verse sentences of moderate length (for Milton) occur in Book II. In the first Beelzebub calls for volunteers to undertake a reconnaissance to Earth; in the second Satan, just beginning that journey, encounters Death and Sin. The unbroken continuity of both these extended sentences serves in itself to outline each of these long-drawn-out moments of suspense in Milton's story. On the one hand, we have that palpable, expectant interval between the moment when Beelzebub finishes speaking and the moment when Satan speaks up and volunteers; on the other, that still, pregnant minute during which the champions of Hell menacingly confront each other.

> This said, he sat; and expectation held
> His look suspence, awaiting who apeer'd
> To second, or oppose, or undertake
> The perilous attempt: but all sat mute,
> Pondering the danger with deep thoughts; & each
> In others count'nance red his own dismay
> Astonisht: none among the choice and prime
> Of those Heav'n-warring Champions could be found
> So hardie as to proffer or accept
> Alone the dreadful voyage; till at last
> *Satan*, whom now transcendent glory rais'd
> Above his fellows, with Monarchal pride
> Conscious of highest worth, unmov'd thus spake.
>   (II, 417–29)

> . . . . Each at the Head
> Level'd his deadly aime; thir fatall hands
> No second stroke intend, and such a frown
> Each cast at th'other, as when two black Clouds
> With Heav'ns Artillery fraught, come rattling on

> Over the *Caspian*, then stand front to front
> Hov'ring a space, till Winds the signal blow
> To joyn thir dark Encounter in mid air:
> So frownd the mighty Combatants, that Hell
> Grew darker at thir frown, so matcht they stood;
> For never but once more was either like
> To meet so great a foe: and now great deeds
> Had been achiev'd, whereof all Hell had rung,
> Had not the Snakie Sorceress that sat
> Fast by Hell Gate, and kept the fatal Key,
> Ris'n, and with hideous outcry rush'd between.
>   (II, 711–26)

Within the framing full stops of each sentence, a heightened or heavy pointing picks out every one of the fleeting but distinct emotions which follow in rapid succession. In the earlier passage we have, first, Beelzebub's flourishing conclusion; then his expectant pause. This is followed by a general silence as all ponder the dangers. Then there is a tenser silence and heightened dismay as each sees his private apprehensions confirmed on the faces of the others. Next comes the dawning certainty that *no* volunteer is going to respond; until at the last possible moment Satan saves the situation by offering himself. Each of these steps is marked by a heavy stop.

Similarly in the second passage one can trace the sequence of minute events. We proceed from the Champions' levelled aim to their frown (this detail is amplified by the metaphor of clouds meeting over the Caspian, suggesting the irresistible, elemental force of the impending encounter). Then to the darkening of Hell by the frown (the metaphor of clouds above the Caspian tacitly carries over into this detail and brings the shock of the encounter a little closer, just as the rapid darkening of the earth is warning of an imminent deluge). Then to the anticipation of another and greater conflict to come with Christ (this by projecting the action into the future suspends it again for a moment and also increases its potential scale and fury). Then at last to the very stroke of swords – when, on the word *now* (as if weapons were in the act of being cast), the whole encounter is suddenly averted by Sin rushing in to separate the combatants. Again a strong stopping marks each step and makes the tense sequence seem a little as if viewed in cinematic

slow motion; the action through being slowed down is made
to appear more deliberate and ominous.

In both passages the strongest stopping is reserved for the
critical moments. In the first passage something like a shock
of dismay is registered by the colons before ": but all sat mute,"
and ": none among the choice and prime . . . ". In the second
passage a comparable punctuation again marks the crisis –
": So frownd the mighty Combatants," and ": and now great
deeds . . . ". The structure of the passage leads us to expect a
continuation of the strong stopping, but instead we have only
a comma before the final clause ", Had not the Snakie Sorceress
. . . Ris'n, . . .". This unexpectedly light stopping at the close
of the sentence has the effect of making the anticipated and
portentous drama trail off somewhat foolishly into anticlimax.

Both of these verse sentences could be broken midway with
some appearance of grammatical improvement. For instance,
full stops might be inserted before : *none* in line 423 and before
: *So frownd* at the end of line 718. Such alterations would be
consistent with those made by many modernized editions of
Paradise Lost. But the full stop is not dramatically appropriate
before the end of either passage, since each forms such a natural
dramatic unit and since in real time each moment described
is so brief as to be indivisible. No more could any of the carefully
graded heavy stops within the framing full stops be altered
without loss to the dramatic content. These passages are not
static pieces of description but presently evolving dramatic
situations, closely defined and shaped by the pointing.

A similar method of a heavily stopped but continuous syntax
is used to outline and shape the course of a retrospective
moment of drama in Milton's story – a tiny narrative within
the narrative. This is the account in Book I of the fall of
Mulciber from Heaven, a tale to which Milton appends, in the
same long-breathed sentence, a denial of the pagan myth, the
Christian emendation and his own moral commentary.

> Nor was his name unheard or unador'd
> In ancient *Greece*; and in *Ausonian* land
> Men call'd him *Mulciber*; and how he fell
> From Heav'n, they fabl'd, thrown by angry *Jove*
> Sheer o're the Chrystal Battlements: from Morn

To Noon he fell, from Noon to dewy Eve,[20]
A Summers day; and with the setting Sun
Dropt from the Zenith like a falling Star,
On *Lemnos* th' *Ægæan* Ile: thus they relate,
Erring; for he with this rebellious rout
Fell long before; nor aught avail'd him now
To have built in Heav'n high Towrs; nor did he scape
By all his Engins, but was headlong sent
With his industrious crew to build in hell.

(I, 738–51)

It is interesting to note how in these longer verse sentences the rhetorical or oratorical pointing may increasingly come into conflict with the natural logic of the syntax. One can see in the above passage that the punctuation as given serves to keep the sentence moving on in those places where it might well have been interrupted by full stops (as at lines 742, 746 and 748). Yet the original punctuation also checks the movement just enough, where the sentence might well flow into a shapeless mass (if a light or no pointing had been used with each *and*), to keep every detail clear and emphatic. No rewriting of the passage – and it is possible to experiment with several which make 'better' English – could retain both the original's clarity of detail and quiet emphasis and at the same time its attractive, slightly breathless impetus, as if the story were crowding into memory and onto the page with equal haste. The tension between pointing and grammar is functional; it has been made to contribute to the dramatic vitality of the narrative.

It is noticeable in this passage, too, that a flexible pointing leaves room for finer manipulations of stops within the defining limits of the verse sentence. Examples of such are the replacing of the expected commas after *day;* and *Erring;* by semicolons, so that the slowness of Mulciber's fall throughout a long summer's day or the violence with which the poet repudiates the pagan error are made to linger or echo in the reader's mind. In just the opposite way, the text's omission of the comma expected following *Sun* rushes the reader along with a quickening pace during the final stage of Mulciber's fall, as that unfortunate deity plunges onto Lemnos like a falling star. In the Manuscript and first edition the actual fall (from the gasp of its beginning at *Battlements:* to the thud of its ending at *Ile:*) is set off by a heavier stopping, colons, within the larger account. Much of the rhythmical charm of the passage, in detail as in larger structure, rests in such delicate interplay between the rhetorical punctuation and conventional syntactical expectations, and evaporates if such interplay is lost.

It might be said that some of the stopping indicated above as 'strong' (especially that in the first and third passages) is not incompatible with the normal seventeenth-century requirements of a heavy, logically distinguishing punctuation. But in *Paradise Lost* there is no consistency of practice observed about grading stops according to grammatical function – whether a clause is subordinate, coordinate, fully independent and so forth. The first two passages show this. The pointing in them as in the third passage is arranged so as to form a natural dramatic climax, though to do so in these cases means that the rule about colon and semicolon with main and dependent members must sometimes be disregarded (see for example lines 420 and 722). The norm of punctuation in *Paradise Lost* tunes our ear to have further expectations beyond those of grammar; it teaches us to listen for dramatic inflections also. These when they occur may actually be sharpened by the contrast or continuum of the reader's more conventional syntactical expectations.

It may seem less easy to define as verse 'sentences' passages which run on for thirty or forty lines (agglomerations, often, of whole periods and sentences in themselves complex and complete). The analogy of the prose paragraph might be appropriate to these longer passages. Like the paragraph, the very long verse sentence includes in its wide compass one extended but unified imaginative area. Or perhaps we might compare Proust's or Henry James' sentences. Like theirs, Milton's take in a whole area of experience or thought or argument. They may compass an entire view, perhaps some great panoramic vista, or one complete event or some particular aspect or stage of either; or even (as in the case of the biblical-historical introduction to Book I) a whole argument or one division of a long argument. As such a sentence progresses, it gathers into its easy confluence all sorts of tributaries: mythological, historical or biblical allusions, metaphors and similes, dramatic digressions and personal comments by the poet. Such bulky yet imaginatively integrated structures are the thirty-two-line account of Satan's flight at

III, 555–87, which begins with Satan's first view of the World from the top of its outer shell and ends with his landing on the Sun, and the forty-line description of Eden's beauties which runs without a major break from IV, 223–63. These extremely long passages are little different in their rhetorical organization from the three verse sentences cited earlier, except that these particular examples draw their effect from a mainly light punctuation varied by an occasional sharper pointing. All the passages alike use syntax to sculpture and recreate the experience instead of merely describing it.

To consider first the passage in Book III. What is represented here is the third lap of Satan's long flight to Earth – his great, swooping plunge from the top of the World down onto the Sun. The passage opens with a glimpse of Satan as he stands on the outer shell of the universe (and also a glimpse of *his* downward view from that point) and it ends with Satan's mid-journey halt on the great Luminary: one unbroken stretch of action, syntactically and narratively complete.

555 Round he surveys, and well might, where he stood
   So high above the circling Canopie
   Of Nights extended shade; from Eastern Point
   Of *Libra* to the fleecie Starr that bears
   Andromeda farr off *Atlantick* Seas
560 Beyond th' *Horizon*; then from Pole to Pole
   He views in bredth, and without longer pause
   Down right into the Worlds first Region throws
   His flight precipitant, and windes with ease
   Through the pure marble Air his oblique way
565 Amongst innumerable Starrs, that shon
   Stars distant, but nigh hand seemd other Worlds,
   Or other Worlds they seemd, or happy Iles,
   Like those *Hesperian* Gardens fam'd of old,
   Fortunate Fields, and Groves and flourie Vales,
570 Thrice happy Iles, but who dwelt happy there
   He stayd not to enquire: above them all
   The golden Sun in splendor likest Heaven
   Allur'd his eye: Thither his course he bends
   Through the calm Firmament; but up or downe
575 By center, or eccentric, hard to tell,
   Or Longitude, where the great Luminarie
   Alooff the vulgar Constellations thick,

That from his Lordly eye keep distance due,
Dispenses Light from farr; they as they move
580   Thir S[t]arry dance in numbers that compute
Days, months, and years, towards his all-chearing Lamp
Turn swift their various motions, or are turnd
By his Magnetic beam, that gently warms
The Univers, and to each inward part
585   With gentle penetration, though unseen,
Shoots invisible vertue even to the deep:
So wondrously was set his Station bright.
There lands the Fiend, a spot like which perhaps
Astronomer in the Sun's lucent Orbe
590   Through his glaz'd Optic Tube yet never saw.

Throughout this passage the syntax, moulded by the pointing, follows the action with exquisite precision, so that at each
moment we can see the event unfolding. In the first six lines two
shorter though complex members (whether clauses or phrases
seems not to matter), both set off by semicolons, give the sense
of Satan's pause as he stops to look about in all directions – first
a sweeping glance right round him, then a long view from East
to West ("Round he surveys, . . . high above . . . Nights extended shade; from Eastern Point . . . to the fleecie Starr . . .
Beyond th' *Horizon*;"). The clause beginning next, ". . . *Horizon*;
then from Pole to Pole . . ." (line 560), starts off as if it is going
to take in another such leisurely view, this time from North to
South. But before that view can be assimilated Satan is already
plunging downward – the comma before ", and without longer
pause" (line 561) giving the reader indeed no time for pause.
Between *; then* in line 560 and *enquire:* in line 571 there is no
major syntactical break. The continuous flow of these twelve
lines and their kaleidoscopic rush of imagery do much to assist
the sense of Satan's rocketing descent. The fluid syntax and
pointing copy the speed with which Satan is moving, itself
indicated in a single line: "shon/Stars distant, but nigh hand
seemd other Worlds, . . .". In that space Satan covers the distance from a far-off view of the stars, such as we might see from
the earth, to the actual presence of the new Worlds; and four
lines later he has shot past and left all behind.

One is saved from confusion in the dazzling flow of description
by the short clause, set off by a heavy pointing, which comes

next and stands out almost independently at the centre of the
passage like a signpost:[21]

>   : above them all
> The golden Sun in splendor likest Heaven
> Allur'd his eye:
>   (571–3)

Satan's guide not less than the reader's; here, as it were, he
orients his flight while still in mid-plunge. The next clause,
similarly short and heavily pointed, also is an orienting clause:

>   : Thither his course he bends
> Through the calm Firmament;
>   (573–4)

Here it can be felt how Satan is braking his headlong plunge
and turning his line of flight toward the Sun, which had not
been his specific goal before. From *Firmament;* in line 574 to the
end of the passage there is again only an even glide with no
major break (except for the slight check of the semicolon before
; they in line 579), the syntax thus keeping pace with Satan's
final rush toward his goal. Then in the last line, with another
short and heavily pointed clause and at last the full stop, Satan
abruptly lands:

>   . . . even to the deep:
> So wondrously was set his Station bright.
> There lands the Fiend, . . .
>   (586–8)

In thirty-two lines there have been only seven stops heavier
than a comma. This is sufficient illustration, if the actual grammatical constructions be examined, that the poem can dispense
with a grammatical punctuation when there is dramatic occasion
to do so.

Now turn to the passage at IV, 223. The contents of this may
seem at first glance very miscellaneous. But one subsequently
notices that the passage opens with the mention of Eden's river
and, after a long intervening description of the garden, returns
at its close to the same river. That one wandering stream, which

as Milton tells us waters all of Eden, now disappearing and now
reappearing in altered form, dispersed into brooks or reunited
into little lakes, seems to run in and out of the passage too,
giving it a thread of continuity; while the *various* views described in the garden, flowers, groves, lawns, valleys, grottoes,
and caves, are as it were revealed in the course of the river's
mazy path. The amorphous syntax, lightly pointed throughout
and almost without major pauses, faithfully represents the
river's meandering progress and the variegated, shifting, blending vistas opening up along its way.

> Southward through *Eden* went a River large,
> Nor chang'd his course, but through the shaggie hill
> 225 Pass'd underneath ingulft, for God had thrown
> That Mountain as his Garden mould high rais'd
> Upon the rapid current, which through veins
> Of porous Earth with kindly thirst up drawn,
> Rose a fresh Fountain, and with many a rill
> 230 Waterd the Garden; thence united fell
> Down the steep glade, and met the neather Flood,
> Which from his darksom passage now appeers,
> And now divided into four main Streams,
> Runs divers, wandring many a famous Realme
> 235 And Country whereof here needs no account,
> But rather to tell how, if Art could tell,
> How from that Saphire Fount the crisped Brooks,
> Rowling on Orient Pearl and sands of Gold,
> With mazie error under pendant shades
> 240 Ran Nectar, visiting each plant, and fed
> Flours worthy of Paradise which not nice Art
> In Beds and curious Knots, but Nature boon
> Powrd forth profuse on Hill and Dale and Plaine,
> Both where the morning Sun first warmly smote
> 245 The open field, and where the unpierc't shade
> Imbround the noontide Bowrs: Thus was this place,
> A happy rural seat of various view;
> Groves whose rich Trees wept odorous Gumms and Balme,
> Others whose fruit burnisht with Golden Rinde
> 250 Hung amiable, *Hesperian* Fables true,
> If true, here onely, and of delicious taste:
> Betwixt them Lawns, or level Downs, and Flocks
> Grasing the tender herb, were interpos'd,
> Or palmie hilloc, or the flourie lap

255 Of som irriguous Valley spread her store,
     Flours of all hue, and without Thorn the Rose:
     Another side, umbrageous Grots and Caves
     Of coole recess, o're which the mantling Vine
     Layes forth her purple Grape, and gently creeps
260 Luxuriant; mean while murmuring waters fall
     Down the slope hills, disperst, or in a Lake,
     That to the fringed Bank with Myrtle crownd,
     Her chrystall mirror holds, unite thir streams.

The few exceptions to this light stopping consist in antithetical
colons or semicolons which serve to suggest how the eye, rambling
easily over the harmonious landscape, is occasionally caught
by a sharper contrast in scene.[22] The following lines illustrate:

> Rose a fresh Fountain, and with many a rill
> Waterd the Garden; thence united fell
> Down the steep glade, . . .
> (229–31)

> Others whose fruit burnisht with Golden Rinde
> Hung amiable, . . . and of delicious taste:
> Betwixt them Lawns, or level Downs, and Flocks . . .
> (249–52)

> Flours of all hue, and without Thorn the Rose:
> Another side, umbrageous Grots and Caves . . .
> (256–7)

> . . . the mantling Vine . . .
> Luxuriant; mean while murmuring waters fall
> Down the slope hills, . . .
> (258–61)

It may also be noticed that this passage, like the one in Book
III, gathers itself together midway in a short, heavily pointed,
nearly independent clause which focusses the whole picture:

> : Thus was this place,
> A happy rural seat of various view;
> (246–7)

Such 'guide' clauses are an important feature of Milton's long
verse sentences; they supply the necessary sharp orientation,

syntactical and narrative, in structures so radically extended that they would without this help soon trail off into slackness or vagueness. In the above instance the guide clause both sums up the picture and gives a clue to the essential unity of the canvas of Eden. Here is the divine Architect's skilful design, of "various view" yet blending softly into a single harmonious whole – a "rural seat" like the discreetly landscaped park and gardens of some English country house.

It is interesting to compare with the first edition's pointing of the above passage, the emended punctuation of an edition such as Richard Bentley's.[23] Bentley breaks up the single long verse sentence into several smaller sentences and also uses a heavier pointing throughout, substituting semicolons or colons for many of the original commas. As a result not only is the overall unity of Milton's canvas partially lost from view, but the particular contrasts in scene indicated by the first edition's more discriminating heavy stops no longer stand out.

In more recent modernized editions of *Paradise Lost* Milton's long descriptive verse sentences are still commonly broken at the 'guide' clause – for example, before ": above them all . . ." (III, 571) and before ": Thus was this place, . . ." (IV, 246). In such places a full stop may be easily substituted for the original colon. But with the breaking up of these extended passages the imaginative unity of their large pictures is inevitably mutilated, and some of the finer registrations of meaning communicated by the carefully graded lesser stops within the framing full stops are also lost. Something else of value may be lost: the unique kinetic quality, the sense of opening vista or unfolding movement or unfolding drama, conveyed by these longest of Milton's sentences. If either of the two passages above were to be divided internally, we might consider what would happen to our sense of the eye's leisurely, sweeping survey over an entire landscape, or to our dizzy sensation of Satan's rocketing descent into the solar universe. Similarly, in the two shorter passages describing Satan, what would happen to our unique sensation of being actually inside developing moments of crisis or panic. Or in the passage quoted afterward, what might be left of that dreamlike feeling of a daylong, graceful fall, arching across a whole summer sky.

VIII

Conclusion

1. *Spelling Variants, Manuscript, Book I, and* 1667

Spellings and spelling corrections within the Manuscript and in the 1667 edition have an obvious bearing on questions concerning Miltonic provenance of punctuation in those texts. There has been some argument for keeping these two questions separate in this study, since Milton's spelling, even more than his punctuation, has been cause of much debate and confusion. It was also said at the outset that the present is not the place to attempt a full survey of Milton's spelling. But even a rapid reading of Book I, with attention to spellings and to spelling corrections in the Manuscript and 1667 texts, will convey some useful impressions.

It appears that by the time of *Paradise Lost* Milton had formulated and there used many distinctive, often prosodically or phonetically significant spellings, even though these were not always consistently followed either in the Manuscript or printed texts. It appears that Milton undoubtedly exercised some influence over the correction of important spellings in the Manuscript and to a lesser degree over corrections in the edition. (There were a considerable number of Miltonic corrections of spelling in the edition, but also, corrections in a contrary direction.) It appears also that, in certain important aspects, the spelling forms in the Manuscript are more characteristic of Milton's practice and more consistently followed than are those in the printed text; certainly the corrections, taken in themselves, are more consistently Miltonic in the Manuscript. In all these matters what evidently happened to Milton's spelling as his text evolved seems not dissimilar to what happened to his punctuation. However, it must be said that the overall picture of spelling changes is more blurred. There is in the texts of *Paradise Lost* a greater proportion of accidental or indifferent usages in spelling than in punctuation: spellings and spelling variations of minor importance, which do not affect either the pronunciation or syllabification or any other important factor of the words concerned. That is to say, there is a smaller proportion of spellings in which Milton might have been really interested: spellings which are either prosodically significant in that they affect the metrical quantities of the lines, or phonetically significant in that they represent the true pronunciations of vowels or consonants (sometimes foreign, or else Milton's peculiar, pronunciations), or significant in some other way, for instance in showing semantic derivations, grammatical distinctions, etc. It is mainly with these more significant spellings that we shall here be concerned.

Although J. T. Shawcross[1] rejects the idea that Milton ever followed any kind of spelling system, the conclusions he earlier published concerning orthography in *Paradise Lost*, his published work on orthography in the texts of Milton's minor poems, and his recent essay on orthography and the text of *Paradise Lost*, go to establish several very interesting facts. These are as follows:

(1) By 1652 (the date of his blindness), and certainly by the date of *Paradise Lost*, Milton had evolved a great many distinctive spellings of words – distinctive enough to enable Shawcross very closely to date Milton's works according to the appearance of certain spellings in his texts.

(2) Study of Milton's autograph and other manuscript and printed works prior to 1652 shows that Milton "generally employed simplified pronunciational spellings" and that "the evolution of certain forms . . . lies in the direction of simplicity, suggestion of pronunciation, or clarity". Shawcross' latest study shows how minutely Milton sometimes discriminated in spelling in order to differentiate between grammatical forms or to ensure clarity of sense or ensure the correct pronunciation or accentuation of words.

(3) In some early printed texts (for example "Lycidas") there is evidence of a certain amount of interference with Milton's characteristic spelling practice, notably by the compositors.

(4) In the 1667 and 1674 texts of *Paradise Lost* there is some evidence (quite a good deal, according to Shawcross' latest data) that "a corrector familiar with Milton's practices . . . proofread both editions". But here too there is evidence of compositorial or other interference with Milton's spelling. Shawcross supports

the partial, "not full authority" of the second over the first edition; and throughout his studies his examples demonstrate in many instances the greater authority of the Manuscript over both editions.

Shawcross has evidently been concerned to confute over-refinements in the interpretation of Milton's spelling (for example, Milton's alleged doubling for 'stress' of final *e* in personal pronouns which fall in accented positions in the verse line). He has also wished to guard against any idea that Milton's usage was ever rigidly fixed. Obviously Milton's spelling could not be rigid if it was evolving and experimental. Some vacillation is also entirely understandable, considering the chaos of English spelling then and the fact that it is at present still far from consistent logically, even though it is standardized. Besides, Milton was no eccentric. Unlike Butler or other contemporaries, he had no wish to foist a grand new improved spelling scheme upon the language. Shawcross is entirely justified in combating any such assumption (though perhaps few Miltonists have actually made such a sweeping one). Shawcross has also wished to show that Milton did not fully control the mechanical minutiae of his texts; his spelling (like his punctuation) was sometimes inter-fered with.

All these are important correctives; but Shawcross probably presses them too far. His own findings, as outlined above, scarcely serve to suggest that Milton did not interest himself in spelling or had no distinctive or significant practices in it, that his peculiar forms entirely failed to get into his texts (including his printed texts), or that he did not considerably influence the correcting of spelling in the written and printed texts of *Paradise Lost*. Further, in the broad chronological evolution toward a simplified, pronunciational spelling which Shawcross detects in forms of words in Milton's works, we may discern a principle of spelling that is flexible and detailed enough to have poetical, as well as linguistic, relevance. It is a principle which, for instance, allows the lengths and vowel sounds of words to be accommodated to metre and rhyme; or which allows for unusual foreign spellings (such as Hebrew, or classical) that can help give an exotic flavour to the diction. These considera-tions are not cancelled out because Milton was not entirely consistent in some of his spelling usages or because many of his phonetic spellings coincided with standard seventeenth-century practices. (In fact, Milton's spelling often seems more fully representational phonetically than his period's or, for that matter, than our own.) The principle of pronunciational spelling can be applied in two quite different ways: so as to provide a logically more consistent spelling (represent the same vowel and consonant sounds always in the same way); or so as to accommodate word lengths and sound values to their changing verse contexts (represent words, or sounds, slightly differently at different times, according as the poet needs to have them heard). Milton uses a pronunciational spelling in both ways; the second implies a somewhat variable usage.

There thus seems nothing, in the very valuable and detailed data which Shawcross has assembled to illustrate Milton's various spelling practices, which compels us to abandon the now old idea that Milton's spelling has some poetical implications. Most earlier poets had made use of alternative spelling forms to fit the rhyme; Spenser, Milton's mentor, did so constantly. Shawcross records an instance of a rhyme-spelling in the manuscript of "Arcades" (the spelling *been*, in place of Milton's more usual *bin*, in order to rhyme with *greene*).[2] It was also standard earlier practice to contract or elide syllables so as to fit the metre; and every study of Milton's prosody has confirmed that elisions and contractions play an important part in his versification.[3] These also depend upon a flexible spelling. One can hardly imagine Milton being indifferent to such stock-in-trade devices of poets; one might indeed expect that with his finely discriminating versification and his distinctive and intelligent spelling, Milton would have been more, not less, alive to the poetical possibilities of spelling variations.

Reading now through spellings and, more especially, spelling changes within the Manuscript, Book I (using Miss Darbishire's facsimiles), and in the 1667 Book I, we may be struck by the following facts.

The Manuscript has a large number of unusual, presumably often Miltonic spellings, as for example in phonetic, or otherwise pronunciational, or occasionally foreign (for instance, Hebrew) forms; also a large number of metrical spellings (words sometimes shortened by one syllable, depending on the quantities of the lines – *Heaven/Heav'n* and its derivatives is a typical example). Some of these Miltonic spellings will appear in the 1667 corrections presently discussed.

Handwritten corrections to the Manuscript introduce a number of distinctive Miltonic forms of the first kind, as for example *rḥime* 16 *etherẹal* 45 (similarly corrected at 285) *vanquishḍt* and *roʷlḍing* 52 (the second, similarly spelt at 671) *wraᵘth* 54 (similarly corrected at 110 and 220) *Cherubᵉ* 157 (similarly corrected at 324; this spelling copies the Hebrew pronunciation) *intransḍ'ᵗ* 301 *Sibmaḥ* 410 *smoᵃkⁱḥḍ* 493 *dreḍd* 589 (an early Milton spelling, though Milton did use both forms) *withḥḥeʳd* 612 (cf. 709 below) *ḍⁱnclose* 617 *woᵒmb* 673 *hundḥḍeʳd]* row of 709 (cf. 1668 errata for 760, *hundreds] hunderds*). There are virtually no instances where the Manuscript corrector corrects away from distinctive Miltonic forms.[4]

The scribal or other handwritten corrections to the Manuscript are also invariably accurate in respect of metrical spelling changes, as at *opposḍ'd* 41 (here a disyllable) *prisoᵒn* 71 (the apostrophe was added to denote a metrical monosyllable, but the corrector evidently forgot to delete the *o*) *Heav ḷin* 104 and *Heavḍn* 136 (metrically in both places monosyllabic; in the first instance a contrary correction is reversed) *buisḥnesse* 150 (disyllable) *thḥ' obscene* 406 (metrical elision to give correctly two syllables) *bord'ring* 419 (apostrophe added to show that there has been a metrical contraction) *Thebḥ's* 578 (to avoid pronouncing the word as a disyllable) *disastḍrous* 597 (three syllables) *Heavᵉns* 612 (the disyllable is correct here) *Op'ḍn* 662 (to show an elided weak syllable).

The 1667 spelling variants show that the correctors of the first edition were less consistent than the Manuscript corrector in following peculiar Miltonic spellings, especially of the phonetic or semantic kind. A number are certainly found in the 1667 text. For example, the following are all retained from the Manuscript: *Siloa's* 11 *rowling* 52 and 671 *Sovran* 246 *Ammiral* 294 *Rabba* 397 *Creet* 514 *Charlemain* 586 *suttle* 727 *Haralds* 752. Some further instances are corrected to unusual foreign or phonetic spellings: *Etna] Ætna* 233 (the diphthongs here and at 721 may indicate the classical derivations of the words) *Cherub] Cherube* 534 *emblaz'd] imblaz'd* 538 *warriors] Warriers* 565 *beleive] beleeve* 631 *Egipt] Ægypt* 721 *folds] foulds* 724. The following changes also are phonetic, but (except for, perhaps, *despare* 126) may be simply editorial modernizations: *wrackt*] *rackt* and *despair*] *despare* 126   *chuse*] *choose* 428   *grundsell*] *grunsel* 460   *mettle*] *mettal* 540 (to distinguish the two meanings). The most consistent phonetic and Miltonic change made by the edition is of final *d* to *t* in a preterite when the letter is so pronounced, as at 331, 429, 568, 609 and 645.

The above represents a not inconsiderable list of Miltonic changes in the first edition. However, a good many distinctive Miltonic forms are not retained in 1667, even though in some cases (as at 16, 54, 110, 220, 589, 617 and 673) they represent corrections earlier made within the Manuscript itself.[5] Among these are: *persues*] *pursues* 15 (similarly altered at 170, 308 and 326)[6]   *rime*] *Rhime* 16   *wrauth*] *wrath* 54, 110 and 220   *buis'nesse*] *business* 150 (metrically wrong also)   *Iland* 205 and *Iles* 521] *Island . . . Isles* (although at 746 the edition retains *Ile*)   *raz'd*] *ras'd* 362   *Horonaim*] *Heronaim* 409 (corrected back again in the 1668 errata)   *Egipt*] *Egypt* 421 (similarly altered at 480)   *lim*] *limb* 426   *past*] *pass'd* 487   *perfet*] *perfect* 550   *travers*] *traverse* 568   *dred*] *dread* 589   *inclose*] *enclose* 617   *woomb*] *womb* 673. The principle of a pronunciational or otherwise representational spelling has been shown to be important to Milton,[7] and the above divergences in 1667 are significant.

Milton may have liked phonetic or pronunciational spelling forms, not only because they were simpler and truer to the spoken language, but because they gave a cleaner quality of vowel and consonant sound to his verse. One wonders if he was at all influenced by the purer pronunciation and phonetically truer spelling of Italian (although Milton would also have found ample English precedent in the phonetic theories of Alexander Gil and others). Such spellings as *rime, suttle, perfet, ammiral,* etc. (all representing current or earlier spoken English, as opposed to the latinizing and sometimes falsely latinizing written spellings being introduced), all find analogous forms in Italian. Certainly, Milton's odd double *rr* and double *cc* pronunciational spellings could suggest the stronger double consonants of Italian. A direct foreign influence is seen in Milton's accurate transliterations of the pronunciations, in their original languages, of foreign loan-words (Hebrew or classical, and names in particular). Such spellings, even if introduced by extension of the principle of spelling phonetically in English, were bound to carry a certain exoticism. The slightly foreign flavour in Milton's spelling may well have been intended in part to produce a little of that deliberate difficulty or remoteness in versification and language which was consciously sought by Tasso, and Milton after him, as part of their programme of *asprezza* and epic grandeur in style. [8]

Metrical spellings (words sometimes contracted by one syllable in order to fit into the decasyllabic line) have of course the most obvious kind of relevance to the verse. The following considerable number of metrical corrections are introduced in 1667. *Heaven* in its various derivatives is correctly contracted at 124, 131, 138, 171, 174 and 361. (However, note that at 124 the word *Heaven*, spelt so in the Manuscript, falls at the end of the line, where Milton frequently allows an extra weak syllable; the edition lets the same spelling stand at the end of line 212.) We have also correctly: *risen*] *ris'n* 211 *evening*] *Ev'ning* 289 *flower*] *Flowr* 316 *given*] *giv'n* 347 *towers*] *Towrs* 499 and 749 *even*] *ev'n* 680. But the edition has not the exactness of the Manuscript in metrical corrections, for the following 1667 spelling changes are quantitatively wrong: *priso'n*] *Prison* 71 *buis'nesse*] *business* 150 *ith'*] *i'th'* 224 (the corrected reading is not so clearly monosyllabic) *followd*] *followed* 238 *powre*] *power* 626 (the Manuscript spelling is of course unclear, and could be confused with *pour*). Thus, as in the case of phonetic spellings, the edition is not consistent in its corrections.

In the above phonetic or metrical spelling corrections in the first edition, we may detect a pattern of change not dissimilar to that evident in punctuation changes made at the same time. Some corrector evidently understood the more obvious metrical application of certain Miltonic spellings (as someone partly understood the rhythmical application of Miltonic punctuation.) To some extent he worked along Miltonic lines himself. But he was not quite so deft as the Manuscript corrector in these poetical matters and (as he did with metrical punctuation) he made a few mistakes. (Or, some third person interfered in a contrary direction in a few instances.) There was possibly more interference still with Milton's unusual phonetic or semantic word forms (just as there was more interference with his unusual, elocutionary pointings). Here the balance of significant change seems to be away from Miltonic practice and toward a standardized usage. This is understandable, since the linguistic and poetical relevance of such forms is much less apparent than is that of metrical spellings. The correctors perhaps understood these unfamiliar forms less well, and found it difficult to arrive at a consistent policy in dealing with them.

Probably the largest body of spelling changes in 1667 is that group in which the edition frankly modernizes. The Manuscript contains a large number of old-fashioned spellings (many of them presumably the scribe's, since the corrector in the Manuscript also occasionally modernizes, for example deleting an occasional doubled final consonant as at 614, or an idle final *e* as at 91, and regularly substituting *i* for the older *y* medially or in a final *ye* syllable). Milton might either have approved of or been indifferent to the bulk of these later modernizations; many of them coincide with his own spellings[9] and with his general preference for a simplified spelling, and most of them do not affect either the correct metrical quantities or any peculiar pronunciations of the words. The 1667 changes in this respect are too numerous to list individually. They are fairly regular in the following respects: removal of idle final *e*; pruning of doubled final consonants *ll*, *nn*, *tt*, *rr*, etc. to single consonants; joining up of compound words written separately in the Manuscript; less regular in altering of final *ye* to *ie*, or *y* internally to *i*, as in modern spelling; correction of medial *ei* or *ea* to *ee* to spell phonetic *ee*; and similar modernizations such as altering of *ou* to *o*, *igh* to *i-e*, hard *c* to *k* or *ck*, etc. These numerous modernizations represent standardized practice of the period and may have had little directly to do with Milton. Hence any statistical calculation of Milton's possible influence over spelling which includes gross numbers of unMiltonic spellings in the Manuscript and gross numbers of simplified or modernized spellings in the first edition may not give a true picture of the texts. Such spellings and spelling changes as the above are poetically neutral, and may be no index to Milton's possible concern over significant spellings in either text.

The above discussion excludes spelling changes in words where Milton's usage has been shown to be vacillating. While a large proportion of the significant variants have been mentioned, there has been no attempt to include every type of spelling change or to discuss spelling exhaustively. The discussion has also excluded certain spelling changes, in both Manuscript and edition, concerning which Milton's correctors, scribal and compositorial alike, seem to have been nearly as confused as his readers. Specifically these are: Milton's alleged spelling for 'stress' (doubling of *e* in personal pronouns, or spelling alternatively *their/thir* when these pronouns fall in accented positions in the metrical line); and what have been termed his phonetic contractions. The question involved in the latter is the use of apostrophe either to indicate contraction of an indeterminate vowel before syllabic *l* or *n*, or to show a long vowel only, in the syllable preceding a contracted preterite ending with final *d* or other consonant. (In the case of a short vowel in the syllable preceding, there would presumably be no apostrophe.) Milton may have had some meaningful intentions in these respects, but if so, his purposes are so inconsistently carried out in both the Manuscript and first edition that analysis seems impossible. The reader may be referred to Miss Darbishire's and to B. A. Wright's detailed discussions of these and similar matters.[10]

2. General Remarks

A brief summary of the main findings of the preceding chapters follows, with some general points arising out of these.

Comparison of the first printed and the manuscript texts of Book I showed that, while the first edition of *Paradise Lost* generally followed Milton's Manuscript closely in details and even sometimes in irregular details of punctuation, it yet also introduced a number of corrections mainly grammatical in intent. Some of these the poet might well have desired had certain obvious oversights been made known to him, while to others he might have been indifferent. Nevertheless, the successive alterations made to the Manuscript copy during the course of the first printing did not always bring the text closer to what Milton seems to have intended. The case is rather the reverse. Whereas the Manuscript pointing generally and its corrections to the pointing specifically (those last corrections entered in another hand into the scribe's fair copy) indicate a rhythmical or rhetorical treatment of the pauses, something which suggests the

poet's hand or influence, such alterations as were introduced by
the first edition seem to be made with more consistent reference
to grammatical regularity. They are changes such as would be
likely to occur to a press corrector or a compositor. Sometimes
it seems as if the edition were trying to regularize the grammar
without violating the rhythmical and rhetorical practices of the
Manuscript. But at other times the edition's corrections run
directly counter to those more poetical principles which the
Manuscript would appear to be following in preference to minor
grammatical exactness. Very occasionally, too, the edition
'corrects' mistakenly – as in adding superfluous stops. In Miltonic
respects, at any rate, the edition shows less consistency in its
style of pointing than does the Manuscript, correcting now in
one manner, now in the opposite; and it is not always easy,
amid the somewhat confused intentions of the edition's own
pointing and the overlay of edition's pointing upon Manuscript's, to discern very clearly what may be Miltonic and
meaningful in the punctuation of the printed poem. There is a
partly analogous situation and a similar difficulty as regards
spellings and spelling variants in the two texts.

A more unambiguous guide is provided by the Manuscript.
In certain instances the Manuscript text contains obvious errors
of punctuation and throughout some passages it is insufficiently
punctuated. Nevertheless, it is clear that someone had paid a
good deal of attention to pointing and the correcting of pointing
(as to other mechanical matters) in the Manuscript, and the
punctuation in that text frequently shows a degree of poetical
delicacy which it is difficult to believe could derive from any one
except the poet. The Manuscript suggests that Milton, if it were
indeed he who was responsible for this pointing, interested himself in punctuation chiefly in so far as it could serve as a poetical
instrument. His poetical intention stands out more clearly
through the sharp contrast between the simple purposefulness
of the Manuscript pointing, incomplete or careless though it
sometimes is, and the more thoroughgoing yet sometimes confusing punctuation of the first edition.

It would appear that Milton uses punctuation in two basic
ways. First, he uses it to help breathe or phrase his lines in an
even, regular fashion, letting his verse move easily and
rhythmically, unencumbered by petty halts and obstructions,

through its steady succession of full lines, half-lines, or units running from midline to midline. The result is the characteristic and firm rhythms we know in *Paradise Lost*: the widely arching movement from line beginning to line end and (overlapping that, almost like a second decasyllabic pattern) from caesura to caesura. This complex, almost contrapuntal rhythmical pattern is set up by the cooperation of metre, syntax and pointing. Second, he uses pointing to assist the dramatic articulation of the verse – to provide those emphases and inflections which in a good reading would be supplied by the voice. These rhythmical and elocutionary manners are also evident in the mature sonnets in Milton's handwritten drafts in the Trinity College Manuscript.

To some extent an even phrasing and adequate emphasis are the concerns of all good punctuation. But in modern punctuation the needs to clarify every shade of meaning and to show all the logical connections and priorities of thought inside the sentence are paramount. For Milton, on the other hand, rhythmical and dramatic considerations are overriding, and grammatical correctness and occasionally even clarity take a secondary place.

The chief means which Milton employs to achieve his special ends in punctuation are these. For an even, regular phrasing, he relies on a severe economy of commas and a carefully selective disposition of all stops, designed to make such punctuation as is used largely coincide with the two natural pauses in the verse line, the caesura and the line ending. This means in practice that many commas must be omitted. And for dramatic emphasis Milton employs a pointing much heavier (or conversely, sometimes much lighter) than that which normal grammar, his or ours, would require – he uses stops in marked contrast to the surrounding context of punctuation.

The first practice is what has been called in this study a "rhythmical", that is, a metrically based punctuation. The second practice is what has rather broadly been called a "rhetorical" pointing, the word "rhetorical" having been used with all the connotations of dramatic, conversational, descriptive or representational effect – pointing, that is, which renders all the effects possible to the speaking voice. For Milton's poetry has always some distinct voice to be heard: whether the voice be

K

that of the fictional characters talking feelingly together, or of the poet-commentator passionately soliloquizing, or of the poet-narrator conveying through the pauses and inflections of his heard words the effects of vigorous movement in the incidents he recounts and even the peculiar impressions and sensuous qualities of the places he describes. Such rhetorical pointing is in a sense also rhythmical in that it momentarily alters the movement of the verse, perhaps introducing the rhythms of speech into the verse; however, a separate word has been preferred, as better distinguishing this sort of punctuation from the metrical kind. The word "oratorical" has also been used, to describe that type of punctuation which brings out oratorical symmetry or pattern (also, a form of rhythm). Whereas rhetorical pointing relies upon some immediate contrast for its effect, the metrical or oratorical types of pointing are more truly rhythmical in that they depend on regular repetitions and create a sequence of regular expectations.

It must be stressed that Milton's punctuation represents no rigid 'system' but a very clever balance or compromise. His punctuation makes sense only if seen as a complex and to some extent shifting set of values, as well as, fundamentally, a relative or contingent set of values.

To say that Milton's punctuation is complex and shifting is only to say that it meets several different needs, and that one need must sometimes take priority over another, according to what is in the forefront of the poet's mind. One underlying function of the punctuation is of course to assist the sense, and in that degree the grammatical structure. Perhaps all but the freest theatrical punctuation must in some degree share such a function; and certainly Milton's pointing does not attempt to dispense with sense or logic. What we have to be prepared for in *Paradise Lost* is that very often small grammatical proprieties may be disregarded if there is good poetical reason. Such a shift from grammar to poetry may be seen when certain minor stops are regularly dispensed with so as not to hinder the broad rhythmical plan of the verse. Such a shift may be seen also when a heavier, or lighter, punctuation than grammar requires is used occasionally to convey certain dramatic inflections or other vivid effects, or when a heavy, partly ungrammatical stopping is regularly used to link related parts in a long verse period. These are the other chief uses of Miltonic punctuation, its metrical, rhetorical and oratorical aspects.

Most often, the punctuation of *Paradise Lost* is so contrived as to meet two or all three of these needs (of the sense, of the rhythmical structure, of the rhetorical/oratorical context) more or less simultaneously. The method of including mainly those grammatically useful stops which are also rhythmically apt is the most brilliant illustration of this kind of coordination of purpose. We may see such a fluid balance of function in more specific contexts; when, for example, the lightly stopped, rhythmical norm of the verse itself becomes a remembered continuum which intensifies the dramatic departure of some more broken pointing. Or when the entire scale of stops in some long descriptive verse sentence is readjusted, so as to permit stopping for specific rhetorical effects and yet preserve some sense of the total architecture of both syntax and event. Such an equilibrium in function is felt, too, when the tension which arises from a recurrent emphatic pointing playing against the natural onward flow of sense and syntax in some extended sentence seems itself to become part of the rhythmical charge or momentum of the verse.

That Miltonic punctuation is not only a complex and shifting but also a relative set of values must be self-evident. It is apparent that any one of the four familiar chief stops can convey some fresh impact only in so far as it occasionally stands out as being used in a different way from the expected. A rhetorical stop may differ relatively to the general weight of punctuation immediately surrounding it, or to what the grammatical context seems to require. The kind of stopping which affords effective contrast in one context may not be identical with that which affords it in another context; nor are we to expect that it should be. In the rhetorical aspect of Miltonic pointing, stops do not have fixed emphatic values, but instead a sensitive shading or grading of stops is constantly taking place.

Milton's style of pointing, then, involves a flexible choice and tactful disposition of stops according to a variety of grammatical and even more of non-grammatical circumstances. Milton, if punctuating in such a way, must often have simply trusted to his ear. The greater variety and freedom of practice in punctuation during the seventeenth century (and even more so in Elizabethan usage, by which he was especially influenced) would have made it natural for him to rely mainly on his ear in such matters. Later readers are not accustomed to this kind of individuality in an area which they tend to regard as almost exclusively a province of grammar, where 'correct' and 'incorrect' usages are rigidly differentiated.

Yet unless we can read *Paradise Lost* with an ear carefully tuned to the complex rhythms and diverse inflections indicated by the fluent original pointing, we shall miss many of Milton's finest poetical nuances. There is that infinitely varied, delicate adjustment of the stops to the exact degree of emphasis required by each phrase and to the dramatic or descriptive demands of the narrative at every moment. There is the sense of Milton's largest syntactical architectonics: of how the supple pointing frames and sculptures event and description in the longest verse sentences. Above all, there is that long, swelling motion of Milton's lines from caesura to caesura: a rhythm counter-pointed against that other basic rhythm of *Paradise Lost*, the regular beat of the five-stress line. This intricate, fluctuating and yet constant pattern is materially shaped by the punctuation. Punctuation thus becomes an important factor in the complex system of interlocking or competing rhythmical energies which gives to Milton's verse both its subtlety and its distinctive drive.

To glance back briefly at punctuation practice in the period before *Paradise Lost*, it was observed that there are important resemblances between Milton's poetic style of punctuation and the fluent and expressive pointing of Elizabethan dramatists and lyricists. Even in non-theatrical Elizabethan prose a rhyth-mical use of punctuation was normal, as was also a patterned, oratorical type of pointing, elements of which again survive into Miltonic and other later practice. Earlier punctuation theory confirms that in these dramatic, metrical and oratorical aspects earlier punctuation was very differently oriented from our own.

On the other hand, the pointing followed in much of the prose and even poetry of Milton's own period was very different from the Elizabethan, and in important ways closer to our own. Grammars and samples of verse and prose taken from various dates of the century stretching from Mulcaster to Caryl suggest that there was a clear evolution in seventeenth-century punctuation away from the rhythmical and dramatic and toward the logical and grammatical. The punctuation prescribed in a standard manual of grammar such as Charles Butler's (1633), or employed in a work coætaneous with *Paradise Lost*, Joseph Caryl's *Exposition . . . upon . . . Job* (1776–7), or used earlier in the 1625 edition of Bacon's *Essays*, is much less rhythmical and expressive and far more formal and logical than is the pointing of *Paradise Lost*. In a sense this later, seventeenth-century punctuation is more rigorously grammatical even than our own. It is at once apparent in Butler or Caryl or the 1625 Bacon that the total number of stops is much greater than in *Paradise Lost* and that the many stops are being used in a different way: for syntactical definition. The main purpose of this later, seventeenth-century pointing seems to be to make a distinction between major and minor components of the sentence and so outline its grammatical organization. A little regard may be paid concurrently to indicating oratorical pattern, usually within the limits of the grammatically coherent sentence.

We might perhaps expect to find that the 1667 pointing corrections to the Manuscript of *Paradise Lost* would be in the logical, heavy, mid-century manner. Yet the first edition's new punctuation, despite its general bias toward grammar, does not suggest a style closely similar to Butler's or Caryl's. The general impression which it conveys is of a style rather lighter, more sparing and more restrained than these authors'; to our eyes, somewhat more modern. The small number of the 1667 corrections would in itself sharply differentiate its style of pointing from the heavy mid-century norm. Details also differ. The 1667 corrector does not, for instance, like strong pointing to mark antithesis. This was a rhetorical device which commonly survived Elizabethan usage until well into the seventeenth century, and it is practised to excess in the style of Wither, Butler or Caryl. Milton uses the device with much more discrimination; but the corrector's antipathy is probably to be accounted for by the prevailing earlier abuse of it. The corrector's greater modernity in this and other respects might hint to us that, by the third quarter of the century, taste in the matter of punctuation was again being modified.

Despite the criticism which has been offered in the present study of the stylistically damping effect of the first edition's pointing corrections, its editorial restraint is perhaps more notable than otherwise, in that early period. Such restraint is visible in the edition's reluctance to alter the punctuation of the Manuscript too radically or too often. The tact of many of its corrections is indicative. For example, nearly two thirds of the commas added, apparently chiefly for purposes of grammatical definition, are selected so as to fall at a natural pause and not interfere with the rhythmical plan of the verse. Restraint is seen equally in the relatively small number of corrections made. Few logically defining heavy stops are added or substituted for commas, although the norm of the period might seem to call for many more. Again, although there are a not inconsiderable number of downpointings of rhetorical stops in Book I, a great many of such marks are also left intact. Only in the pointing of epic similes are changes made consistently enough to obscure the style of the original Manuscript. Even the sixty-five commas inserted into the Manuscript text represent an average of only one comma added every eleven lines. The 1667 text might easily have added four or five times as many minor stops before bringing the punctuation of *Paradise Lost* even remotely to resemble the peculiarly deliberate, almost halting manner of Butler or Caryl. The changes made by the first edition serve to throw into relief, not to obliterate, Milton's distinctive practice.

David Masson remarked that the punctuation of the first edition of *Paradise Lost* was based on a "system of compromise between clause-marks and pause-marks" – meaning, one takes it, that the punctuation was intended to be half logical or outlining and half rhythmical or for poetical intonation. As he expressed the latter elements, the pointing has some "regard for the vocal pauses convenient in reading".[11] His remark is particularly pertinent to the final corrected punctuation of the first edition, which seems so much a careful balance between the distinctive poetical style of the Manuscript, Book I, and the necessities imposed on the printer by the logic and conventions of seventeenth-century grammar. If the printer was prepared to allow such a compromise, in substantial measure accepting a style of pointing which was by now quite atypical of the period, and in part accommodating the press corrections to this style, these facts would in themselves seem to indicate that there was something in the style of the original Manuscript which he had reason to respect – that the original punctuation had some Miltonic authority. This inference is strengthened by the fact that the printer seems largely to have left Caryl's punctuation alone too. The punctuation of Caryl's *Job* also is somewhat individual – not at all like the pointing of *Paradise Lost*, nor yet quite like the 1667 corrections, but much closer to the heavy mid-century manner. Samuel Simmons clearly was a man who had some respect for the stylistic preferences of his authors.

3. *Editing*

Some final questions suggest themselves and indeed are difficult to avoid. The questions are whether, if there is a Miltonic style of punctuation in *Paradise Lost*, the punctuation of the poem should in some way be revised or reconstructed in accordance with it. And if the punctuation should not be revised, then on which of the three original texts produced during the author's lifetime, or to what degree on each, are we to depend?

These are editorial questions, and not altogether in place in a primarily critical study such as the present one. The problems of editing *Paradise Lost* are multiple, not single, and punctuation is only one of many matters involved in deciding upon a text. Spelling similarly has to be taken into consideration, and there are other smaller matters of style and presentation as well. An editor may feel constrained to adopt a policy which is consistent throughout. But in so far as one can discuss the editing of punctuation apart from other textual questions in the poem, the following opinions might be expressed.

Modernization of Milton's pointing should really be out of question. To modernize is to surrender, at the outset, some of the original savour of the poem's style: to blunt the fineness of Milton's discrimination in prosody and rhetoric. Nor does modernization seem in any way necessary; the first edition carried out all that was needed for intelligibility. Any extensive attempt to reconstruct Milton's punctuation, on the other hand, is likely to present considerable difficulties. It would be more difficult to restore punctuation than, for instance, to restore some of Milton's most distinctive spellings to the printed text or to correct a few extant metrically defective spellings.

It might perhaps be feasible in a very limited way to restore some of the Manuscript's most characteristic usages (for example, the emphatic pointing with epic similes), when these appear to be lacking in the printed texts. It might also be possible to delete a few unmetrical minor stops, or even to reduce the numbers of metrical commas used in connection with certain minor constructions (appositives, coordinates, qualifying phrases, etc.), in places where the phrasing of the verse seems too broken. But no hard and fast standard could be adopted for such alterations. Changes would have to be made not only with reference to parallel usages elsewhere in *Paradise Lost* and Milton's early poems, but with constant reference to the immediate contexts, rhythmical or dramatic, of the passages in question. And even proceeding with restraint and caution, it would be easy to oversimplify Miltonic practice. The punctuation of *Paradise Lost* is, even in the Manuscript of Book I where the main stylistic lines are clearer, so complex and flexible in operation, apparently fulfilling several different needs and contingent upon a number of widely differing circumstances, and throughout all twelve Books it often is so personal, depending on the poet's taste, tact and fineness of ear, that any programme of alteration could be at best only an approximation rather than a true reconstruction of Miltonic practice. In addition, there is the problem that the pointing in the first and second editions is apparently composite in nature, an evident amalgam of two or more differing hands and purposes. The question then arises how to allow for such latitude as Milton might have chosen to exercise in, sometimes, and in some matters, compromising with the rather different ideas of the press concerning pointing. All in all, there would be a considerable risk that in any systematic programme of reconstruction the original punctuation (composite, complex, even ambiguous though it sometimes is) might lose as much as it gained.

If reconstruction may not be the best course, then in what degree are we to depend upon the punctuation in each of the original texts? There are at least three separate factors to be balanced against each other here. We have above all to consider the fresher and distincter stylistic flavour of the pointing in the Manuscript of Book I. We have to allow for the fact that the two editions of 1667 and 1674 in certain limited and sometimes unexceptionable ways improved upon the punctuation, the first introducing some corrections of conspicuous oversights, and the second, possibly, a few Miltonic emendations. And we have to guard against the fact that each of the three original texts in its turn introduced some mistakes – the Manuscript and 1674, apparently, chiefly through carelessness, and 1667 through misguided good intentions. Each of the three texts therefore holds something of value, but no one can be relied on fully.

The following might then seem a reasonable compromise to hope for. In Book I the larger part of the Manuscript's punctuation should be retained, enough fully to display its original style. In the other eleven Books the bulk of the extant (partly emended) punctuation of the two editions should be preserved. But when variants occur within the first or between the two first editions, those readings should be chosen which are closer to the style of the Manuscript (due allowance of course being made for mechanical or other error, where this can really be determined). There will obviously be cases where what is the best reading, as between the two later or even all three texts, lies in doubt. In such cases our choice between variants should be guided not only by what is better grammar or clearer sense but equally by our general feeling about the poem's style. The question should be asked, and answered from our experience of the Manuscript, how the poet might have tended to punctuate in a certain kind of rhythmical or rhetorical or other particular context. Any forms which might be characteristic of Milton's peculiar practices merit attention. Readings which assist the verse structure or which improve the rhetorical impact of the poetry have a claim and perhaps a priority over those which only slightly support the sense or grammar. The Manuscript can be used as a constant yardstick in these matters.

An edition which included punctuation on such a basis, even if it were slightly inconsistent in the practices followed as between Book I and the other Books, would at least have some historical value in indicating the evolution of the text and the different kinds of pointing practice followed in it and in the period. It might be of additional use and interest if such an edition also could (instead of emending) draw attention in textual notes to suspect pointings or constructions, that is, to those which seem unMiltonic in their style. Equally so, if it could indicate passages which particularly well illustrate characteristic Miltonic usages.

If the punctuation of the Manuscript, Book I, has special value for the textual scholar as a tool to explore and help unravel the text of *Paradise Lost* (and others of Milton's poems), its value is not lacking for the critic and general reader. Milton's distinctive style of pointing in the Manuscript can, if used as a mental gauge, help the reader to recover the contextual significance of many odd or difficult or apparently lacking pointings throughout *Paradise Lost* (and, probably, in others of the poems and prose works). In this process the reader will be helped more fully to grasp the rhythmical subtleties and finer inflections of Milton's verse. He will be able to distinguish some main elements in the formation of Milton's versification and rhetorical techniques, and will so acquire a valuable insight into the whole growth of Milton's epic style and into its linguistic background. An understanding of the original punctuation will help him to read any of Milton's texts with a more discerning and responsive (occasionally too a more critical) ear and eye. It must certainly help him to read *Paradise Lost* more satisfactorily: with a clearer perception of the many strata and strands in its text, with greater understanding of much which at first sight appears to be eccentric or erroneous in the poet's manipulations of syntax, and with enhanced appreciation of the mature and complex art underlying Milton's "easie" and "unpremeditated verse".

Notes

Notes to Chapter I

[1] *The Manuscript of Milton's Paradise Lost, Book I* (Oxford, 1931), pp. xxv–viii. See for example the scribal spelling changes at I, 612 *Heav̰ns* and 597 *disast‖rous.*

[2] *Proof-Reading in the Sixteenth Seventeenth and Eighteenth Centuries* (London, 1935), p. 54. See chaps. I and II of this work for a general survey of the treatment of punctuation in author's copy and in printer's copy and proofs.

[3] The extant manuscripts of Milton's minor poems are reproduced photostatically and transcribed in H. F. Fletcher's edition, *John Milton's Complete Poetical Works*, Vol. I: *Poems . . . 1673; Poems . . . 1645 . . .* (Urbana, Ill., 1943). Fletcher follows W. A. Wright's transcriptions in *Facsimile of the Manuscript of Milton's Minor Poems, Preserved in the Library of Trinity College, Cambridge* (Cambridge, 1899). Autograph quotations in the present study are taken from the original manuscript in Trinity College Library. However, page numbers follow Wright's and Fletcher's renumberings (in general 2–3 pp. lower than the Manuscript). This will be more convenient to the reader, who is likely to be referring to one or the other facsimile. Scratched-out words in the Trinity Manuscript have been indicated by italics; briefer corrections in the Manuscript of *Paradise Lost*, Book I, are given facsimile, or as much so as possible.

[4] See sec. V, "The Punctuation," of "General Essay on Milton's English," in D. Masson's edition, *The Poetical Works of John Milton* (London, 1874), I, ciii–iv.

[5] An earlier study of the punctuation in the texts of *Comus* up to 1645 is that of J. S. Diekhoff, "The Punctuation of *Comus*," *PMLA*, LI (1936), 757–68.

[6] See the discussion in chap. VIII, 1.

Notes to Chapter II

[1] *Shakespearian Punctuation* (Oxford, 1911). This and others of Simpson's general remarks are quoted from pp. 8–11.

[2] See Introd., sec. on "Dramatic Punctuation," in *A New Shakespeare Quarto: The Tragedy of King Richard II . . .* (1598), ed. A. W. Pollard (London, 1916), pp. 23–30; also by this author, *Shakespeare's Fight with the Pirates . . .* (Cambridge, 1920), pp. 88–93. A. C. Partridge, *Orthography in Shakespeare and Elizabethan Drama . . .* (London, 1964), chaps. 14, 15 and App. VIII: "The Historical Development of Punctuation Marks."

[3] Charles C. Fries, "Shakespearian Punctuation," in *Univ. of Michigan Publications, Language and Literature*, Vol. I: *Studies in Shakespeare, Milton and Donne* (New York, 1925), 65–86. Fries supplies a full bibliography of the discussion on elocutionary punctuation up to that date. Walter J. Ong, "Historical Backgrounds of Elizabethan and Jacobean Punctuation Theory," *PMLA*, LIX (1944), 349–60.

[4] P. Simpson (in *Shakespearian Punctuation*), C. Fries (*op. cit.*) and A. C. Partridge (*op. cit.*) considered the earlier "time-value" system of punctuation

almost entirely in terms of its elocutionary possibilities (Fries with negative conclusions). W. Ong seemed to hint at the wider rhythmical possibilities of the system when, in the article cited (p. 354), he described earlier punctuation as "a device *serving primarily the exigencies of breathing* in discourse" (i.e. in oratory). (For some similar hints, see the earlier article by P. Simpson, "The Bibliographical Study of Shakespeare," *Oxford Bibliographical Society Proceedings and Papers*, I [1922–6], pp. 33–41 on punctuation.) Such a 'breathing' system of punctuation as Ong describes would inevitably create a regular succession of pauses, rhythmical in its effect. However, Ong's discussion was confined to theory of pointing and did not show actual practice; also, he did not connect the 'breathing' punctuation he described either with oratorical design and symmetry in written prose or with metrical structure in verse, evident though it is that a natural connection exists in both aspects. Other scholars (A. W. Pollard, ... *Quarto* ... *of King Richard II*; J. Shawcross, "Establishment of a Text of Milton's Poems through a Study of *Lycidas*," *PBSA*, LVI (1962), 317–31; R. Alden, "The Punctuation of Shakespeare's Printers," *PMLA*, XXXIX [1924], 557–80) note the metrical use of punctuation in Elizabethan verse without enlarging on the structural significance of such usage or on the kind of variations it may be given. But in the structural functions of metrical punctuation in verse (or of analogous rhythmical punctuation in prose) lies an answer to the question put by Fries, one which typifies the scepticism of the entire group of scholars who have disagreed with Simpson's views: "... there must be found some means to account for ... the later progress from that [alleged] elocutionary principle back to structural [Fries means, grammatical] considerations after the Elizabethan era" (*op. cit.*, p. 85). It might be replied, that structural considerations were never absent from Elizabethan punctuation; that punctuation merely developed from a looser outlining mainly of the rhythmical structure to a stricter outlining of grammatical and syntactical structure. This was a natural transition as grammar became both more fixed and more sophisticated in the seventeenth century, and as 'plain' and 'correct' writing superceded 'rhythmical' or 'ornate' prose in popularity.

[5] Canto XXIX, st. 7, from Add. MS 18920 of the Brit. Mus.; as quoted by Simpson, *Proof-Reading* . . . , pp. 74–5.

[6] See *Shakespeares Sonnets* . . . *1609*, ed. in facsimile by Sidney Lee (Oxford, 1905), Sonnets 33, 35, 54. See also the two texts of *King Richard II*: the 1598 Quarto, ed. by A. W. Pollard, and the 1623 Folio, in Sidney Lee's facsimile edition, *Shakespeares Comedies, Histories, & Tragedies* . . . *1623* (Oxford, 1902).

[7] See E. Simpson, "A Note on Donne's Punctuation," *RES*, IV (1928), 295–300; also *A Study of the Prose Works of John Donne* (Oxford, 1948). H. J. C. Grierson, ed., "The Text and Canon of Donne's Poems," in *The Poems of John Donne* (London, 1912), II, especially pp. cxxi–iv on the punctuation.

[8] *A Maske (Comus)*: Trin. MS; 1634; 1637; 1645; 1673. All these texts may be read in Fletcher's Vol. I. The first quotation follows the Trinity Manuscript but the others have been taken from, respectively, pp. 322, 281, 203, 67, of Fletcher's edition. The scratched-out words in the Trinity MS are indicated by italics. The quotation from Simpson is from *Shakespearian Punctuation*, pp. 17–18.

[9] Opening of introduction to *Pierce Penilesse his Supplication to the Divell*, by Tho. Nash (1592). In Brit. Mus. copy (photostat facsimile Cambridge Univ. Library), no title page, p. numbered only as sig. A.

[10] Bodleian MS e Musaeo 131, pp. 1, 2. As reprinted in "A Note on Donne's

Punctuation," p. 298. See *A Study of the Prose Works* . . . , pp. 160–4, for further discussion of this manuscript.

[11] The quotation follows E. T. Campagnac, ed., *Mulcaster's Elementarie* (Oxford, 1925), reprinted with the original punctuation, p. 166. Mulcaster has a brief chapter (XXI) on punctuation.

[12] See *The Arte of English Poesie* (1589), ed. G. D. Willcock and A. Walker (Cambridge, 1936), II, iv(v), 73–6.

[13] Howell names only the three stops of classical rhetoric: comma, colon and period. See "Of the points of Words and Sentences," in *A New English Grammar* . . . , London . . . , 1662, p. 78. Daines (*Orthoepia Anglicana*, 1640) mentions semicolon but merely gives it a further time value, making it represent a length of pause halfway between those of comma and colon. See later discussion and note 16 below.

[14] Introd. to *The English Grammar* of Ben Jonson, as reprinted in *Ben Jonson*, ed. C. H. Herford, Percy and Evelyn Simpson: Vol. II (Oxford, 1925), pp. 431–2.

[15] A. Baugh, *A History of the English Language*, 2nd rev. ed. (London, 1959), p. 295.

[16] *Simon Daines' Orthoepia Anglicana, 1640*, English Linguistics, 1500–1800, Facsimile Reprints (Menston, England, 1967), pp. 69–75. The chapter on punctuation was partly reprinted by C. Fries, *op. cit.*, pp. 78–9.

[17] The passages cited follow the original texts as reprinted in *The Works of John Milton*, ed. F. A. Patterson, 18 vols. (New York, 1931–8). The references, in the same order as the examples were quoted, are to: (*Of Ref.*) III, pt. 1, 1–3; (*Church-gov't.*) III, pt. 1, 181–2; (*Divorce*) III, pt. 2, 367–8; (*Hist. Br.*) X, p. 2, lines 2 and 3; (*M. Buc.*) IV, p. 14, line 21; (*Tenure*) V, p. 4, lines 4 to 7; *ibid.*, p. 8, line 8; (*Eik.*) V, p. 64, line 21; *ibid.*, p. 63, line 15; (*C. Book*) XVIII, p. 176, line 9; *ibid.*, p. 135, line 9, p. 152, line 5 and p. 168, line 6; *ibid.*, p. 167, line 6 and p. 195, line 20. On the printing and spelling of Milton's prose tracts see Darbishire, *The Poetical Works of John Milton*, Vol. I: *Paradise Lost* (Oxford, 1952), pp. xvi–xvii.

[18] *Religio Medici*, in *The Works of Sir Thomas Browne*, ed. G. Keynes, 2nd edition (London, 1964), I, 11. The punctuation of Keynes' edition is based on the text of the 1643 edition, authorized by Browne.

[19] See E. M. W. Tillyard, *The Miltonic Setting, Past and Present* (London, 1947), p. 128.

Notes to Chapter III

[1] The quotations are taken from "The Epistle Dedicatorie" to *The Holy Bible: A Facsimile . . . of the Authorized Version . . . 1611*, introd. by A. W. Pollard (Oxford, 1911), pp. numbered sigs. $A_{2(v)}$ and A_3; and the first page of the text of Genesis (I, 1–5) p. numbered sig. A.

[2] *The Authorized Edition of the English Bible (1611), its Subsequent Reprints and Modern Representatives* (Cambridge, 1884), pp. 81–2.

[3] P. Simpson takes up questions concerning Jonson's style of pointing in different works and at different times, and the degree to which Jonson may have supervised the punctuation in his printed works or revisions of it in subsequent editions in: *Proof-Reading*, pp. 11–12; *Ben Jonson*, V (Oxford, 1937), pp. xv and 7–9 (for the corrections made to the 1616 *Volpone*); and *Ben Jonson*, IV (Oxford, 1932), 6–17 (for the proof corrections to the Quarto *Cynthia's Revels*).

[4] *Shakespearian Punctuation*, p. 56.

[5] *Volpone*, III, 1 (1616 Folio), as reprinted in *Ben Jonson*, V, 66–7. This edition retains the original punctuation of 1616, as supervised by the author. The passage is one quoted by Simpson.

[6] "Epithalamion: or, a Song . . . ," *Under-Woods* (1640 Folio), as reprinted in *Ben Jonson*, VIII (Oxford, 1947), 256.

[7] *Timber: or, Discoveries* (1640 Folio), as reprinted in *Ben Jonson*, VIII, 563.

[8] *The English Grammar* . . . , by Charls Butler . . . , Oxford . . . , 1633. The quotations are taken from the brief subsection "Of Primary Points simple," pp. 58–60. Spellings have been modernized, because of Butler's peculiar phonetic notation.

[9] *Works of . . . Milton*, I, civ–v.

[10] Chap. IX, "Of the Distinction of Sentences," in Book II, "Of Syntaxe," as reprinted in *Ben Jonson*, VIII, 551–3. The quotations are taken from this brief section. See also Simpson's discussion in his introduction to this work, *Ben Jonson*, II, 431 ff.

[11] *The English Grammar*: *Ben Jonson*, VIII, 553.

[12] See Simpson, *Shakespearian Punctuation*, p. 56.

[13] "Of Expence" (XXVIII), in *The Essayes or Counsels, Civill and Morall*, of Francis Lo. Verulam . . . , Newly written, London . . . , 1625, pp. 164–5.

[14] See *Essayes, Religious Meditations, Places of perswasion and disswasion*, by Francis Bacon, from the First Edition of 1597, exactly reprinted (London, 1924), pp. 7$_{(v)}$–8.

[15] *The History of the Pestilence (1625)*, ed. J. Milton French (Cambridge, Mass., 1932). The quotations are taken from pp. 4–5 of French's transcription. Wither's spelling abbreviations have not been followed, nor have his italics or other type faces.

[16] *Britain's Remembrancer. Containing a Narration of the Plague lately past* . . . , by Geo: Wither . . . , 1628, p. 15.

[17] See *ibid.*, "A Premonition," p. numbered as sig. B$_{3(v)}$.

[18] *An Exposition with Practical Observations upon the Book of Job* . . . , printed by Samuel Simmons . . . , London, 1676–7. The quotations are taken from Caryl's Vol. I, the preface "To the Christian Reader . . . ," pp. numbered A$_2$–A$_{2(v)}$, and (example 4) the "Exposition . . . ," column 15. Italics and other type faces in Caryl's preface have not been followed.

[19] See the sec. on "Samuel Simmons, Printer," in H. F. Fletcher's Vol. II, *The First Edition of Paradise Lost* (Urbana, Ill., 1945), pp. 106–9.

Notes to Chapter IV

[1] See H. Darbishire, ed., *Paradise Lost*, pp. xx-xxiii, and also *The Manuscript of . . . Book I*, pp. xxxvii-xlvii. M. Y. Hughes, ed., *John Milton: Paradise Lost* (New York, 1935), pp. xiv–xv. B. A. Wright, ed., *Milton's Poems*, Everyman (London, 1956), pp. xiii–xix.

[2] See "The Punctuation of *Comus*," p. 768. Diekhoff through the tenor of his discussion frequently hints at the dominance of the rhythmical principle of punctuation over the grammatical in *Comus*. However, the structure of his analysis is such as to imply that all three elements, the grammatical, the rhetorical and the rhythmical, are of equal importance in Milton's use. This leaves no way of explaining how the three principles interdepend or why they sometimes appear to clash in *Comus*. Diekhoff also seems to assume that most or all of the grammatical improvements to the punctuation in the 1637 and 1645 editions necessarily derived from the poet. This although he notes that the

"consistent progression from the manuscript to the edition of 1645 toward fuller and heavier [i.e., grammatically more correct] stopping" (p. 760 n.) is a tenor of change which sometimes acts in direct opposition to the correct rhythms of the verse (e.g., see Diekhoff's examples and discussion on p. 763). Some of these pointing changes seem incomprehensible if the poet's. Much less evident inconsistency would appear in Milton's practice if, possibly, some of the more uncompromisingly grammatical corrections in the printed editions had been due to printer's or other interference with the punctuation. The usage in the Trinity Manuscript suggests that in Milton's own practice the rhythmical principle usually dominates in punctuation.

³ John T. Shawcross, "Establishment of a Text of Milton's Poems . . . ," pp. 317–31. Earlier views questioning Milton's control over numerous minor changes made during the printing of *Paradise Lost* were forcefully expressed by D. Stillman and also J. H. Hanford, who on Miss Darbishire's own evidence challenged the superiority of many 1667 readings over the Manuscript's. See D. Stillman, "Milton as Proof Reader," *Mod. Lang. Notes*, LIV (1939), 353–4; and J. H. Hanford, App. E., "Milton and his Printers," in *A Milton Handbook*, 4th ed. (New York, 1954), pp. 390–400.

⁴ See also my earlier study of the punctuation variants, 1667, *Paradise Lost*, Book I, from the Manuscript: Mindele Black (Mindele Treip), "Studies in the Epic Language of *Paradise Lost*," doctoral dissertation (Radcliffe College/Harvard University, 1956), chap. III, "Pointing," pp. 170–248.

⁵ T. Banks ("Miltonic Rhythm; A Study of the Relation of the Full Stops to the Rhythm of *Paradise Lost*," *PMLA*, XLII [1927], 140–5), using the 1667 text as his basis, discussed the use of medial full stops or colons in combination with accentual variations to indicate the opening and close of the verse periods and so to convey a sense of 'sentence structure' in *Paradise Lost* (that is, of oratorical structure superimposed on the verse structure). J. Diekhoff, answering ("Terminal Pause in Milton's Verse," *St. Phil.*, XXXII [1935], 235–9), asserted that Milton intended instead that his verse should be read with a pause at the end of each line. Diekhoff noted but did not explain the preponderance of medial over end-of-line punctuation in both the Trinity Manuscript and 1667 *Paradise Lost*. It is probable that, as Banks thought, the illusion of oratorical or speech structure in Milton's verse is particularly related to midline punctuation. One should add that it is not only the preponderance of medial full stops and colons which assist the effect but the preponderance of all kinds of stops internally, especially commas. However, there is no real conflict between Diekhoff's and Banks' views. Both rhythmical movements, that based on stressed medial pauses and that based on our unassisted sense of the full line, seem intended, and counterpoint each other. The verse period (a larger, embracing rhythmical pattern) may finish at either the middle or the end of the line: that is, merge into either movement.

⁶ J. H. Hanford, *A Milton Handbook*, pp. 312–23.

⁷ Douglas Bush, *John Milton: A Sketch of his Life and Writings* (London, 1965), pp. 179–81.

⁸ Cf. B. A. Wright, *Milton's Poems*, Introd., pp. xiii and xvii.

Notes to Chapter V

¹ *The Manuscript of . . . Book I*, nn. to ll. 13 and 29; also the Introd., sec. entitled "The Manuscript Described," pp. xv–xxiii. Quotations from the Manuscript of Book I follow the collotypes in Miss Darbishire's edition.

² *song,* 13 *state,* 29 *Creator,* 31 *Angells,* 38 *peeres,* 39 *discernes,* 78

crime, 79　*hope,* 88　*Heav'n,* 104　*indeed,* 114　*good,* 163　*end,* 164　*wave,*
193　*Lee,* 207　*flood,* 312　*strand,* 379.

[3] After *Confounded/* 53　*So|/* 644　and possibly *Ahaz* 472. See also *The Manuscript of . . . Book I,* nn to ll. 53 and 542. Once, at l. 521 (see Darbishire's n.), a medial comma is deleted, but the mark is obviously misplaced.

[4] In all instances of parallel quotations, the readings of the Manuscript are given first and the readings of the first edition follow. Readings from the 1667 and 1674 eds. of *Paradise Lost* follow the photographic facsimiles of these texts as reproduced in H. F. Fletcher's Vol. II and Vol. III: *The Second Edition of Paradise Lost* (Urbana, Ill., 1948).

[5] *Fire,* 48　*Arch-Enemy,* 81　*Enterprize,* 89　*low,* 137　*ire,* 148　*sure,* 158　*Thunder,* 174　*rage,* 175　*tell,* 205　*Fire,* 234　*Mate,* 238　*round,* 285　*Chivalrie,* 307　*Gold,* 372　*male,* 422　*King,* 444　*King,* 471　*Cliff,* 517　*fear'd,* 628　*taught,* 685　*high,* 733　*Eve,* 743.

[6] *fall,* 76　*him,* 85　*Conquerour,* 143　*Gods,* 240　*Heav'n,* 270　*Moon,* 287　*Afloat,* 305　*Creator,* 369　*Jehovah,* 487　*Streets,* 501　*courage,* 530　*these,* 630　*Herarchie,* 737　*power,* 753.　The comma before parenthesis at 143 is grammatically acceptable, parenthesis often being taken in earlier practice as a tone mark rather than a pause.

[7] Ed. 1 *Thou O Spirit,*] Ed. 2 *Thou, O Spirit,* (in some copies). The added comma of edition 2 is rhythmically an impediment. Possibly for this reason it was omitted during proof correction. (On this variant see Fletcher, III, 80, n. to l. 17.)

[8] See *The Manuscript of . . . Book I,* n. to l. 60.

[9] After *Powers,* 128　where the added comma wrongly turns a restrictive into a non-restrictive clause; *slumber,* 377　which is entirely redundant; and *man,* 573　where the addition assists a confusion in sense.

[10] Ed. 1 *him, that made them,*] Ed. 2 *him that made them,* . . . . Ed. 2 seems finally to get the pointing and phrasing right.

[11] *The Manuscript of . . . Book I,* n. to l. 79.

[12] The edition's second comma could possibly be justified as rhetorically stressing *crime, . . .*; similarly another, unmetrical, addition at *heard,* 331.

[13] Unless at 295 the compositor missed the comma enclosed in the flourish of the *h.* The instances are: *spirit,* 146　*works,* 201　*he,* 245　*with,* 295　*Though,* 394　*Argob,* 398　*thence,* 404　*faithfull,* 611.

[14] At: *Abysse,* 21　*God,* 42　*mercy,* 218　*sufferance,* 366　*Heav'n,* 651. Possibly at 21 the compositor missed the faint comma.

[15] Any rhythmical plan of punctuation necessarily involves a large proportion of omitted stops; cf. the analysis of omitted punctuation in the Manuscript (see chap. IV, sec. 1) and in the 1674 text (see App. C, sec. 6).

Notes to Chapter VI

[1] See *The Manuscript of . . . Book I,* nn. to ll. 36 and 338, and Fletcher, ɪII, 85, n. to l. 114. The hand corrections show at 338 full stop written over comma; at 114 comma altered to semicolon; and at 36 colon changed to semicolon. No hand corrections of spelling are recorded in quotations in text or notes, chap. VI.

[2] Ed. 1, state 1 (1 copy) *views,*] state 2 (most) *views,* . . . . See App. B.

[3] Only three downpointings by the edition are certainly wrong grammatically. MS *downfall. Since*] Ed. *downfall;* 116; the semicolon muddles the proposition which follows. MS *fate;*] Ed. *Fate,* 133; the Manuscript's semicolon was required to indicate the end of the long vocative address which began at

line 128 *O Prince,* .... MS *pure;*] Ed. *pure,* 425; the edition's comma would have been better put, if at all, in place of the semicolon after *both;* 424.

⁴ For some brief remarks on certain of Milton's uses of rhetorical stops, see H. Darbishire, ed., *Paradise Lost,* pp. xx–xxii, and *The Manuscript of* . . . *Book I,* pp. xl–xli. See also B. A. Wright's edition, pp. xv–xix.

⁵ Miss Darbishire's note (*The Manuscript of* . . . *Book I*) for 362 says that the upper dot is accidental, and she gives no note for 467.

⁶ Cf. to example one: MS *occasion:*] Ed. *occasion,* 178   MS *Mansion;*] Ed. *Mansion,* 268   MS *smoakd:*] Ed. *smoak'd;* 493. In the line preceding 493 the edition leaves unchanged a colon 'correctly' marking an independent clause; but after *smoakd:* in line 493 it reduces rhetorical colon introducing a *yet* or antithetical clause. (Cf. also the similar usage *various: wondring* at V, 89.) Cf. to example two: MS *Mankind;* . . . *heav'n;*] Ed. *Mankinde,* . . . *Heav'n,* 36–7   MS *empire; that*] Ed. *Empire, that* 114.   Cf. to example three: MS *Mount;*] Ed. *Mount,* 15   MS *pure;*] Ed. *pure,* 425   MS *Azotus;*] Ed. *Azotus,* 464   MS *sounds.*] Ed. *sounds:* 540   MS *retreat;*] Ed. *retreat,* 555   MS *custome;*] Ed. *custome,* 640   MS *sweet:*] Ed. *sweet,* 712.

⁷ MS *bane*] Ed. *bane.* 692. 1667 also gives a full stop for: MS *seate*] Ed. *seat.*] Ed. 2 *seat?* 634,   but since the edge of the page is here torn in the Manuscript, one cannot tell whether the full stop had been given originally.

⁸ MS *Compeer:*] Ed. *Compeer.* 127

⁹ MS *he,* . . . *fal'n*] Ed. *he;* . . . *fall'n!* 84. Possibly in this line the compositor missed or merely ignored an existing scribal correction of semicolon to comma after *he,* ....

¹⁰ MS *him,*] Ed. *him;* 56   MS *deep,*] Ed. *Deep;* 152   MS *evill,*] Ed. *evil;* 165.

¹¹ MS *lustre,*] Ed. *lustre;* 97. The dot over the comma had been struck out in the Manuscript, as at line 84.

¹² *delayes. So stretcht out*] Ed. *delayes:* 208   MS *smoake. Such resting*] Ed. *smoak:* 237   MS *wheeles. so thick bestrown*] Ed. *Wheels,* 311   MS *Nile. So numberless*] Ed. *Nile:* 343.

¹³ Similarly, there is nothing wrong with the full stops before the *So* parts of the comparisons at VIII (Ed. 2, IX) 676 and at IX (Ed. 2, X) 436 which Miss Darbishire, following along the printer's lines, reduces to colons in her edition. Her changes betray an inconsistency, since she recognizes Milton's special use of the full stop before the first part of a comparison (see *The Manuscript of* . . . *Book I,* p. xxxix).

¹⁴ MS *imbowre: or scatterd sedge*] Ed. *imbowr;* 304   MS *beames; or from*] Ed. *Beams,* 596.

¹⁵ MS *course: they*] Ed. *course,* 786. It has earlier been mentioned that once or twice only the edition heightens the pointing in such cases – 202 and 771.

¹⁶ MS *in hew; as when*] Ed. *in hue,* 230   MS *the wing; as when*] Ed. *wing,* 332   MS *nook: As in an Organ*] Ed. *nook,* 707.

¹⁷ See Darbishire, *The Manuscript of* . . . *Book I,* p. xxxix, and B. A. Wright, "Note on *Paradise Lost,* I. 230," *RES,* XXIII (1947), 146–7. See also Miss Darbishire's *Paradise Lost,* where she follows the Manuscript's pointing in ll. 229–30 but accepts the first edition's alterations to ll. 237 and 238.

Notes to Chapter VII

¹ Cf. Donne's use of emphasizing comma (chap. II, 3); similarly Simpson's illustrations of the same device in the Elizabethans (see *Shakesperian Punctuation,* pp. 26–31).

² Miss Darbishire in her edition of *Paradise Lost* changes the semicolon of line

L

285 to comma. But cf. the identical use of the semicolon for emphasis, Manuscript example 3, chap. VI, 1. Cf. also the use of emphasizing semicolon by the Elizabethans, as shown by Simpson, *Shakespearian Punctuation*, pp. 62–5.

[3] Cf. Manuscript example 4, chap. VI, 1.

[4] Ed. 1 *ground*] Ed. 2 *ground*, ... The comma of edition 2 may have been added to call attention to the pun.

[5] See Manuscript examples 6 to 8, chap. VI, 1.

[6] See Manuscript example 1, chap. VI, 1; also Bk. I, 84 in the edition's pointing.

[7] As may be seen in the editions of Darbishire and B. A. Wright, who make this change. Yet Miss Darbishire retains the similar heavy pointing at V, 89 in the passage about Eve's dream.

[8] As Miss Darbishire does in her edition.

[9] Miss Darbishire reduces this expressive colon to semicolon in her edition. But this is a typical and consistent Miltonic usage. To it and the three parallel instances at II, 929–40, cf. the use of a heavy, rhetorical pointing to convey qualification, suspension of thought, contrast or antithesis, in Manuscript examples 1, 2 and 5, chap. VI, 1; also the Manuscript's distinctive pointings, again reduced by the first edition, at ll. 178 and 493.

[10] See Simpson, *Shakespearian Punctuation*, pp. 74–7.

[11] Ed. 1, state 1 *Mæonides*] state 2 *Mæonides,*] Ed. 2 *Mæonides,*

[12] *Shakespearian Punctuation*, pp. 82–3.

[13] See Manuscript examples 6–8, chap. VI, 1.

[14] Among numerous parallel examples to the five given in the text of a light, rhetorical pointing are: Satan's peremptory address, II, 979–80; his indignant, breathless speech at V, 769–81 (Ed. 2, 772–84); Adam's impetuous, whispered exhortation to Eve, V, 17–25; his and Eve's exchanges, V, 35–7 and VIII (Ed. 2, IX) 947–50. In this passage the commas of lines 949–50 simulate, during the course of the speaker Adam's conversation, the speech of a third person, God. Cf. also the dramatic account of Messiah's rushing progress, VI, 760–6.

[15] E.g. Miss Darbishire substitutes a heavier pointing for most of the light rhetorical pointings quoted, putting colon or semicolon in place of comma after: *prison*, IV, 824   *ensue*, V, 679 (Ed. 2, 682)   *smiles*, VIII (Ed. 2, IX), 480. She also replaces five of the light pointings cited in n. 14 above, substituting semicolons at: *profound*, II, 980   *Calls us*, V, 21   *Ascended*, . . . *Eagle-wing'd*, VI, 762–3   *Favors*, VIII (Ed. 2, IX), 949. Yet she retains a similar light stopping at IV, 313–14 because, as she notes, it is dramatically appropriate in context.

[16] *Shakespearian Punctuation*, pp. 17–18; see also chap. II, 2.

[17] III, 399; V, 163; VI, 14; VI, 595; VIII (Ed. 2, IX), 849; VIII (Ed. 2, IX), 1014.

[18] Miss Darbishire, who perhaps did not notice the slight differentiation between Milton's pointing of major and minor antitheses, heightens to semicolon or colon many antithetical or reiterative commas, among them those at: II, 676   III, 209   and VI, 200; III, 399   V, 163   V, 353   VI, 14   VI, 251   VI, 595   VI, 774; VIII (Ed. 2, IX), 849; also, from the examples next discussed in the text, one at III, 246 and one at VIII (Ed. 2, IX), 949. She alters others as well, e.g. the stop at IV, 370.

[19] Ed. 1 *long?*] Ed. 2 *long;*

[20] Ed. 1 *Battlements:*] Ed. 2 *Battlements;* 742;   Ed. 1 *Eve,*] MS *eeve* 743.

[21] Cf. the use of semicolon to set off a significant phrase, Manuscript example 4, chap. VI, 1; also the parallel use of the semicolon at V, 293–6 and of colon at V, 89 and X (Ed. 2, XI), 80.

[22] Cf. the use of semicolon and colon to indicate qualification, sharp contrast or change, or antithesis, Manuscript examples 1, 2 and 5, chap. VI, 1. Cf. also the use of colon at II, 598 and throughout the passage at II, 929 ff.

[23] *Milton's Paradise Lost. A New Edition* (London, 1732).

Notes to Chapter VIII

[1] Quotations and references (in order of appearance) are from or to the following of Shawcross' studies: (1) "Milton's Spelling: its Biographical and Critical Implications," *Dissertation Abstracts*, XXII (1961), 567–8. (2) *Ibid.*; "What We Can Learn from Milton's Spelling," *HLQ*, XXVI (1962–3), 361; "Orthography and the Text of *Paradise Lost*," *Language and Style in Milton*, ed. R. D. Emma and J. T. Shawcross (New York, 1967), pp. 127–8, e.g. (3) "Establishment of a Text of Milton's Poems through a Study of *Lycidas*," pp. 317–31. (4) "Milton's Spelling . . . ," p. 568; "Orthography and the Text of *Paradise Lost*," p. 150.

B. A. Wright (*Milton's Poems*, Introd., pp. vii–xxxii), also has important discussions of Milton's spelling and its poetical implications.

[2] "Orthography and the Text of *Paradise Lost*," p. 138. Shawcross also notes apparent "eye-rhymes" in early Milton MSS: see "Orthography . . . ," p. 137.

[3] Shawcross' most recent conclusion seems too extreme: ". . . the minutiae of spelling" are no "necessary part of [Milton's] technique as a metrical artist" ("Orthography . . . ," p. 150). In this article Shawcross allows that Milton's use of sometimes contracted preterite endings relates partly to metre (p. 133). The only piece of evidence which Shawcross records to show that Milton did not use other kinds of syllabic contractions for metre (or the only piece I can find directly bearing on this point) is that Milton writes indifferently, *heaven* or *heavn* in *Comus*, even though he both times pronounces the words as a monosyllable ("Orthography . . . ," p. 143). This particular illustration is of doubtful value, since the reading *heaven* in the first draft of the passage quoted from *Comus* appears to depend on W. A. Wright's or Fletcher's transcription of lines so heavily scored out, in the original, as to be nearly illegible (see Fletcher, I, p. 423, l. [14]). In so far as the letters of the word in question can be read at all, their formations appear to correspond exactly with *heavn* (correctly, monosyllabic) in the second draft of the same passage (see Fletcher, I, p. 420, l. 41). Wright occasionally mistranscribes the Trin. MS pointing, Fletcher following.

[4] Shawcross notes one or two trifling instances, in spellings concerning idle final *e*, where the Manuscript corrects away from Milton's practice ("Orthography . . . ," p. 122).

[5] See p. 125 above.

[6] Shawcross ("Orthography . . . ," p. 137), says that the spelling *per* . . . is not demonstrably Milton's. But at least, it copies his intended pronunciation.

[7] See e.g. Miss Darbishire's edition of *Paradise Lost*, Introd., pp. xxiii–xxxv, and *The Manuscript of . . . Book I*, Introd., pp. xxv–xxxvii.

[8] See F. T. Prince, *The Italian Element in Milton's Verse* (Oxford, 1954), pp. 36–40.

[9] Milton tended to simplify spellings, including doubled end consonants, but he had a few meaningful exceptions (one was his doubled final *r*) and some of these were apparently ironed out in the 1667 text (see Shawcross, "Orthography . . . ," pp. 125; 128). Seventeenth-century usage was and for that matter modern usage still is far from consistent on these matters.

[10] See nn. 7 and 1 above.

[11] *Works of . . . Milton*, I, civ–vi.

Variant Pointings 1667, Book I, from Manuscript, Book I

The list which follows has been drawn up by collation of the Manuscript, Book I, as reproduced in Miss Darbishire's collotype facsimiles, with the 1667 text as reproduced in H. F. Fletcher's photographic facsimiles. Two hitherto undetected instances (lines 362 and 467) where the Manuscript contains a semicolon but the 1667 and all later editors (including Miss Darbishire and Fletcher) give commas are listed at the end of the table, "Stops Reduced." These supply further instances of the 1667 text's tendency to standardize heavy rhetorical punctuation in Milton's manuscript. Apart from these cases, the list presented agrees with Miss Darbishire's, except at lines 505 and 776. The Manuscript distinctly shows a full stop and comma respectively in these places, and Miss Darbishire's printed transcriptions are incorrect. Only one variant pointing (line 569) is found between copies of Book I, 1667, studied by Miss Darbishire and Fletcher. The Manuscript readings are shown first.

List of Variant Pointings 1667, Bk. I, from Manuscript, Bk. I

Commas Added	Commas Deleted or Omitted
7 Oreb] *Oreb,*	21 Abysse,] Abyss
7 Sinai] *Sinai,*	42 God,] God
17 Spirit] Spirit,	59 kenne,] kenn
18 pure] pure,	146 spirit,] spirit
48 fire] Fire,	201 works,] works
60 wilde] wilde,	218 mercy,] mercy
68 deluge] Deluge,	245 he,] hee
76 fall] fall,	295 with,] with
79 power] power,	362 raz'd,] ras'd
81 Arch-enemy] Arch-Enemy,	366 sufferance,] sufferance
85 him] him,	383 seats,] Seats
89 enterprize] Enterprize,	383 after,] after
128 powers] Powers,	394 Though,] Though
133 strength] strength,	398 Argob,] *Argob*
133 chance] Chance,	404 thence,] thence
137 low] low,	611 faithfull,] faithfull
143 conquerour] Conquerour,	651 Heav'n,] Heav'n
148 ire] ire,	783 fountain,] Fountain
158 sure] sure,	

Commas Added—contd.

174 thunder] Thunder,
175 rage] rage,
205 tell] tell,
234 fire] Fire,
238 Mate] Mate,
240 Gods] Gods,
270 Heav'n] Heav'n,
285 round] round,
287 moon] Moon,
305 Afloat] Afloat,
307 chivalry] Chivalrie,
331 heard] heard,
346 nether] nether,
369 Creator] Creator,
370 him] him,
370 them] them,
372 gold] Gold,
377 slumber] slumber,
387 yea] yea,
409 Horonaim] *Heronaim,*
422 male] male,
439 Astarte] *Astarte,*
444 king] King,
465 Ascalon] *Ascalon,*
471 King] King,
487 Jehovah] *Jehovah,*
501 streets] Streets,
507 renown'd] renown'd,
517 cliff] Cliff,
530 courage] courage,
573 man] man,
613 oakes] Oaks,
628 fear'd] fear'd,
630 these] these,
631 beleive] beleeve,
631 losse] loss,
685 taught] taught,
700 prepar'd] prepar'd,
702 lake] Lake,
716 freeze] Freeze,
733 high] high,
737 hierarchy] Herarchie,
743 eeve] Eve,
753 power] power,
781 Elves] Elves,
796 seat's] seat's,

Heavy Stops Reduced

  15 Mount;] Mount,
  36 Mankind;] Mankinde,
  37 heav'n;] Heav'n,
  66 dwell;] dwell,
  67 all:] all;
114 empire;] Empire,
116 downfall.] downfall;
131 Fearless;] Fearless,
133 fate;] Fate,
178 occasion:] occasion,
208 delayes.] delayes:
230 hew;] hue,
237 smoake.] smoak:
268 Mansion;] Mansion,
297 azure;] Azure,
304 imbowre:] imbowr;
311 wheeles.] Wheels,
318 spirits:] spirits;
332 wing;] wing,
337 obai'd;] obeyd
343 Nile.] *Nile*:
425 pure;] pure,
464 Azotus;] *Azotus*,
493 smoakd:] smoak'd;
540 sounds.] sounds:
555 retreat;] retreat,
569 views;] views;/views,
592 brightnesse;] brightness,
596 beames;] Beams,
640 custome;] custome,
656 eruption;] eruption,
707 nook:] nook,
712 sweet:] sweet,
786 course:] course,

Stops Heightened

  56 him,] him;
  84 he,] he;
  97 lustre,] lustre;
127 Compeer:] Compeer.
152 deep,] Deep;
165 evill,] evil;
202 stream;] stream:
229 fire,] fire;
238 feet:] feet.
771 clusters,] clusters;

Other Changes

  84 fal'n] fall'n!
183 dreadfull!] dreadful?
380 aloof.] aloof?
634 seate] seat.

---

362 memoriall;] memorial,
467 Rimmon;] *Rimmon*,

I. *Variant Pointings in States of* 1667

The variants listed in Appendix A were (all but one at I, 569 in signature C) press changes introduced, as far as present known states of the first edition reveal, either when the poem was edited at the press or when the compositors set the formes. Some corrections were also made later, after the first sheets had been pulled; or as we would now say, "in proof." As was customary in earlier printing, the printer of *Paradise Lost* did not discard the first uncorrected sheets but had them bound up along with corrected ones. These later punctuation variants are very much fewer in number than the earlier set of changes. Thus, only the one proof change is recorded in Book I, five in III, three in IV, thirteen in V, and an odd one in some of the other Books: about 2·8 changes per Book, as compared with at least 130 initial changes made in Book I alone. The proof changes could therefore have little effect on the overall style of punctuation of the poem. However, they are of interest as a possible index to any intentions Milton might have had concerning punctuation during the printing. It would seem that these later press changes are similar to the earlier ones and not distinctively Miltonic in character.

The list of punctuation proof changes appended is drawn up partly out of the collations made by Fletcher and Miss Darbishire (see Fletcher's textual notes and lists in "The Signatures," II, 139–55, and his more complete collations in Vol. III, his edition of the 1674 text; also Darbishire's lists in App. II, "Copies of . . . First Edition . . . ," *Paradise Lost*, pp. 313–22); and partly out of direct comparison of facsimiles of known alternative states of the first edition, as published by Fletcher in Vol. II (earlier states shown first). Differences which are not true variants are not included. Only one variant has been found (III, 35) which is not included in Miss Darbishire's lists or in Fletcher's lists in Vol. II, but this omission is rectified in the textual note to that line in Fletcher's Vol. III. The copy of the 1667 edition (first title page) in the Trinity College Library follows uncorrected or only partly corrected states in signatures L outer and Q inner: that is, it does not include about one third of the punctuation variants listed here.

The changes made in the completely reset signatures Vv and Z in 1669 are listed and discussed separately. The punctuation changes made in 1669 in general have not the same careful character as those now in question. In his edition of the 1667 text Fletcher prints complete photographs of the two reset signatures, and an independent list of variants has been compiled by collation of these with his facsimiles of the 1667 printing (earlier states shown first).

DISCUSSION

The signatures in which the punctuation was most heavily altered in proof are L, Q and S. In the case of these three one may be fairly certain that what appear to be the corrected versions of punctuation are in fact the later states, since, at the same time that the pointing was revised, the pages were also tidied up in various small, mechanical ways (see Fletcher, II, 144–8).

L adds a heavy stop once and twice heightens stops: *impure*] *impure;* III, 630   *accostes;*] *accostes.* III, 653   *groane;*] *goane :* IV, 88. Of these corrected pointings only the first (semicolon to introduce comparison) is a rhetorical usage, although one not peculiar to Milton in the period. The second (colon to introduce speech) conforms to the typographical conventions adopted by the edition and the third (colon to introduce independent clause) is consistent with seventeenth-century grammar. Once in L a comma is added at the end of a line, it is difficult to say whether for emphasis, grammar or metre, possibly for all these reasons: *relapse*] *relapse,* IV, 100. Conversely, once a comma falling unrhythmically in the line is deleted: *renewing,*] *renewing* III, 729. But in the same line a pointing is reduced which, though grammatically too heavy, could be thought useful in breathing the long period: *Heav'n;*] *Heav'n,* III, 729. Thus of the six changes in L two have some rhythmical significance; two if not three are intended chiefly for grammar (one change being a downpointing of the kind made in larger numbers earlier by the edition); and only one change may be a distinctively rhetorical pointing of the kind illustrated in chapter VI, 1. The second edition does not incorporate any of these proof changes in L, although it follows all the others which are listed here (save for IV, 720).

In Q and S (Book V) three proof changes consist in the deletion of grammatically unwanted but metrical commas: *within,*] *within* 710 (Ed. 2, 713)   *Harp,*] *Harp* 151   *raies,*] *Raies* 301. In five other instances commas are added. Two of these (*works*] *works,* 153 *Heavens*] *Heavens,* 156) help to articulate the sense but double metrical pauses within one line, in the first case in connection with a vocative where Milton's habit is to leave out the stop. The comma added at 156 is not retained in a third and finally altered state of Q. Two further added commas (*battel*] *battel,* 725 [Ed. 2, 728]   *Morning*] *Morning,* 743 [Ed. 2, 746]) are rhythmically inept, although that at 743 may be needed to avoid a slight ambiguity. Another comma added in Q, grammatically unimportant, is an undoubted impediment to the rhythm:

> From hence, no cloud, or, to obstruct his sight,
> Starr interpos'd, however small he sees,
> (257–8)

The comma inserted after *cloud,* is highly obstructive to the phrasing of the line. One might guess that in the original manuscript copy for Book V a lighter pointing here had been matched by a lighter pointing also in the first half of line 257 (no comma originally after *hence,...*) Similarly, a light pointing is still evident in line 258 (no comma after *small*). Thus the eight changes concerning commas in Q and S seem to be intended primarily for grammar and sense; rhythm is frequently interfered with.

Three other changes in Q and S are obviously for grammar: *do:*] *do.* 121　*needs*] *needs;* 302　*Lord,*] *Lord:* 608. In the first instance the full stop concludes a "sentence" but probably breaks up an intended period. The other two changes, to semicolon or colon in order to separate coordinate or independent clauses, are needed corrections.

A few further changes occur in the following signatures. Most are obvious grammatical corrections to clarify the sense, but the changes in H and Oo are also rhythmically apt. One change in Cc seems a mistake.

C: *views;*] *views,* I, 569. An inept downpointing, disregarding the Manuscript's reading and general style (see ex. 7, chap. VI, 1).

H: *Mæonides*] *Mæonides,* III, 35. Grammatically and rhythmically an improvement.

O: *stood.*] *stood,*] Ed. 2 *stood* IV, 720. A needed correction of error.

R: *Tastes;*] *Tastes,* V, 335　*change;*] *change,* V, 336. The first is needed grammatically. In the second case either reading might be grammatically correct, but the earlier one is more consistent with the heavy, blocking-out style of punctuation in the poem.

Cc: *serene.*] *serene,* VII, 818　*Live*] *live,* VII, 819. The first is a needed correction of error, the second possibly a metrical pointing (though grammatically superfluous) or else a mistake.

Nn: *misery.*] *misery,* IX, 982. A needed correction of error.

Oo: *pray let me,*] *pray, let mee* X (Ed. 2, XI), 32　*linkt,*] *linkt;* X (Ed. 2, XI), 139. Both are needed for the sense, but the change at line 32 is also a great rhythmical improvement and is interesting because it is coupled with the doubling of final *e* (possibly for stress?) at the line ending, in the same phrase.

CONCLUSIONS

Most of the twenty-seven proof changes in the 1667 edition are clearly inspired by grammar. A few changes involving commas in L, Q and S and occasionally in other signatures suggest some secondary attention to the rhythmical structure of the verse; on the other hand, some added commas impede the rhythm. The relative numbers of proof changes of different categories or kinds is very similar to that noted in the earlier printer's changes for Book I (see Appendix A). About twice as many commas are inserted as deleted in proof, and there are more downpointings than heightened pointings in proof (though not so many more as in the earlier changes). Again as in the earlier corrections, only one of the heightened pointings in proof (III, 630) is a distinctive rhetorical usage like the heavy pointings found in the Manuscript, Book I. All the other heavier pointings are merely changes for better grammar or typographical form. Downpointings in proof are also obvious corrections of grammatical or typographical error, or else are reductions of rhetorical stops. All the tendencies noted in the earlier press corrections thus appear in the proof corrections as well; these later changes are if anything more exclusively grammatical than the earlier ones.

J. H. Hanford wrote that he could not point to a single clear author's change in minor matters (and exclusive of the errata) in the 1667 text (see "The Manuscript of *Paradise Lost*", p. 316). One would not like to be so definite as this about Milton's negative part in the press corrections. He did after all direct a few verbal changes in proof (as at I, 505 and 603), and someone certainly corrected at least some spellings along Miltonic lines and corrected punctuation with some apparent understanding of the structural and rhythmical principles Milton applied. Nevertheless, it is a fact that there are very few punctuation changes in the 1667 printed text which seem distinctively or peculiarly Miltonic in style.

Of the proof changes, only two could feasibly suggest the poet's actual intervention: III, 630 (semicolon put before *as* in a comparison) and X (Ed. 2, XI), 32 (comma moved back to the caesura to clarify the meaning; but this change is also a rhythmical improvement and is coupled with the doubling of *e* in *me* at the end of the same line – possibly for stress). Similarly, the only earlier printing change which stood out as possibly the author's own was the heightening of the stop before a simile at I, 771. The deletion of one unmetrical comma in proof at III, 729 (and the few similar deletions in the earlier press changes), as grammatically unconventional uses of punctuation, might suggest the author's influence. On the other hand, the much more frequent addition in both proof and earlier press corrections of commas which are both grammatically appropriate and also metrically placed is more uncertain evidence of author's intervention. Such changes, primarily grammatical, could have been made by any good corrector or by a corrector influenced only in a general way by Miltonic practice. A few passages in which the additions stress medial pauses may somewhat more strongly suggest Miltonic influence.

As far as can be judged from their small number, the proof changes thus represent a style of pointing in no significant way different from the earlier punctuation changes made at the press. They appear to be merely a continuation of the same process of correction. There is nothing at all in them to show that Milton corrected punctuation any more thoroughly in proof (the natural place) than at the preceding stages of printing; and there is only very little in them to suggest that he might have been personally responsible for pointing corrections at either stage. What both the earlier printer's corrections and the proof changes suggest, rather, is an intelligent, systematic and careful corrector or compositor, who was working chiefly with an eye to good grammar and consistent typographical form but possibly with some limited understanding of the rhythmical basis of Miltonic punctuation. Such understanding if it existed did not extend to subtleties, nor was it consistently displayed; and the corrector showed distinctly less sympathy with the elocutionary or rhetorical aspects of Miltonic punctuation.

Such a corrector would not be incompatible with Moxon's ideal compositor: ". . . he reads his *Copy* with consideration; that so he may get himself into the meaning of the *Author*, and consequently considers how to order his Work the better . . . . As how to make his *Indenting, Pointing, Breaking, Italicking*, etc., the better sympathize with the *Authors* Genius, and also with the capacity of the Reader." (See sec. 22, para. 5 of *Mechanick Exercises . . . [1683–4]*, 2nd. ed., ed. H. Davis and H. Carter [London, 1962], p. 212.) Milton might perhaps have exercised some restraint or indirect influence over such a corrector. Milton might also have been more directly responsible for a very few punctuation changes made during the printing. But any idea that the fairly homogeneous revision of punctuation undertaken during the early stages of the printing and continued into the proof reading was supervised by the poet himself seems not to fit the evidence of the variants.

Alternatively to the hypothesis of a single, enlightened corrector, we must allow for several at the press. One might have been cautiously regularizing punctuation (but with regard to Miltonic rhythm and structure), he or another perhaps also making the odd specific change as directed by the poet; while another reader, or the compositor, to some extent interfering with the work of the first and with the poet, would have been correcting typography, standardizing unconventional rhetorical punctuation, and adding commas needed for grammar but not always rhythmically apt. Fortunately, these revisions were not far-reaching enough to do more than illuminate the significant differences in the style of the original.

List of Variant Pointings, States of 1667

Commas Inserted

III,   35 *Maeonides*] *Maeonides*,
IV, 100 relapse] relapse,
 V, 153 works] works,
 V, 156 Heavens] Heavens,/
          Heavens
 V, 257 cloud] cloud,
 V, 725 (Ed. 2, 728) battel]
          battel,
 V, 743 (Ed. 2, 746) Morning]
          Morning,
VII, 819 (Ed. 2, VIII, 182) Live]
          live,
 X,   32 (Ed. 2, XI) pray] pray,

Commas Deleted

III, 729 renewing,] renewing
 V, 151 Harp,] Harp
 V, 301 raies,] Raies
 V, 710 (Ed. 2, 713) within,]
         within
 X,   32 (Ed. 2, XI) me,] mee

Stops Reduced

 I, 569 views;] views,
III, 729 Heav'n;] Heav'n,
IV, 720 stood.] stood,
 V, 335 Tastes;] Tastes,
 V, 336 change;] change,
VII, 818 (Ed. 2, VIII, 181)
          serene.] serene,
IX, 982 (Ed. 2, X) misery.]
          misery,

Stops Heightened

III, 653 accostes;] accostes.
IV,   88 groane;] groane:
 V, 121 do:] do.
 V, 608 Lord,] Lord:
 X, 139 (Ed. 2, XI) linkt,]
          linkt;

Other Changes

III, 630 impure] impure;   V, 302 needs] needs;

II. *The* 1669 Reset *Z and Vv Signatures*

These two completely reset signatures, probably printed in 1669 to make up a deficiency of stored pages for the sixth issue, have been pronounced by Fletcher and Miss Darbishire to be of little value. The later states are certainly very carelessly printed in mechanical and other respects, the Z signature (Book VII) especially.

In the latter, one gross example of compositorial carelessness is the substitution in line 25 of *tongues;* for *dayes,* – the compositor's eye picked up the word from the next line and wrongly repeated it. There are numerous spelling mistakes and misreadings as well; the sheets could scarcely have been proofread. Milton's characteristic spellings are not followed and the change *watrie*] *watery* at 234 is metrically wrong; so also at 136 the change *th' Omnipotent*] *the Omnipotent.*

The larger part of the punctuation changes consists of commas omitted, most of them accidentally, as the contexts establish. Nearly all the omitted commas were caesural stops. Perhaps because midline stops do not stand out on the page as well as commas placed at the ends of lines, the compositor, reading hastily, failed to notice some. At any rate he certainly was not kept on his guard by any appreciation of the importance of midline punctuation to Milton's verse structure. The other changes are erroneous too. At 56 the downpointing of colon spoils an antithesis. The colon at 183, similarly reduced, had been effective in suggesting the rhythmical punctuation of the 1611 Bible, copied elsewhere by Milton. The only possible improvement to the pointing in the Z signature is *Heav'n,*] *Heav'n;* 162 – a suitably heavier pointing for syntactical partitioning and emphasis. Omission of a few commas (as at 93, 122 and 220) might be defended, but the context of carelessness makes all omissions suspicious.

The Vv signature (Book X) also shows signs of poor printing, but it contains fewer gross errors and makes fewer changes in the punctuation. We find four omissions of needed commas at 1429, 1479, 1499, 1540 (Ed. 2, XII: 537, 587, 607 and 648). But three lines contain an important correction: line 1493 (Ed. 2, XII, 601) had an incorrect full stop at the end, which the later state changes to comma to make a continuous sentence, at the same time adding a comma at the middle of line 1495 (Ed 2, XII, 603) after *unanimous,* . . . . Whoever made this and the associated correction knew what sense Milton intended. But a corrector who understood Milton's rhythms would in addition to these two changes have removed the comma after *sad,* at the end of line 1495. The partly corrected reading of the Vv signature did not get into the 1674 edition.

The variants next listed are my collations from Fletcher's alternative facsimiles. Miss Darbishire's list of variants in Z is incomplete in quite a number of particulars of punctuation.

List of Variant Pointings Z and Vv Signatures 1669, from 1667 First Printing

Commas Deleted	Commas Inserted
VII, 1 *Urania,*] *Urania*	X (XII), 1495 (603) unanimous]
3 Following,] Following	unanimous,
11 Father,] Father	
19 Dismounted,] Dismounted	
36 rapture,] rapture	
39 Heav'n lie,] Heav'nlie	
40 Goddess,] Goddess	
41 Arch-angel,] Arch-Angel	
52 admiration,] admiration	
83 knowing,] knowing	
93 begun,] begun	
97 works,] works	
122 King,] King	
139 fail'd,] fail'd	
144 many,] many	
151 done,] done	
156 innumerable,] innumerable	
171 goodness,] goodness	
207 moving,] moving	
220 *Chaos,*] *Chaos*	
223 Creation,] Creation	
236 infus'd,] infus'd	
X (XII), 1429 (537) on,] on	
1479 (587) thee,] thee	
1499 (607) Descended,] Descended	
1540 (648) slow,] slow	

Stops Reduced	Stops Heightened
VII, 56 confusion:] confusion,	VII, 162 Heav'n,] Heav'n;
183 peace:] peace;	
X (XII), 1447 (555) fixt:] fixt;	
1493 (601) Mankind.] Mankind,	

APPENDIX C

Variant Pointings 1674 from 1667

1. The variants of the second edition of *Paradise Lost* have been discussed by H. F. Fletcher ("Comparison of the 1674 and 1667 Texts" and "Summary," *op. cit.*, III, 50–9) and more briefly by H. Darbishire ("Introduction," *The Manuscript of . . . Book I*, pp. xliv–vii). Punctuation variants were considered by these scholars, but not as a class in themselves nor apart from other minor variants such as spellings, capitalizations, line numbering, type faces and so on. Punctuation is a matter of greater stylistic consequence than some of these and needs to be considered separately.

The appended list of punctuation variants is drawn up out of Fletcher's collations in the textual notes to his edition of the 1674 text, these having been checked against his photographs of the relevant pages in both editions and his photographs of alternative states of pages. The list is intended to include only true punctuation variants (where type has been altered from 1667 or marks left out); cases of apparent variants which Fletcher interprets as due to mechanical irregularities in the printing (faint or broken type, etc.) have not been listed. However a few doubtful cases (according to Fletcher) have been listed but not included in the discussion. A few instances where 1674 follows earlier, uncorrected states of 1667 (III, 630, 653; III, 729, twice; IV, 88, 100) are not listed as variants. The readings of 1667 are given first. The list shows distribution of changes by Books. Nearly all variants listed enter the discussion.

The 1674 text, as Fletcher observed, is a difficult one. However, it is here thought that some meaningful tendencies can be discerned in its overall pattern of punctuation changes.

Fletcher's two main conclusions regarding all the 1674 minor variants were: (1) The numbers of changes remain nearly constant by Books, though lessening somewhat after the first two Books; and the punctuation and spelling become "better patterned . . . to Milton's vagaries" in the later Books. (2) The compositor and press corrector were probably responsible for as much of the state of the text, in minor matters, as Milton and his friends or helpers (Vol. III, pp. 57, 59).

2. As regards punctuation only, a count shows that the numbers of changes do remain not far off constant throughout the first eight

Books (taking the divided 1674 Books VII and VIII as one, and XI and XII as one); but in fact the smallest number of changes occurs in Book III, and the largest in Books IX, X, and XI/XII. (The figures run: Bk. I, 14; Bk. II, 15; Bk. III, 7; Bk. IV, 15; Bk. V, 11; Bk. VI, 15; Bks. VII/VIII, 11; Bk. IX, 25; Bk. X, 17; Bks. XI/XII, 20.) There is no evident improvement of any kind in punctuation toward the end of the poem. Book IX contains the largest number of probable errors, while Books I and XI are possibly the best corrected; however, there is not much to choose between Books, since all contain numerous mistakes.

There are in all some 150 changes in punctuation (purposive changes and also errors or faults) made in the 1674 text, according to Fletcher's collations, as compared with a slightly larger number of changes of which we know in 1667 (133 early press changes for Book I, plus twenty-eight proof changes for the whole poem). Some comparisons can therefore be made on a proportional basis between the styles of the pointing variants in the two editions (the ratio of each type of change to approximately 150 or 160), although in effect we shall be comparing the style of 1667, Book I only, with the style of 1674 throughout the poem. It should be stressed that the 150 variants of 1674, distributed over the entire poem, are hardly a sufficient number to affect the general style of its punctuation. Fewer than ten changes per Book could not make much difference to the text. The 1674 changes are interesting mainly because their total number is just sufficient to enable us to make some general inferences about the character and style of the second edition's pointing, as compared with that of 1667 and with the general habits of punctuation in the Manuscript.

There appear to have been virtually no changes to the punctuation in proof in 1674; Fletcher records only one punctuation variant between states of that edition (I, 17), and there may have been another intended change in type already set at I, 370. This absence of proof correction is in keeping with the generally less careful character of the 1674 punctuation.

As to Fletcher's second conclusion. The punctuation changes of 1674 do present an immediate impression of being in no uniform style, or of containing sharp inconsistencies in style. Much more uniformity was evident in 1667, where the orientation of the punctuation changes was fairly consistently grammatical (with some secondary attention to rhythm, and a few mistakes mainly of omission). There was also more consistency in the general style of pointing in the Manuscript of Book I, which seemed primarily rhythmical and rhetorically expressive in intention, although sometimes heedless of grammatical form. If the compositor or press corrector were responsible for part of the punctuation changes in 1674 (as seems certain), it would appear that these were not the same persons who had been working during the 1667 printing. Several factors point to this conclusion: the larger amount of mechanical error in the type than in 1667; the larger number of errors due obviously to compositorial carelessness in typesetting; and an occasional preference, in minor grammatical matters, for a more modern form or usage (see section 5). Possibly also the rather different distribution or pattern of the changes (see section 4) has some relevance here.

3. Faulty type is seen in 1674 in, for example, the large number of italic colons set; faint or broken marks, some of which could be misread (Fletcher records these in his textual notes, and a few instances are also given in the list below, e.g. I, 776; II, 392; XII, 29 [Ed. 1, X, 921]); and errors due to 'foul case', that is, definite but unintended changes in the punctuation. Wrong face, damaged type, etc. occur in the 1667 text, but (speaking of the punctuation only) seem to be present in smaller numbers. Changes due most likely to foul case (more easily detected in changes involving heavier stops) occur in 1674 in possibly fourteen instances. There are: IV, 934; VI, 368; VIII, 223 (Ed. 1, VII, 860); IX (Ed. 1, VIII), 356, 951, 1098; X (Ed. 1, IX), 271, 706 – all these, needed periods reduced. Again: VI, 346; VIII, 466 (Ed. 1, VII, 1103); IX (Ed. 1, VIII), 745; XI (Ed. 1, X), 233, 335, 710 (706) – these, stops wrongly heightened, or heavy stops incorrectly altered to question mark. 1667, Book I, shows very few or no pointing errors due apparently to foul case (in fact little typographical error of any kind in its punctuation). Its reduced full stops, for example, are always those associated with epic similes; these changes form part of the systematic regularizing of rhetorical punctuation by the first edition. Other alterations to heavy stops in 1667, Book I, and instances where stops are heightened contain only one doubtful change (I, 380) which could be due to foul case. However, 1667 did set or follow a few wrong stops in other Books, for example: heavy stops for commas at IV, 720; V, 335; VII, 818 (Ed. 2, VIII, 181); IX (Ed. 2, X) 982 – these were corrected in proof, 1667; and superfluous colon, or period for comma, at V, 538, 633; VIII (Ed. 2, IX), 206 – these errors were rectified in 1674.

Errors due probably to carelessness in setting the type in 1674 are seen in the large number of stops dropped or in some cases mistakenly inserted. Obviously needed heavy stops are forgotten at least five times, at: II, 53; III, 92, 515; V, 617; X (Ed. 1, IX), 762. These omissions are balanced by only one addition, at VI, 405, of a needed full stop. 1667, Book I, shows no such gross oversights of

M

punctuation given in the Manuscript. Dropped commas occur more frequently still in 1674; that is, marks are omitted which seem needed for the sense and often for the rhythm too. Compared with only four or five doubtful omissions of commas in the early corrections for 1667, Book I, we find more than twenty questionable omissions of commas in 1674. There is no certainty that some of these deletions were not intended, but most give the appearance of being oversights. Thus we have: I, 362, probably 635 (depending on how the sense is taken); II, 981, probably 232 (rhythmically very necessary), also 310; III, 298; IV, 720; VI, 140, 568; VIII, possibly 307 (Ed. 1, VII, 944), almost certainly 602 (Ed. 1, VII, 1239); IX (Ed. 1, VIII), 581 (space set but no comma), 979; X (Ed. 1, IX), possibly 48, more certainly 215, 338, 380 (needed to avoid a misreading), 787, 835; XII, 46 (Ed. 1, X, 938), 238 (Ed. 1, X, 1130), 539 (Ed. 1, X, 1431), 550 (Ed. 1, X, 1442). We have to consider in parallel with this group a further group of omitted commas in 1674 which could be purposive. This will be discussed in section 6.

Commas which are apparently mistakenly inserted occur not so frequently as the above omissions, but still more frequently than in 1667. It sometimes seems as if the end of the line has irrelevantly caught the compositor's eye. There is a clear example of error due to this cause at VI, 568, where the comma in 1667 given after *words,* is wrongly moved two words forward to follow *scarce,* at the end of the line. (Cf. to this the wrong reading of 1667, corrected in 1667 proof, at X [Ed. 2, XI], 32.) In some further instances grammatically unwanted commas are added at the end of the line, either deliberately to mark the metrical pause without regard to the sense, or because the compositor (or corrector) failed to read on past the line ending, not noting how in typical Miltonic fashion the sense carries over to the next caesura. Thus II, 658, 973; III, 95; IV, 131. Similarly a comma is added, perhaps only to stress the caesura, at IV, 946. Commas added at IV, 586 and X (Ed. 1, IX), 3 are probably also purely metrical. If these seven stops are intended as metrical markings, they are crudely metrical. The pauses thus emphasized are not important, the stops mostly interfere with the sense, and all but one double pauses within the line. The additions would be more characteristic of some early printer's practice (see the remarks on punctuation variants in the Shakespeare Folio, 1623, chap. II, 2 above) or of an ignorant scribe's than of the poet's. In the 1667 text several such clumsily metrical markings are removed, such changes agreeing with the prevailingly grammatical tenor of the 1667 emendations. (These are, *viz.,* from the Manuscript text at I, 146, 201, 245, 295; and, in proof, from earlier states, at V, 151, 301, 710 [Ed. 2, 713].) In only one or two cases are purely metrical marks added in 1667 (I, 377, and VII, 819 [Ed.2, VIII, 182] – probably an error in proof). 1674 removes clumsy metrical marks at I, 88; VII, 20; and XI (Ed. 1, X), 137. While mainly metrical stops are occasionally to be found in the Manuscript of Book I, they are usually less obtrusive. But the rhythmical punctuation of the Manuscript normally functions in the reverse way, by omitting unmetrical, grammatical stops rather than by inserting metrical, ungrammatical stops.

4. Perhaps the most striking difference between the 1674 and the 1667 punctuation variants is the different pattern or distribution of the changes. This fact raises the important question of whether the 1674 changes show any stylistic differences from the new punctuation in 1667.

Whereas the 1667 text showed about three and one-half times as many commas added as deleted or dropped during the first press corrections (and twice as many commas added as removed in later proof changes), 1674 shows very nearly the opposite: the appended list indicates about twice as many commas taken or left out of the 1674 text as put into it. And whereas 1667 showed only about one third as many stops heightened as heavy stops reduced, 1674 shows less disinclination to introduce heavier punctuation. The appended list indicates some fifteen stops heightened as against twenty-five stops reduced. (Unlike 1667, the cases where stops are heightened in 1674 are not all merely grammatical changes – see section 8.) Of course account must be taken of the fact that many of the 1674 changes are not purposeful, whereas most of those in 1667 appeared to be so. But even excluding from the above comparisons the more obvious instances of mechanical error in the type or of compositorial error in 1674 (see section 3), the picture is not much altered. A more conservative count shows in 1674 a maximum of some forty-two commas intentionally removed as against the thirty-two (or more probably only twenty-five) apparently purposeful additions of commas to the text; and possibly seventeen meaningful downpointings as against possibly eleven meaningfully heightened pointings.

The distribution of the 1674 punctuation changes therefore suggests a pattern of pointing which might be closer to that of the Manuscript of Book I than is the case with 1667. The rhythmical and elocutionary styles of the Manuscript depended chiefly on a light pointing or the frequent omission of commas for fluency, coupled with the occasional contrasting use of a particularly heavy pointing for rhetorical stress; such tendencies might seem to be repeated in 1674, judging from the relative ratios of changes in the above breakdown. On the other hand, the largely grammatical emendations of 1667 showed just the opposite tendencies, far more commas put into the text and heavy stops reduced than the reverse.

5. We must now consider more closely, how many of the possibly purposeful changes of 1674 seem to be grammatical in intention and how many appear to be rhythmical or rhetorical in intent, and how the various kinds of changes made compare with those of 1667 and with the general style of pointing in the Manuscript, Book I.

A small number of intended punctuation changes in 1674, like a similar number in 1667, are obvious corrections of grammatical errors or omissions. So we have question mark substituted for period at I, 634; unwanted colon deleted at V, 633; needed full stop or needed semicolon added at VI, 405 and XI (Ed. 1, X), 142; incorrect full stop reduced at V, 538 and IX (Ed. 1, VIII), 206. Further we find, as in 1667, a few commas replaced by heavier stops for more correct syntactical division at: IV, 465; V, 631; IX (Ed. 1, VIII), 319; similarly colon replaced by full stop at VII, 337. We also find, as in 1667, a few grammatically superfluous commas (mostly metrical marks) deleted at I, 88; VI, 423 (comma before parenthesis); VII, 20; XI (Ed. 1, X), 137.

However, not all the obvious corrections for grammar in 1674 run strictly to the pattern of 1667. For instance, it appears that the 1674 compositor several times forgets the established practice of both Manuscript and first edition of using full stop to introduce speech, and inconsistently sets a comma instead, as in modern practice: V, 506; VI, 620; IX (Ed. 1, VIII), 272, 1016, 1162; XI, 552 (Ed. 1, X, 548). (Once, however, 1674 gives the more usual period to introduce speech, replacing a semicolon: XI, 683 [Ed. 1, X, 679].) Also following modern practice, 1674 takes comma out before parenthesis at VI, 423, whereas 1667 put comma in before parenthesis at I, 143 (accepted earlier practice). Again as in modern practice, 1674 more often deletes than gives comma before *and*, especially before the final one of a sequence of items: I, 465 (a return to the MS reading); II, 559, 949; IX (Ed. 1, VIII), 1056. These instances contrast with comma put in at only IX (Ed. 1, VIII), 116. The 1667 text, typically more concerned with minute grammatical definition, five times in Book I puts commas in before *and* or *or* – at I, 133 (twice), 346, 465, and also III, 35 (a proof change). The 1674 and modern usage in this context happen, perhaps fortuitously, to coincide with the Manuscript's or Milton's preference for lighter, more fluent (rhythmically grounded) punctuation.

6. What attention to rhythm may be evident in the 1674 pointing variants, and does the practice of 1674 in rhythmical matters follow 1667 or the Manuscript of Book I?

One fairly numerous group of changes in 1674, of a mixed grammatical-rhythmical character, closely parallels the largest group of changes in the 1667 edition. Commas are added primarily for grammar but also so as to fall at a metrical pause: I, 94, 96, 112; II, 1000; III, 335; IV, 274, 344, 553, 885; V, 545, 840 (Ed. 1, 837); IX (Ed. 1, VIII), 114, 147, 634, 841; X (Ed. 1, IX), 829, 974; XII, 21 (Ed. 1, X, 913). In the above nineteen changes the balance oscillates somewhat between grammar and poetical considerations. A few changes noticeably improve the rhythmical or even the rhetorical articulation of the verse, along with the logical (e.g. II, 1000; IX [Ed. 1, VIII], 114; X [Ed. 1, IX], 974; again IV, 885; IX [Ed. 1, VIII], 147). A few changes (e.g. IX [Ed. 1, VIII], 147) seem logically imperative. But in many cases metrical pauses are doubled within the line in contexts which do not seem to need such detail in the punctuation for any special reasons of rhythm, stress or intelligibility: e.g. at I, 112; IV, 344, 553; V, 545; IX (Ed. 1, VIII), 634, 841; X (Ed. 1, IX), 829; XII, 21 (Ed. 1, X, 913). All this is much as it was in 1667, except that the comparable group of changes was larger then (some fifty of the total sixty-five added commas). A few further added commas (1674) of only slight grammatical value actively interfere with the metre: I, 529, 563 (these two commas might be for stress); V, 553; IX (Ed. 1, VIII), 116. It is noticeable that there are fewer such rhythmically obtrusive stops added in 1674 than 1667, where for Book I some twelve metrically clumsy additions were earlier cited, plus two or three more inept commas added in the proof changes.

Deletions of commas in 1674 (see also sec. 3) suggest a more specific concern with rhythmical structure, somewhat along the lines of the Manuscript of Book I. Whereas only three or four deletions of unmetrical commas appeared in 1667 (three in the earlier press changes for Book I, possibly one more in proof at III, 729), in 1674 we find ten possibly deliberate omissions of unmetrical commas. Of these, nine occur at: I, 370, 465; II, 19, 247; III, 332; IX (Ed. 1, VIII), 668, 1002, 1159; X (Ed. 1, IX), 332. It seems of some significance that I, 370 and 465 return to the original Manuscript readings. One further change at I, 17 (deletion of an unmetrical comma earlier added by the 1674 corrector or compositor), similarly returns to the original Manuscript reading. (It is possible also that the deletion of comma at I, 370 – space set but no comma given – was a deliberate change to type already set.) The 1674 readings at I, 370; III, 332; and IX (Ed. 1, VIII), 1159 constitute very characteristic Miltonic pointings. All ten deletions seem modelled on the Manuscript's light style.

There is in addition to the above deletions a large and intriguing marginal group of omitted commas in 1674. All of these had fallen at a pause; none of them is much missed for the sense. As a group, this has no parallel in the changes of 1667. Here we may have a deliberate lightening of the punctuation, somewhat along the lines of the Manuscript, though withholding one of two metrical stops in a line. These are usually unimportant defining stops in some minor construction. The natural pauses of the verse line then supply the want of the missing stops. Such omissions occur at: I, 694; II, 323; IV, 53, 194, 294, 949; V, 4; VI, 483, 785, 846; VII, 151; VIII, 313 (Ed. 1, VII, 950), 451 (Ed. 1, VII, 1088), 600 (Ed. 1, VII, 1237); IX (Ed. 1, VIII), 393, 638, 1056, 1087; X (Ed. 1, IX), 132, 523, 837, 973; XI (Ed. 1, X), 355, 669 (Ed. 1, X, 665); XII, 542 (Ed. 1, X, 1434). Of course some of these twenty-five omissions may be compositor's oversights. On the other hand, most of them offer a suggestive parallel to the basic habit, evident in the Manuscript of Book I or in Milton's autograph sonnets, of omitting a second metrical and defining comma (especially at a line ending) in the interest of more fluent rhythmical structure.

Certain kinds of very subordinate, parenthetical, or brief sentence elements offer the readiest means for such economy. Qualifying phrases, brief relatives, appositives, vocatives or interjections, short compounds or coordinates, etc., can easily be presented only half defined by the pointing – defined sometimes at one end of the construction or sometimes at the other end, or not defined at all, just as is most convenient for the rhythmical structure. Especially suggestive of Miltonic habits of pointing were these of the above instances: IV, 194; VII, 151; VIII, 313 (Ed. 1, VII, 950); XII, 542 (Ed. 1, X, 1434) – stop omitted at the line ending in connection with an appositive or some similar construction (pointing only at the end of such constructions). Again: IX (Ed. 1, VIII), 393, 1056, 1087; X (Ed. 1, IX), 132, 837 – comma omitted fairly consistently at the line ending, but once internally, in connection with compounds or coordinates (pointing only at one [either] end of the construction).

Scanty, withheld, metrical pointing in such contexts is a basic habit not only in the Manuscript but even in the printed texts. Excellent examples are the two passages, unaltered from first to second editions, at IV, 268–71 and VIII (Ed. 2, IX), 124–5. The possibility should therefore not be disregarded that the above twenty-five odd instances in 1674, or some of them at least, may represent an attempt by someone correcting along the author's lines to prune away a little of the excessive punctuation introduced by the first edition. 1667 shows no similar attempt, or perhaps only one comparable instance (I, 404).

7. It is interesting to compare with the light rhythmical or structural punctuation discussed in section 6, a group of hand-written corrections to the punctuation found by Fletcher particularly in copy 19 collated by him. Fletcher thinks that these alterations may

have been entered at the printing house after the printing work was completed (see his Vol. III, notes to the lines cited below and note to Bk. II, 190). In that case these penned corrections would have been a belated substitute, apparently executed in only the one copy, for proof corrections to the punctuation (of which one only appears in variant states of 1674: I, 17). As Fletcher points out, there is no definite evidence as to the derivation of these penned corrections. But they are notable for their astuteness. The changes characteristically involve not only the adding or deleting of stops but the shifting of stops to the midline, in a way which often clears up a difficulty in the sense at the same time as it reformulates the rhythm, emphasizing the forward surge of the verse. Some of these handwritten corrections are cited below (1674 printing shown first):

Together both with next to Almightie Arme,	[Arme]
Uplifted imminent one stroke they aim'd . . .	[imminent,]
(VI, 316–17)	

when the most High	
Eternal Father from his secret Cloud,	[Father, . . . Cloud]
Amidst in Thunder utter'd thus his voice.	[Amidst,]
(X [Ed. 1, IX], 31–3)	

for now were all transform'd	
Alike, to Serpents all as accessories	[First: Alike to
To his bold Riot:	Serpents,
(X [Ed. 1, IX], 519–21)	Then: Alike, to
	Serpents all,]

The evident improvement to both sense and rhythm in all these changes recalls such printed variants as in proof, 1667: X (Ed. 2, XI), 32–3, or 1674: X (Ed. 1, IX), 973–4. Such corrections illustrate how, in Miltonic usage, punctuation and syntax both cooperate with the verse structure to produce at once the desired forward rhythms and the clearest and easiest flow of the sense. The style of the above pen corrections might serve as a guide to a few still existing cruxes in the poem, where repunctuation along Miltonic lines, stressing midline pointing as the pivot of rhythm and sense, might sometimes clear a difficulty. Examples are X (Ed. 1, IX), 581–2, where this kind of emendation (as proposed earlier by Pearce: see Fletcher's Vol. III, note) would seem to offer the best reading. Similarly XII, 601–3 (Ed. 1, 1493–5), where the wrong readings have been perpetuated through later editions, despite the partial correction by the 1669 reset Vv signature (see Appendix B).

8. Lastly, do the 1674 variants suggest any attention to rhetorical or elocutionary principles of punctuation, which were evident in the

Manuscript of Book I especially in the use of a heavy or emphasizing type of stopping? Such a rhetorical orientation was conspicuously lacking in the 1667 text, where some thirty-six earlier downpointings for Book I (plus three more in the proof corrections) revealed a systematic attempt to regularize the Manuscript's unconventional emphatic stopping. In 1674 we find, among a much smaller number of downpointings, some reductions of pointings which probably had been intended as rhetorical stops. These occur at: I, 742 (colon indicating suspension is reduced); III, 113, VI, 73, IX (Ed. 1, VIII), 1059 (heavy stops introducing similes or comparison are reduced); IV, 208, V, 624, VI, 812, XI, 712 (Ed. 1, X, 708) (a heavy, blocking-out type of punctuation is reduced). Some of these changes may reflect the 1674 preference for slightly more modern, lighter grammatical forms. Where two forms might be logically acceptable (the one according to earlier grammar, the other according to later usage), 1674 often tends to choose the lighter and to us more familiar pointing. This preference is evident in possibly the following of the above cited downpointings in 1674: IV, 208; VI, 812; XI, 712 (Ed. 1, X, 708]); also in other 1674 changes as cited in section 5.

In contrast to the several instances of reduced rhetorical stops cited above, we find as many or more cases in 1674 where stops are rhetorically heightened (the reverse of the 1667 pattern). Thus we find: IX (Ed. 1, VIII), 319 (semicolon substituted to mark antithesis); XI, 684 (Ed. 1, X, 680) (colon given probably for emphasis); VI, 666 (emphasizing comma added, but the mark is also metrical); IX (Ed. 1, VIII), 949 (semicolon substituted for question mark, probably to bring out oratorical pattern); II, 924 (semicolon used to mark an element in a comparison); VI, 891, VIII, 575 (Ed. 1, VII, 1212), XI, 736 (Ed. 1, X, 732) (heightening of stops to block out the narrative more emphatically). All but one of these revised pointings are ungrammatical. Those at VI, 891 and XI, 736 (Ed. 1, X, 732) are notably appropriate to their dramatic context, carrying echoes of the "colometric" style of punctuation of the Bible (See chap. VII, I).

A few other 1674 heightened pointings (at IV, 465; V, 631; VII, 337) seem to have been introduced primarily for more correct syntactical division. Almost all of the heightened pointings of 1667 were of this kind or were introduced for other obvious grammatical reason. There should also be mentioned two instances where the punctuation is lightened in 1674 (commas removed), perhaps to give speed and a sense of dramatic urgency: II, 675, 697. However, deletions at II, 559 and 949 spoil dramatic emphasis.

1674 thus shows one group of mainly unconventional changes,

some of which are evidently, others possibly, rhetorical in purpose and similar in style to that of the Manuscript, Book I; and another quite incompatible group of changes which, like the 1667 down-pointings, are anti-rhetorical or grammatical in purpose.

CONCLUSIONS

A general survey of the 1674 punctuation variants gives an impression that they are much less uniform in character than those of 1667. Almost all of the 1667 changes in pointing were grammatically oriented, wholly or in part. Even such changes as notably improved the rhythmical structure were usually also grammatically acceptable. Except for a few inappropriate additions of commas (sometimes in difficult contexts), and a few omissions of commas possibly overlooked by the compositor, 1667 contains very little typographical and very little grammatical error in its new punctuation. In keeping with this grammatical concern, 1667 shows almost no new pointings which are specifically rhetorical in purpose and only a very few pointings (deletions of unmetrical commas) which seem exclusively rhythmical. That is, there are almost no changes which are grammatically unorthodox though possibly desirable from other points of view. Conversely, grammar apparently being given a priority in 1667, rhythmical and rhetorical considerations are not infrequently flouted in the first edition's punctuation. From one point of view, the grammatical, the 1667 punctuation changes are homogeneous. They are compatible with the work of a single intelligent corrector or compositor, not unaware of certain aspects of Miltonic style but working mainly and more consistently for good grammar and typographical form, and hence sometimes against Miltonic principles.

The 1674 punctuation variants seem more mixed than this. They show on the one hand more gross inaccuracies and mechanical faults than are seen in 1667, yet on the other hand a smaller proportion of rhythmical and rhetorical infelicities and possibly in some instances a rather more specific concern for rhythmical fluency and rhetorical expressiveness. The 1674 variants seem to contain three distinct strata or groups, apparently little related to each other, or frankly incompatible.

First, there is a large group of almost certain errors, due either to mechanical causes or to the compositor's ignorance or carelessness (foul case or wrong stops set for other reasons; dropped or misplaced stops; superfluous stops or crudely metrical stops added; etc.). Most of these must have originated during the actual setting of the type.

Next, there is as in 1667 a group of mainly grammatically oriented changes (commas added, a number of them accommodated to the verse structure, but this is not consistent; heavier stops added, adjusted or reduced; a few grammatically unwanted stops deleted). Most of these changes are such that they could as well have originated with a press corrector as anyone else – apparently a corrector of slightly different grammatical habits from the 1667 corrector. This group of changes is conspicuously smaller than in 1667. Then it formed the main bulk of the variants, whereas in 1674 it comprises a little more than a third.

Lastly, there is a third group of grammatically unorthodox changes, some evidently, others possibly, rhythmical and rhetorical in intention. These changes if purposive could have derived only from the poet. (This group comprises unmetrical though otherwise 'correct' commas deleted, excessive metrical punctuation lightened, stops unconventionally added or heightened for rhetorical effect.) This group is relatively large, nearly one third of the variants. In style it is incompatible with the conventional second group of corrections, and similarly it disagrees with the main body of grammatical corrections in 1667. The style of this group is suggestive, rather, of the pointing of the Manuscript of Book I. It does not seem reasonable to assume that all of these possibly Miltonic changes in 1674 are the product of chance or inadvertence in the printing, though some may be. Besides occurring in considerable number, many of these variants conform rather closely to distinctively Miltonic usages of punctuation in special contexts (as seen in the Manuscript, Book I, or in some of Milton's autograph poems). Three of the variants in Book I also return to Manuscript readings.

These three distinct groups of variants in 1674 could conceivably have originated not only with different persons but at different periods during the preparation of the second edition. The mechanical faults and gross errors would have been the latest group, arising with the compositor (apparently not the same compositor who was working in 1667, judging from the greater number of such mistakes). The more grammatical corrections could have derived from the press or any corrector commissioned to check the printer's copy before the typesetting. Milton of course could himself have had some of the more flagrant grammatical errors and omissions in the 1667 text corrected in his revised copy before sending it to the printer. However, there is nothing in most of this second group of wholly or partly grammatical corrections to make us think that they must have derived from the poet; and there are occasional rhythmical or rhetorical insensitivities in this group which suggest that many of the changes did not derive from Milton.

On the other hand, the third and more unconventional group of changes from their nature might more feasibly have originated with Milton. These changes could have been directed by him during the actual printing, but, if the poet's, would more likely have been written into the copy of the 1667 edition which Milton is thought to have used when preparing his text for the second edition. Into this copy he caused to be marked not only the new Book divisions, new lines and words and revised lines, but also much slighter changes concerning forms of words, spelling, elision and similar matters designed to correct the metrical quantities and emphases of the verse. In conjunction with such fine changes he might have introduced a number of equally fine changes to the punctuation (a few, as in Book I, merely restoring Manuscript readings), similarly designed to improve the rhythms and rhetorical inflections of his verse.

There may thus be a natural explanation of the seemingly odd circumstance that the second edition, despite its considerable numbers of gross errors or faults, yet shows some more distinctively Miltonic characteristics of punctuation than does the first edition, which is far more meticulous and homogeneous in its punctuation. We know (because we can check them against the Manuscript copy for Book I that was used by the printer) that all the variants which appeared in the printed 1667 text were changes made at the press. This is not the case with 1674, where the printed variants include both press changes and author's corrections made earlier. If the more Miltonically styled punctuation variants of 1674 (those in the unconventional third group, of kinds not found or not prominent in 1667) are possibly to be taken as preceding the other printed variants in date and having little connection with them, then the balance of the second edition's new punctuation does not appear so very different from the new punctuation of 1667. Any differences then lie in minor matters of grammatical form, due to the probable presence of a different compositor or corrector from the 1667, and in the greater degree of carelessness of the later edition, due no doubt to the fact of its being a cheaper edition over which less trouble was taken.

Either it was the case that this third group of changes was of earlier date, or else we must suppose that unusual, Miltonically styled emendations to the punctuation were being introduced during the printing in direct opposition to other, more conventional types of corrections being made at the same time, while both sets of changes were being interfered with by the persistent lapses of the compositor. It would seem unlikely that Milton took greater pains thus to impose his peculiar habits of punctuation on the 1674 than on the 1667 printing. He could of course have had a better agent acting for him at the press than before. But in any case, there are only the two details of type changes in 1674 (at I, 17, a proof change, and possibly at 370) which might confirm intervention along Miltonic lines during the actual printing process. There is equally little stylistically to suggest Milton's personal intervention in punctuation corrections during the 1667 printing.

List of Variant Pointings 1674 *from* 1667

	Bk. I	Bk. II	Bk. III
Commas *Added*	17 Thou] Thou,/Thou 94 those] those, 96 inflict] inflict, 112 power] power, 529 worth] worth, 563 view] view,	658 howl'd] howl'd, 973 way] way, 1000 defend] defend,	95 fall] fall, 335 dwell] dwell,
Commas *Deleted* *or* *Omitted*	88 hope,] hope 362 memorial,] memorial 370 him,] him 465 *Ascalon,*] *Ascalon* 635 me,] mee 694 Kings,] Kings	19 next,] next 232 hope,] hope 247 Heav'n,] Heav'n 310 heav'n,] heav'n 323 sure,] sure 559 Will,] Will 675 fast,] fast 697 scorn,] scorn 949 wings,] wings 981 Directed,] Directed	298 hate,] hate 332 Hell,] Hell

Stops
Reduced
	742 Battlements:]
	    Battlements;
		392 resolv'd;]
		    resolv'd,
		    (1674 possibly
		    faint semicolon)
			113 Fate;] Fate,

Stops
Heightened
	776 giv'n,] giv'n.
	    (1674 possibly
	    smashed comma)
		924 City,] City;	

Other
Changes
	634 seat.] seat?	53 now.] now	92 pervert;]
			    pervert
			515 Heav'n.]
			    Heav'n

	Bk. IV	Bk. V	Bk. VI

Commas
Added
	131 comes] comes,
	274 Spring] Spring,
	344 Pards] Pards,
	553 Speares] Speares,
	586 walks] walks,
	885 *Satan*] *Satan,*
	946 Angel] Angel,
		538 serve] serve,
		545 eare] eare,
		553 me] me,
		840 (Ed. 1, 837)
		    Powers] Powers,
			568 scarce] scarce,
			666 ground]
			    ground,

	Bk. IV	Bk. V	Bk. VI
Commas Deleted or Omitted	53 burthensome,] burthensome 194 Life,] Life 294 Severe,] Severe 720 stood,] stood 949 Leader,] Leader	4 light,] light	140 limit,] limit 423 fight,] fight 483 us,] us 568 words,] words 785 Foes,] Foes 846 Wheels,] Wheels
Stops Reduced	208 Earth:] Earth, 934 untri'd.] untri'd,	506 repli'd.] repli'd, 538 serve.] serve, 624 seem:] seem,	73 tread;] tread, 368 Maile.] Maile, 620 mood.] mood, 812 mee;] mee,
Stops Heightened	465 love,] love;	631 Desirous,] Desirous;	346 Reines,] Reines; 891 high;] high:
Other Changes		617 all.] all 633 flows:] flows	405 mov'd] mov'd.

	Bk. VII	Bk. VIII (Ed. 1, VII)	Bk. IX (Ed. 1, VIII)
Commas Added			114 round] round, 116 Hill] Hill, 147 Created] Created, 634 Fire] Fire, 841 crown] crown,
Commas Deleted or Omitted	20 Erroneous,] Erroneous 151 Heav'n,] Heav'n	307 (Ed. 1, 944) Fruit,] Fruit 313 (Ed. 1, 950) appeer'd,] appeer'd 451 (Ed. 1, 1088) wish,] wish 600 (Ed. 1, 1237) me,] me 602 (Ed. 1, 1239) actions,] actions	393 *Pomona*,] *Pomona* 581 Fenel,] Fenel 638 attends,] attends 668 comely,] comely 979 thee,] thee 1002 lowr'd,] lowr'd 1056 righteousness,] righteousness 1087 broad,] broad 1159 Nay,] Nay

N

	Bk. VII	Bk. VIII (Ed. 1, VII)	Bk. IX (Ed 1, VIII)
Stops Reduced		223 (Ed. 1, 860) formes.] formes,	206 Flour.] Flour,
			272 reply'd.] reply'd,
			356 forbid.] forbid,
			951 Foe.] Foe,
			1016 move.] move,
			1059 more.] more,
			1098 unclean.] unclean,
			1162 reply'd.] reply'd,
Stops Heightened	337 good:] good.	466 (Ed. 1, 1103) warme,] warme;	319 Love,] Love;
		575 (Ed. 1, 1212) shows;] shows:	745 Fruits,] Fruits.
Other Changes			949 long?] long;

	Bk. X (Ed. 1, IX)	Bk. XI (Ed. 1, X)	Bk. XII (Ed. 1, X)
Commas Added	3 Serpent] Serpent,		21 (Ed.1, 913) Feast] Feast,
	829 vain] vain,		
	974 dying] dying,		
Commas Deleted or Omitted	48 rests,] rests	137 found,] found	46 (Ed. 1, 938) lost,] lost
	132 constraint,] constraint	355 confirmd,] confirmd	238 (Ed. 1, 1130) desire,] besaught
	215 feet,] feet	669 (Ed. 1, 665) exploded,] exploded	539 (Ed. 1, 1431) groaning,] groaning
	332 Hee,] Hee		542 (Ed. 1, 1434) aid,] aid
	338 them,] them		550 (Ed.1, 1442) love,] love
	380 things,] things		
	523 monsters,] monsters		
	787 place,] place		
	835 bear,] bear		
	837 desir'st,] desir'st		
	973 heart,] heart		

	Bk. X (Ed. 1, IX)	Bk. XI (Ed. 1, X)	Bk. XII (Ed. 1, X)
Stops Reduced	271 aid.] aid,	551 (Ed. 1, 548) up.] up, (Milton's change: line revised)	29 (Ed. 1, 921) Earth;] Earth, (1674 possibly faint semi-colon)
	706 *Libecchio.*] *Libecchio,*	552 (Ed. 1, 548) repli'd.] repli'd, 712 (Ed. 1, 708) chang'd;] chang'd,	
Stops Heightened		335 Earth,] Earth. 683 (Ed. 1, 679) *Michael*;] *Michael*. 684 (Ed. 1, 680) saw'st;] saw'st: 736 (Ed. 1, 732) order;] order:	13 (Ed. 1, 905) few,] few; (misreading of smudge over comma in 1667)
Other Changes	762 not:] not	142 descends] descends; 233 coming;] coming? 710 (Ed. 1, 706) punishment;] punishment?	

Frequencies of Punctuation Marks in Passages of Early Authors Quoted

The following table shows that the Elizabethan and Jacobean authors between 1582–1616 employ a lower total number of stops per hundred words, and a much smaller proportion of heavy stops relative to commas, than do the authors cited after 1616. From Jonson, 1616, to Caryl, 1676, the period of the middle century, there is a rise in the total number of stops used from the earlier average of $15\frac{1}{2}$–16 to a later average of twenty (or twenty-seven, excluding Daines and Browne), and also a sharp rise in the relative number of heavy stops to commas, Bacon and Wither (1625) using heavy stops in nearly equal numbers to commas, while Butler has more heavy stops than commas.

The exceptions to this general pattern are, in the later period, Daines and Browne, whose pointing is light, and in the earlier period, Harington and the 1611 Bible (text of the translation). Harington shows a rather high total number of stops, and both he and the 1611 translation use a higher proportion of heavy stops. The latter is because both are using frequent colon for metrical punctuation. That the heavy pointing of these two texts is not a logically differentiating pointing is indicated by the complete absence of semi-colons. Daines and Browne, whose punctuation approximates to that of the other Elizabethan writers cited, in fact are writing a rhythmical type of prose comparable to the earlier, and Daines of course is an advocate of rhythmical punctuation.

The table stresses that Milton's punctuation approximates to the Elizabethan pattern rather than to that of his own period. In total number of stops used Milton's pointing is sparse even by Elizabethan standards; he uses rather more heavy stops, proportionately, than some though not all Elizabethan writers, some of these of course being rhetorical stops. That is, there is quite a sharp contrast between his normally sparing and fluent, rhythmical punctuation and his not infrequent use of heavy or emphatic punctuation. The 1673 *Poems*, a bad text in many ways, alters the balance of Milton's Manuscript punctuation drastically, adding many commas so as to bring it into line with the higher total usages of the period, and obliterating the contrast between his heavy pointing and sparing use

Frequencies of Punctuation Marks in Passages of Early Authors Quoted

Date	Author	Number of Words in Passage	Number of Stops in Passage				Commas per 100 Words	Heavy Stops per 100 Words	Total Stops per 100 Words
			Comma	S.c.	Colon	F. Stop or other			
1582	Mulcaster	156	19		1	4	12	3	15
1591	Harington	44	6		1	2	13	7	20
1592	Nash	97	11		3	1	11	4	15
1609	Shakespeare: Sonnet 33	108	11	1	2	2	10	4½	14½
1611	Authorized Version: Epistle Dedicatorie	294	26	3	2	3	9	2½	11½
	Translation	72	6		3	4	8	10	18
1612	Donne	237	37		1	4	15½	2	17½
1616	Jonson: Volpone	185	36	9	2	3	19½	7½	27
1625	Bacon	167	15	4	4	6	9	8	17
1625	Wither: verse	115	12	4	5	2	10½	9½	20
1628	Wither: verse	102	12	5		3	12	8	20
1633	Butler (all Biblical extracts)	140	18	15	2	6	13	16½	29½
1641	Daines	348	31	5	4	7	9	4½	14
1643	Browne	201	22	3	2	1	11	3	14
1676	Caryl: example 5	119	18	4	1	1	15	5	20
—	Milton: Sonnet 11, Trin. Coll. MS	119	9	2		3	7½	4	11½
—	Comus, Trin. Coll. MS	36	4			3(2)	11	8½(6)	19½(17½)
1634	Comus, Bridgewater MS	36	6		1		16½	2½	19½
1673	Comus, Poems 1673	36	9			2	25	6	30½
—	P. Lost, MS Bk. I, lines 29–61	245	16	5	2	4	6	4½	10½
1667	P. Lost, first ed., I, 29–61	245	17	4	2	4	7	4	11
—	P. Lost, MS Bk. I, lines 296–325	241	24	2	2	5	10	3½	13
1667	P. Lost, first ed., I, 296–325	241	28	3		4	11½	3	14½

of commas. The 1667 edition of *Paradise Lost*, on the other hand, makes very little total change in Milton's punctuation, lightening the heavy stopping occasionally and adding a few more commas. It is noteworthy that the frequencies of stops in *Paradise Lost* (MS and 1667 texts) are very similar to those in some of Milton's autographs, for example, Sonnet 11, Trinity Manuscript. The frequencies of stops in the passage quoted from the Trinity Manuscript *Comus* are somewhat higher, although still well within the Elizabethan pattern. This passage is an exceptionally heavily pointed one in the Manuscript text of *Comus*.

For the purpose of tabulation, only that punctuation in association with ellipses (three spaced dots) is counted which follows, with no letter space preceding, the word before the ellipsis. For example, four spaced dots thus. . . . indicate counted full stop followed by ellipsis; whereas four spaced dots thus . . . . indicate ellipsis up to the end of a sentence, the full stop not counted. Similarly comma with ellipsis thus, . . . is counted, but not comma after ellipsis, thus . . . , (the punctuation sometimes being quoted so to show the rhythmical contours of the sentence).

Bibliography of Works Consulted

I. Works of Milton

MILTON, JOHN. Paradise Lost, First Book. Manuscript. New York: Pierpont Morgan Library.

——. The Milton Manuscript (Manuscript of Milton's Minor Poems). Cambridge: Trinity College Library, R. 3. 4.

——. Paradise Lost: a Poem written in Ten Books. By John Milton. London: . . . Peter Parker . . . Robert Boulter . . . , 1667. (First title page.) Cambridge: Trinity College Library, Capell S. 10.

——. Richard Bentley, ed., Milton's Paradise Lost. A New Edition. Annotated. London: Printed for Jacob Tonson, 1732.

——. Helen Darbishire, ed., The Manuscript of Milton's Paradise Lost, Book I. Reproduced in collotype and transcribed. Oxford: Clarendon Press, 1931.

——. Helen Darbishire, ed., The Poetical Works of John Milton. With introduction. 2 vols. Oxford: Clarendon Press, 1952–5. Including Vol. I: Paradise Lost, 1952.

——. Harris Francis Fletcher, ed., John Milton's Complete Poetical Works. Reproduced in photographic facsimile: A critical text edition. 4 vols. Urbana: University of Illinois Press, 1943–8. Including: Vol. I, Poems . . . 1673; Poems . . . 1645; With . . . Manuscript Copies, and Their Collations, 1943; Vol. II, The First Edition of Paradise Lost, 1945; Vol. III, The Second Edition of Paradise Lost, 1948; Vol. IV, The 1671 Edition of Paradise Regained and Samson Agonistes, 1948.

——. Merritt Y. Hughes, ed., John Milton: Paradise Lost. New York: The Odyssey Press, 1935.

——. David Masson, ed., The Poetical Works of John Milton. With Introduction. 3 vols. London: Macmillan and Co., 1874.

——. Frank Allen Patterson et al., eds., The Works of John Milton. 18 vols. New York: Columbia University Press, 1931–8.

——. B. A. Wright, ed., Milton's Poems. With Introduction. Everyman. London: J. M. Dent, 1956.

——. William Aldis Wright, ed., Facsimile of the Manuscript of Milton's Minor Poems, Preserved in the Library of Trinity College, Cambridge. Transcribed. Cambridge: University Press, 1899.

II. Earlier Works

BACON, FRANCIS. *Essayes. Religious Meditations. Places of perswasion and disswasion.* From the First Edition of 1597. Exactly reprinted. Haslewood Books. London: Westminster Press, 1924.

——. *The Essayes or Counsels, Civill and Morall* . . . . Newly written. London: printed by John Haviland, 1625.

BIBLE. *The Holy Bible: A Facsimile* . . . *of the Authorized Version* . . . *1611*, Introduced by A. W. Pollard. Oxford: University Press, 1911.

BROWNE, THOMAS. *The Works of Sir Thomas Browne.* Edited by Geoffrey Keynes. Second edition. 4 vols. London: Faber & Faber Ltd., 1964.

BUTLER, CHARLES. *The English Grammar, or The Institution of Letters, Syllables, and Words, in the English tongue.* Oxford: printed by William Turner, 1633.

——. *Charles Butler's English Grammar (1634).* Reprinted and edited by A. Eichler. Neudrucke Frühneuenglischer Grammatiken, 4. Halle a.S.: Max Niemeyer, 1910.

CARYL, JOSEPH. *An Exposition with Practical Observations upon the Book of Job.* . . . 2 vols. London: Printed by Samuel Simmons . . . , 1676; 1677.

DAINES, SIMON. *Simon Daines' Orthoepia Anglicana, 1640.* A Scolar Press Facsimile: English Linguistics, 1500–1800, No. 31. The Scolar Press, Ltd.: Menston, Eng., 1967. Chapter on punctuation partly reprinted by C. Fries, "Shakespearian Punctuation" (see bibliography, part III).

DONNE, JOHN. *Biathanatos.* Bodleian MS e Musaeo 131. Partly reprinted by E. Simpson, "A Note on Donne's Punctuation" (see bibliography, part III).

——. *The Poems of John Donne.* Edited . . . with introductions . . . by Herbert J. C. Grierson. 2 vols. London: Oxford University Press, 1912.

HARINGTON, JOHN. *Orlando Furioso of Ariosto.* Additional MS 18920, Brit. Mus. Partly reprinted by P. Simpson, *Proof-Reading* . . . , and W. W. Greg, "An Elizabethan Printer and his Copy" (see bibliography, part III).

HOWELL, JAMES. *A New English Grammar* . . . . London: Printed for T. Williams . . . , 1662.

JONSON, BEN. *Ben Jonson* (Life and Works). Edited by C. H. Herford, Percy and Evelyn Simpson. 11 vols. Oxford: Clarendon Press, 1925–52. Including Vol. VIII: *The English Grammar*, 1947.

MOXON, JOSEPH. *Mechanick Exercises on the Whole Art of Printing (1683–4.)* Reprinted and edited by Herbert Davis and Harry Carter. Second edition. London: Oxford University Press, 1962.

MULCASTER, RICHARD. *Mulcaster's Elementarie* (1582). Exactly reprinted and edited by E. T. Campagnac. Oxford: Clarendon Press, 1925.

NASH, THOMAS. *Pierce Penilesse his Supplication to the Divell* (1592). No title page. British Museum copy. Photostated and bound (with Samuel Daniel's *A Defence of Rhyme*), in Cambridge University Library.

PUTTENHAM, GEORGE. *The Arte of English Poesie*. Ed. Gladys Willcock and Alice Walker. Cambridge: University Press, 1936.

SHAKESPEARE, WILLIAM. *A New Shakespeare Quarto: The Tragedy of King Richard II*. Printed for the third time by Valentine Simmes in 1598. Reproduced in facsimile, . . . with introduction by Alfred W. Pollard. London: B. Quaritch, 1916.

——. *Shakespeares Comedies, Histories, & Tragedies*. . . . Facsimile of The First Folio Edition 1623, from the Chatsworth Copy . . . . Introduction by Sidney Lee. Oxford: Clarendon Press, 1902.

——. *Shakespeares Sonnets*, ... Facsimile of the First Edition, 1609, from the copy . . . in the . . . Bodleian Library. Introduction by Sidney Lee. Oxford: Clarendon Press, 1905.

WITHER, GEORGE. *Britain's Remembrancer. Containing A Narration of the Plague lately past* . . . . (London): Imprinted for . . . John Grismond, 1628.

——. *Britain's Remembrancer (1628)*. Two parts. Exactly reprinted. Spenser Society Publication. Manchester: Charles Simms, 1880.

——. *The History of the Pestilence (1625)*. Transcribed and edited by J. Milton French. Cambridge, Mass.: Harvard University Press, 1932.

III. Later Books or Articles

ALDEN, RAYMOND M. "The Punctuation of Shakespeare's Printers," *PMLA*, XXXIX (1924), 557–80.

AMES, JOSEPH. *Typographical Antiquities: Being an Historical Account of Printing in England* . . . . London: W. Faden, 1749.

BANKS, THEODORE H., Jr. "Miltonic Rhythm; A Study of the Relation of the Full Stops to the Rhythm of *Paradise Lost*," *PMLA*, XLII (1927), 140–5.

BAUGH, ALBERT C. *A History of the English Language*. Second revised edition. London: Routledge & Kegan Paul, Ltd, 1959.

BLACK, MINDELE (Mindele Treip). "Studies in the Epic Language of *Paradise Lost*". Ph.D. dissertation: Radcliffe College/Harvard University, 1956.

BUSH, J. DOUGLAS. *John Milton: A Sketch of his Life and Writings*. London: Weidenfeld and Nicolson, 1965.

DARBISHIRE, HELEN. "The Printing of the First Edition of *Paradise Lost*," *The Review of English Studies*, XVII (1941), 415–27.

DIEKHOFF, JOHN. "Milton's Prosody in the Poems of the Trinity Manuscript," *PMLA*, LIV (1939), 153–83.

——. "The Punctuation of Comus," *PMLA*, LI (1936), 757–68.

——. "Terminal Pause in Milton's Verse," *Studies in Philology*, XXXII (1935), 235–9.

——. "The Text of Comus, 1634–1645," *PMLA*, LII (1937), 705–27.

——. "The Trinity Manuscript and the Dictation of *Paradise Lost*," *Philological Quarterly*, XXVIII (1949), 44–52.

EMMA, RONALD D. *Milton's Grammar*. Studies in English Literature, Vol. II. The Hague: Mouton & Co., 1964.

EVANS, ROBERT O. "Proofreading of *Paradise Lost*," *Notes And Queries*, 200 (1955), 383–4.

FRIES, CHARLES C. "Shakespearian Punctuation." *Studies in Shakespeare, Milton and Donne*. University of Michigan Publications, Language and Literature, Vol. I. New York: The MacMillan Co., 1925. Pp. 65–86.

GARROD, H. W. "Milton's Lines on Shakespeare," *Essays and Studies by Members of the English Association*, XII (1926), 7–23.

GREG, W. W. "An Elizabethan Printer and his Copy," *The Library* (4th series), IV (1923–4), 102–18.

HANFORD, JAMES HOLLY. Appendix E: "Milton and his Printers." *A Milton Handbook*. Fourth edition. New York: Appleton-Century-Crofts, 1954.

——. "The Manuscript of *Paradise Lost*," *Modern Philology*, XXV (1927–8), 313–17.

HONAN, PARK. "Eighteenth and Nineteenth Century English Punctuation Theory," *English Studies*, XLI (1960), 92–102.

LEE, SIR SIDNEY, ed. *The Year's Work in English Studies, 1919–1920*. London: Oxford University Press, 1921. Pp. 64–7.

McKERROW, RONALD B. *An Introduction to Bibliography for Literary Students*. Oxford: Clarendon Press, 1927.

ONG, WALTER J. "Historical Backgrounds of Elizabethan and Jacobean Punctuation Theory," *PMLA*, LIX (1944), 349–60.

PARTRIDGE, A. C. *Orthography in Shakespeare and Elizabethan Drama: A Study of Colloquial Contractions, Elision, Prosody and Punctuation*. London: E. Arnold, 1964.

PERSHING, JAMES H. "The Different States of the First Edition of *Paradise Lost*," *The Library* (4th series), XXII (1941–2), 34–66.

PLOMER, HENRY R. *A Dictionary of . . . Booksellers and Printers . . . 1641–1667*. London: Bibliographical Society, 1907.

——. *A Dictionary of . . . Printers and Booksellers . . . 1668–1725*. Oxford: University Press (for the Bibliographical Society), 1922.

——. *A Short History of English Printing, 1476–1898.* Second edition. London: K. Paul, Trench, Trübner, 1915.

POLLARD, ALFRED W. *Shakespeare's Fight with the Pirates, and the Problems of the Transmission of his Text.* Second edition. Cambridge: University Press, 1920.

PRICE, HEREWARD T. "Grammar and the Compositor in the Sixteenth and Seventeenth Centuries," *JEGP*, XXXVIII (1939), 540–8.

PRINCE, F. T. *The Italian Element in Milton's Verse.* Oxford: Clarendon Press, 1954.

SCRIVENER, F. H. A. *The Authorized Edition of the English Bible (1611), its Subsequent Reprints and Modern Representatives.* Cambridge: University Press, 1884.

SHAWCROSS, JOHN T. "Establishment of a Text of Milton's Poems through a Study of *Lycidas*," *The Papers of the Bibliographical Society of America*, LVI (1962), 317–31.

——. "Milton's Spelling: its Biographical and Critical Implications," *Dissertation Abstracts*, XXII. Ann Arbor, Michigan: Univ. Microfilms Inc., 1961. Pp. 567–8.

——. "One Aspect of Milton's Spelling: Idle Final 'E'," *PMLA*, LXXVIII (1963), 501–10.

——. "Orthography and the Text of *Paradise Lost*." *Language and Style in Milton: A Symposium in Honor of the Tercentenary of 'Paradise Lost'*, ed. Ronald David Emma and John T. Shawcross. New York: Frederick Ungar, 1967.

——. "What We Can Learn from Milton's Spelling," *The Huntington Library Quarterly*, XXVI (1962–3), 351–61.

SIMPSON, EVELYN M. "A Note on Donne's Punctuation," *The Review of English Studies*, IV (1928), 295–300.

——. *A Study of the Prose Works of John Donne.* Second edition. Oxford: Clarendon Press, 1948.

SIMPSON, PERCY. "The Bibliographical Study of Shakespeare," *Oxford Bibliographical Society Proceedings and Papers*, I (1922–6), 19–53.

——. *Proof-Reading in the Sixteenth Seventeenth and Eighteenth Centuries.* London: Oxford University Press, 1935.

——. *Shakespearian Punctuation.* Oxford: Clarendon Press, 1911.

STILLMAN, DONALD G. "Milton as Proof Reader," *Modern Language Notes*, LIV (1939), 353–4.

TILLYARD, E. M. W. *The Miltonic Setting, Past and Present.* London: Chatto & Windus, 1947.

WRIGHT, B. A. "Note on *Paradise Lost*, I. 230," *The Review of English Studies*, XXIII (1947), 146–7.

Index